About this Book

The Enemy of Nature faces the harsh but increasingly inescapable conclusion that capitalism is the driving force behind the ecological crisis, and draws the radical implications. Joel Kovel – noted scholar and author, also public speaker and green campaigner – indicts capitalism, with its unrelenting pressure to expand, as both inherently ecodestructive and unreformable. He argues against the reigning orthodoxy that there can be no alternative to the capitalist system, not because this orthodoxy is weak, but because submission to it is suicidal as well as unworthy of human beings. Kovel sees capital as not just an economic system but as the present manifestation of an ancient rupture between humanity and nature. This widening of scope is given theoretical weight in the second part of the work, which develops a positive synthesis between marxism, ecofeminism and the philosophy of nature. Then Kovel turns to 'what is to be done?' He criticizes existing ecological politics for their evasion of capital, advances a vision of ecological production as the successor to capitalist production, and develops the principles for realizing this, as an 'ecosocialism', in the context of anti-globalization politics. He sees, prefigured in present struggle, the outlines of a society of freely associated producers for whom the earth is no longer an object to be owned and exploited, but the source of intrinsic value.

The Enemy of Nature is written in the spirit of the great radical motto, 'be realistic – demand the impossible!' Its author dares to think the unthinkable – we have a choice: capitalist barbarism and ecocatastrophe, or the building of a society worthy of humanity and nature.

About the Author

Joel Kovel has been Alger Hiss Professor of Social Studies at Bard College, in Annandale, New York since 1988. He was awarded a Fellowship at the John Guggenheim Foundation in 1987. In 1998, Kovel was a New York candidate for the US Senate, and in 2000 he was a candidate for nomination for President of the United States, on both occasions representing the Green Party. He lectures widely and has appeared on radio and television broadcasts in the USA, Canada, the UK, South Africa and Australia. Since the 1960s, he has published numerous journal articles on topics related to psychoanalysis and psychiatry (his original area of study), as well as politics and ecology.

His recent books include:

- *Red Hunting in the Promised Land* (Second Edition, Cassell, London, 1997)
- *History and Spirit* (Second Edition, Essential Books, 1998)
- *In Nicaragua* (Free Association Books, London, 1988)
- *The Radical Spirit: Essays on Psychoanalysis and Society* (Free Association Books, London, 1988)
- *White Racism: A Psychohistory* (Second Edition, Columbia University Press, New York, 1984).
- *The Age of Desire* (Second Edition, Columbia University Press, New York, 1981).

THE ENEMY OF NATURE
The end of capitalism or the end of the world?

Joel Kovel

Fernwood Publishing Ltd
NOVA SCOTIA

Zed Books Ltd
LONDON • NEW YORK

The Enemy of Nature: The end of capitalism or the end of the world? was first
published by Zed Books Ltd, 7 Cynthia Street, London N1 9JF, UK and
Room 400, 175 Fifth Avenue, New York, NY 10010, USA, and in Canada
by Fernwood Publishing Ltd, PO Box 9409, Station A, Halifax, Nova
Scotia, Canada B3K 5S3, in 2002.

Distributed in the USA exclusively by Palgrave, a division of St Martin's
Press, LLC, 175 Fifth Avenue, New York, NY 10010, USA

Second impression, 2002

Cover designed by Andrew Corbett
Set in Monotype Baskerville and Univers Black by Ewan Smith, London
Printed and bound in the United Kingdom
by Bookcraft Ltd, Midsomer Norton

A catalogue record for this book is available from the British Library
Library of Congress Cataloging-in-Publication Data: available

National Library of Canada Cataloguing in Publication Data
Kovel, Joel, 1936—
The enemy of nature : the end of capitalism or the end of the world?
Includes bibliographical references and index.
ISBN 1-55266-069-9
1. Capitalism—Environmental aspects. 2. Environmentalism. I. Title.
HC79.E5K68 2002   363.7   C2001-903587-X

ISBN 1 84277 080 2 cased
ISBN 1 84277 081 0 limp

Contents

Preface

Growing numbers of people are beginning to realize that capitalism is the uncontrollable force driving our ecological crisis, only to become frozen in their tracks by the awesome implications of the insight. Considering that the very possibility of a future revolves around this notion, I decided to take it up in a comprehensive way, to see whether it is true, and if so, how it came about, and most importantly, what we can do about it.

Here is something of how this project began. Summers in the Catskill Mountains of New York State, where I live, are usually quite pleasant. But in 1988, a fierce drought blasted the region from mid-June until well into August. As the weeks went by and the vegetation baked and the wells went dry, I began to ponder something I had recently read, to the effect that rising concentrations of gases emitted by industrial activity would trap solar radiation in the atmosphere and lead to ever-growing climatic destabilization. Although the idea had seemed remote at first, the ruin of my garden brought it alarmingly close to home. Was the drought a fluke of the weather, or, as I was coming to think, was it a tolling bell, calling us to task for a civilization gone wrong? The seared vegetation now appeared a harbinger of something quite dreadful, and a call to action. And so I set out on the path that led to this book. Thirteen years later, after much writing, teaching and organizing, after working with the Greens and running for the US Senate in 1998 and seeking their presidential nomination in 2000, and after several drafts and false starts, *The Enemy of Nature* is ready to be placed before the public.

It would have been understandable to shrug off the drought as just another piece of odd weather (and, indeed, nothing that severe has occurred since). But I had for some time been disposed to take a worst-case attitude with respect to anything having to do with the powers-that-be; and since industrial activity was close to the heart of the system, so were its effects on

Imperialism

climate drawn into the zone of my suspicion. US imperialism had got me going, initially in the context of Vietnam and later in Central America, where an agonizing struggle to defend the Nicaraguan revolution against Uncle Sam was coming to a bad end as the drought struck. The defeat had been bitter and undoubtedly contributed to my irritability, but it provided important lessons as well, chiefly as to the implacability displayed by the system once one looked below its claims of democracy and respect for human rights.

Here, far from the pieties, the effects of capital's ruthless pressure to expand are encountered. Imperialism was such a pattern, manifest politic-ally and across nations. But this selfsame ever-expanding capital was also the superintendent and regulator of the industrial system whose exhalations were trapping solar energy. What had proved true about capital in relation to empire could be applied, therefore, to the realm of nature as well, bringing the human victims and the destabilizations of ecology under the same sign. Climate change was, in effect, another kind of imperialism. Nor was it the only noxious ecological effect of capital's relentless growth. There was also the sowing of the biosphere with organochlorines and other toxins subtle as well as crude, the wasting of the soil as a result of the Green Revolution, the prodigious species losses, the disintegration of Amazonia, and much more – spiralling, interpenetrating tentacles of a great crisis in the relationship between humanity and nature.

From this standpoint there appears a greater 'ecological crisis', of which the particular insults to ecosystems are elements. This has further im-plications. For human beings are part of nature, however ill at ease we may be with the role. There is therefore a human ecology as well as an ecology of forests and lakes. It follows that the larger ecological crisis would be generated by, and extend deeply into, an ecologically pathological society. Regarding the matter from this angle provided a more generous view. No longer trapped in a narrow economic determinism, one could see capital not only as a material arrangement, but more deeply, as a pathological way of being cancerously lodged in the human spirit. And if it is a whole way of being that needs changing, then the essential question 'what is to be done?' takes on new dimensions. Ecological politics becomes much more than managing the external environment. It takes on, rather, a frankly revolutionary aspect. And since the revolution is against the capital that is nature's enemy, the struggle for an ecologically just and rational society will be the logical successor to the socialism that agitated the last century and a half before sputtering to an ignominious end. The great question now becomes whether this 'next-epoch', ecological socialism could overcome the flaws that haunted and brought down the original version.

A big problem hanging over these ideas is that very few people take them seriously. I have been acutely aware from the beginning of this project that the above theses are at a great distance from so-called mainstream opinion. How could it be otherwise in a time of capitalist triumph, when by definition reasonable folk are led to think that just a bit of tinkering with market mechanisms will see us through our ecological difficulties? And as for socialism, why should anyone with an up-to-date mind bother thinking about such a quaint issue, much less trying to overcome its false starts?

These difficulties extend over to the fragmented and divided left side of opinion, whether this be the 'red' left that inherits the old socialist passion for the working class, or the 'green' left that stands for an emerging awareness of the ecological crisis. Socialism, though ready to entertain the idea that capital is nature's enemy, is less sure about being nature's friend. It needs to be said that most socialists, though they stand for a cleaner environment, decline to take the ecological dimension seriously. They support a strategy where the worker's state will clean up pollution, but are unwilling to follow the radical changes that an ecological point of view implies as to the character of human needs, the fate of industry, and the question of nature's intrinsic value. Meanwhile, Greens, however dedicated they may be to rethinking the latter questions, resist placing capital at the centre of the problem. Green politics tend to be populist or anarchist rather than socialist, hence Greens envision an ecologically sane future in which a suitably regulated capitalism, brought down to size and mixed with other forms, continues to regulate social production. Such was essentially the stance of Ralph Nader, whom I challenged in the 2000 presidential primary, with neither intention nor hope of winning, but only to keep the message alive that the root of the problem lies in capital itself.

We live at a time when those who think in terms of alternatives to the dominant order risk exclusion from polite intellectual society. During my youth, and for generations before, a consensus existed that capitalism was embattled and that its survival was an open question. For the last twenty years or so, however, with the rise of neoliberalism and the collapse of the

one needs an opponent in order to clarify one's own position

Soviets, the system has acquired an aura of inevitability and even immortality. It is quite remarkable to see how readily the intellectual classes go along, sheeplike, with these absurd conclusions, disregarding the well-established lessons that nothing lasts for ever, that all empires fall, and that a twenty-year ascendancy is scarcely a blink in the flux of time. But the same mentality that went into the recently deceased dot.com mania applies to those who see capitalism as a gift from the gods, destined for immortality. One would think that a moment of doubt would be introduced into the official scenario by the screamingly obvious fact that a society predicated on endless expansion must inevitably collapse its natural base. However, thanks to a superbly effective propaganda apparatus and the intellectual defects wrought by power, such has not so far been the case.

Change, if it comes, will have to come from outside the ruling consensus. And there is evidence that just such an awakening may be taking place. Cracks have been appearing in the globalized edifice through which a new era of protest is emerging. When the World Trade Organization is forced to hold its meeting in Qatar in order to avoid disruption, or fence itself in inside the walled city of Quebec, or when the president-select, George W. Bush, is forced by protestors at his inauguration to slink fugitive-like along Pennsylvania Avenue in a sealed limousine, then it may fairly be said that a new spirit is in the air, and that the generation now maturing, thrown through no choice of their own into a world defined by the ecological crisis, are also beginning to rise up and take history into their own hands. *The Enemy of Nature* is written for them, and for all those who are beginning to recognize the need to break with the given in order to win a future.

An attitude of dissension conditioned me to see the 1988 drought as a harbinger of an ecologically ruined society. But that was not all I brought to the task. I was also working at the time on my *History and Spirit*, having been stirred by the faith of the Sandinistas, and especially their radical priests, to realize that a refusal is worthless unless coupled with affirmation, and that it takes a notion of the whole of things to gather courage to reach beyond the given. There is a wonderful saying from 1968, which should guide us in the troubled time ahead: to be realistic, one demands the impossible. So let us rise up and do so.

Many people helped me on the long journey to this book – too many, I fear, for them all to be included here, especially if one takes into account, as we should, the many hundreds I met during the political campaigns that provide much of its background. But there is no difficulty in identifying its chief intellectual influence. Soon after I decided to confront the ecological crisis, I decided also to link up with James O'Connor, founder of the journal *Capitalism, Nature, Socialism*, and originator of the school of ecological Marxism that made the most sense to me. It proved one of the most felicitous moments of my career and led to a collaboration that is still active. As my mentor in matters political-economic and toughest critic, but mostly as a dear friend, Jim's presence is everywhere in this volume (although the disclaimer must be underscored that its errors are mine alone). I have been indebted throughout to the *CNS* community for giving me an intellectual home and forum, and for countless instances of comradely help. This begins with Barbara Laurence, and includes the New York editorial group – Paul Bartlett, Paul Cooney, Maarten DeKadt, Salvatore Engel-Di Mauro, Costas Panayotakis, Patty Parmalee, Jose Tapía and Edward Yuen – along with Daniel Faber and Victor Wallis, of the Boston group, and Alan Rudy.

A number of people have taken the trouble to give portions of the manuscript a close reading during various stages in its gestation – Susan Davis, Andy Fisher, DeeDee Halleck, Jonathan Kahn, Cambiz Khosravi, Andrew Nash, Walt Sheasby and Michelle Syverson – and to them all I am grateful. I am further grateful to Michelle Syverson for the active support she has given this project during its later stages.

Among those who have helped in one way or another at different points of the work, I thank Roy Morrison, John Clark, Doug Henwood, Harriet Fraad, Ariel Salleh, Brian Drolet, Leo Panitch, Bertell Ollman, Fiona Salmon, Finley Schaef, Don Boring, Starlene Rankin, Ed Herman, Joán Martinez-Alier, Daniel Berthold-Bond and Nadja Milner-Larson. Mildred Marmur provided, once again, stalwart support and practical guidance through that sector of the real world that will always baffle me. And to Robert Molteno and the people at Zed, thanks for the help and the opportunity to join the honourable list of works they have shepherded into existence.

I would also take the opportunity to give thanks to Bard College, my academic home since 1988, and to its administration, especially Leon Botstein and Stuart Levine, as well as its faculty, staff (in particular, Jane Dougall), and students, for all the support – material, intellectual and spiritual – over the years. In a time of declining tolerance for dissident views, it was an extraordinary piece of luck for me to find Bard, and this project would have been far lonelier and more arduous without it.

Last and as ever, not least, except in the ages of its younger members, I thank the family that sustains me. This begins with my wife and soulmate, DeeDee, and extends to those who represent the children of the future for whom the battle must be fought: Solmaria, Rowan, Liam, Tolan and Owen.

November 2001

The grim shadow over our future cast on September 11, 2001 occurred between the composition of The *Enemy of Nature* and its release, and could not be incorporated into its argument. Yet its significance is such as to call for some brief observations.

First, because much of this book was written during a period of rampant economic growth, its main theme, that of the relentless expansive pressure of capital, might seem less important given the current brutal downturn of the world economic system. However, the same basic principles hold. For the pressure itself is what counts, whether or not it succeeds in imposing growth. Capital is a crisis-ridden system, and although there is never any clean correlation between crises in the economy and those of ecology, the integrity of ecosystems is sacrificed at either end of the economic cycle. *Boom of Bust* When the economy grows, sheer quantity becomes the dominating factor; while when, as now, it heads downwards, the diminution in growth acts as a signal causing environmental safeguards to be loosened in order to restore accumulation. *Business as usual*

Second, the crisis posed by fundamentalist terror and that posed by global ecological decay share certain basic features. As we will see in the following pages, the ecological crisis is like a nightmare in which the demons released in the progressive domination of nature on a world scale come back to haunt the master. But something of the same holds for terrorism. Fundamentalism's rebellion is often seen as being against modernity, but this only begins to matter in the context of imperialism, that is, the progressive domination of *humanity* on a world scale. In the species of imperialism known as globalization, the dissolution of all the old ways of being is part and parcel of forcibly imposed 'free trade'. Fundamentalisms arise within disintegrating peripheral societies as ways of restoring the integrity of ravaged communities. The project becomes irrational because of the hatred induced by powerlessness, and as it does, turns towards a pattern of terror and counter-terror in a cycle of vengeance.

The dialectics of terror and ecological disintegration are joined in the regime of oil. This constitutes, on the one hand, the chief material dynamic of the ecological crisis, and on the other, the organizing principle for imperial domination of those lands where the conflict is being fought out. Petroleum fuels industrial society, and the growth of the West is necessarily a growth in the exploitation and control of those lands where it is most strategically located. As these happen to be largely Islamic, so is the stage set for the great struggle now unfolding.

This is not the place to take up the conduct of this struggle except to say that it needs to be joined at the root of its causes. From this perspective, resolving the ecological crisis and freeing humanity from terror – including, to be sure, the terror inflicted by the superpower on its victims – are two aspects of the same process. Both require the overcoming of empire, which requires the the undoing of what generates imperialism over nature and humanity. It is an illusion to think that this can be achieved without a profound restructuring of our industrial system, and, by implication, our whole way of being. The grip of imperialism, whether of oil or otherwise, cannot be broken within the terms of the current order. Hence what is required to overcome global warming and the other aspects of the ecological crisis also goes for terror. A world must be built that does not *need* the fossil fuel economy, a world, as is argued in what follows, beyond capital.

For everything that lives is Holy *William Blake*

All that is holy is profaned *Karl Marx*

To my grandchildren: Owen, Tolan, Liam,
Rowan and Solmaria

Part I
The Culprit

1 Introduction

In 1970, growing fears for the integrity of the planetary ecology gave rise to a new politics. On 22 April, the first 'Earth Day' was announced, since to become an annual event of re-dedication to the preservation and enhancement of the environment. Remarkably, the newly aroused citizens became joined by certain members of the elites, who, organized into a group called 'The Club of Rome,' even dared to announce a theme never before entertained by persons of power, which appeared as the title of their 1972 manifesto, 'The Limits to Growth'.[1]

Thirty years later, Earth Day 2000 featured a colloquy between Leonardo di Caprio and President Bill Clinton, with much fine talk about saving nature. The anniversary also provided a convenient vantage point for surveying the results of three decades of 'limiting growth'. Thus, at the dawn of a new millennium, one could observe that:

1972 "Limits to Growth"

- human population had increased from 3.7 billion to 6 billion (62%);
- oil consumption had increased from 46 million barrels a day to 73 million;
- natural gas extraction had increased from 34 trillion cubic feet per year to 95 trillion;
- coal extraction had gone from 2.2 billion mctric tonncs to 3.8 billion; *worse pollution + not oil*
- the global motor vehicle population had almost tripled, from 246 million to 730 million;
- air traffic had increased by a factor of six;
- the rate at which trees are consumed to make paper had doubled, to 200 million metric tons per year;
- human carbon emissions had increased from 3.9 million metric tons annually to an estimated 6.4 million – this despite the additional impetus to cut back caused by an awareness of global warming, which was not perceived to be a factor in 1970;

"facts" w/o sources

- as for this warming, average temperature increased by 1° Fahrenheit – a disarmingly small number that, being unevenly distributed, translates into chaotic weather events (seven of the ten most destructive storms in recorded history having occurred in the last decade), and an unpredictable and uncontrollable cascade of ecological trauma – including now the melting of the North Pole during the summer of 2000, for the first time in 50 million years, and signs of the disappearance of the 'snows of Kilmanjaro' the year following;
- species were vanishing at a rate that has not occurred in 65 million years;
- fish were being taken at twice the rate as in 1970;
- 40 per cent of agricultural soils had been degraded;
- half of the forests had disappeared;
- half of the wetlands had been filled or drained;
- one-half of US coastal waters were unfit for fishing or swimming;
- despite concerted effort to bring to bay the emissions of ozone-depleting substances, the Antarctic ozone hole was the largest ever in 2000, some three times the size of the continental United States; meanwhile, 2000 tons of the substances that cause it continue to be emitted every day;[2] and
- 7.3 billion tons of pollutants were released in the United States during 1999.[3]

Most of these tendencies are accelerating. And they all are manifestations of what is proclaimed by every responsible and authoritative source to be the best of news, namely, that the world gross economic product has increased in the 30 years since the enunciation of the 'Limits to Growth' by almost 250 per cent, from 16 to 39 trillion dollars.

We need to add human costs to the picture, for during this phase of unparalleled prosperity:

- Third World debt increased by a factor of eight;
- the gap between rich and poor nations, according to the United Nations, went from a factor of 3:1 in 1820, to 35:1 in 1950; 44:1 in 1973 – at the beginning of the environmentally sensitive era – to 72:1, roughly two-thirds of the way through it, and no one would deny that this shocking ratio has increased since;
- between 1990 and 1998, per capita income declined in 50 countries.

One – Russia – has undergone the most catastrophic set of developments ever witnessed in a nation not invaded in war, with such declines
in life expectancy and rises in birth defects that the country will be
depopulated in a century or so if the rate continues;

- 1.2 million women under the age of 18 enter the global sex trade each
  year; and
- 100 million children are homeless and sleep on the streets.

There is, of course, much more. But my purpose is not to bludgeon the
reader with statistics, only to make a point that is there for every sentient
person to see, yet is continually both ignored and misunderstood. Let me
put it plainly.

As the world, or to be more exact, the Western, industrial world, has
leapt into a prosperity unimaginable to prior generations, it has prepared
for itself a calamity far more unimaginable still. The present world system
in effect has had three decades to limit its growth, and it has failed so
abjectly that even the idea of limiting growth has been banished from official
discourse. Further, it has been proved decisively that the internal logic of
the present system translates 'growth' into increasing wealth for the few and
increasing misery for the many. We must begin our inquiry, therefore, with
the chilling fact that 'growth' so conceived means the destruction of the
natural foundation of civilization. If the world were a living organism, then
any sensible observer would conclude that this 'growth' is a cancer that, if
not somehow treated, means the destruction of human society, and even
raises the question of the extinction of our species. A simple extrapolation
tells us as much, once we learn that the growth is uncontrollable. The
details are important and interesting, but less so than the chief conclusion
– that irresistible growth, and the evident fact that this growth destabilizes
and breaks down the natural ground necessary for human existence, means,
in the plainest terms, that we are doomed under the present social order,
and that we had better change it as soon as possible if we are to survive.

One wants to scream out this brutal and plain truth, which should be on
the masthead of every newspaper and the station-identification of every
media outlet, the leading issue before Congress and all governmental organizations, the focus of every congregation and the centrepiece of every
curriculum at all levels of education … but is nothing of the kind. Yes,
endless attention is paid to the crisis, a great deal of it useful, some of it

trivial, and some plainly harmful. But where is the serious, systematic reflection of the brutal truth – that humanity is in the hands of a *suicidal regime*, which scarcely anyone thinks it either possible or desirable to fundamentally change? Where is the rational dissection of this system's assault on nature, and the derivation of a plan to really change it – not to regulate this or that, or to resort to prayer or inward change, but actually to address the cancer and lay out the lineaments of a cure?

I should hope, here. In any case, that is my goal, and if what I have to say is not true in every detail, or even sadly mistaken, at least it can serve to push the debate about fundamentals along. I have no quarrel with many of the virtuous and sensible environmental schemes put forward these days. My quarrel is only with the judgement that holds that piecemeal reforms are all that is needed. My grievance is against the attitude that refuses to look at the problem as a whole and to contemplate radical change. For if the argument laid out above has even the slightest claim on plausibility – and it deserves repetition that the mass of evidence is such as to place the burden of proof on those who would deny it – then its implications need to be spun out without regard for how unfashionable or unsettling these may be. If there is no effective discourse on the logic of the system's growth, and the world now sits blandly in smug denial, or even uneasily in morbid contemplation, taking the word of greenwashers and conmen of all kinds instead of facing the ecological crisis squarely, then a work is needed that strives just for such a discourse. I have written *The Enemy of Nature*, therefore, not because there is a lack of address to our environmental woes, but because scarcely any of the innumerable works devoted to the subject develop the following implications from what has been sketched out above:

- That the 'reigning system' in question is capitalism, the dynamism of which, capital, is a strange beast indeed, not at all accessible to common sense, and extending far beyond its usual economic implications.
- That the 'growth' in question is essentially capital expressing its innermost being.
- That this is incorrigible; thus to seriously limit capital's expansion throws the system into deep crisis. For capital, it must always be 'Grow or Die!' It follows that capital cannot be reformed: it either rules and destroys us, or is destroyed, so that we may have a lease on life.
- That these implications demand of us that we rethink the question of

revolution, now generally thought of as lying quietly in the dustbin of history. I would argue, instead, that capital's combined ecodestructivity and incorrigibility forces open the prospect of a total revolution, which I would call *ecosocialist*, related to but distinct from the socialisms of the past century.

• That it is incumbent upon us to imagine the contours of such a revolution and spell them out, notwithstanding the currently miserable state of radical forces.

Now it may be that the times are changing. Perhaps the long downturn of resistance is coming to a close, because capital, having achieved globalization, can no longer rein in the contradictions stemming from its domination of nature and humanity, so that people everywhere break loose from the system. There are great signs to this effect, chiefly in the worldwide outbreak of demonstrations taken against the unholy trinity of global capital – the IMF, the World Bank and the WTO.[4]

Although *The Enemy of Nature* was begun well before the events in Seattle shook the world in 1999, it is, I believe, responsive to the same historical forces. It asks of those protesting globalization to consider where the logic of their actions points. How, in other words, do we go beyond the first stages of confronting the system? In what sense can the regime of capital be checked, if it can no more stop its unrelenting expansion than a man can voluntarily stop breathing? Are we ready to think through capital's overthrow and its replacement with a new kind of society based on a new kind of production? Are we ready, spurred by a dawning awareness that this crisis cannot be resolved within the existing system, to rethink this system in all its aspects, and really change it? These broad questions, and some of the innumerable issues arising from them, are addressed in the chapters to come.

The work is divided into three parts. In the first, 'The Culprit', we indict capital as what will be called the 'efficient cause' of the ecological crisis. But first, this crisis itself needs to be defined, and that is what the next chapter sets out to do, chiefly by introducing certain ecological notions through which the scale of the crisis can be addressed, and by raising the question of causality. The third chapter, 'Capital', lays out the main terms of the indictment, beginning with a case study of the Bhopal disaster, and proceeding to a discussion of what capital is, and how it afflicts ecosystems intensively, by degrading the conditions of its production, and extensively, through ruthless expansion. The next chapter, 'Capitalism', follows up on this by considering the specific form of society built around and for the production of capital. The modes of capital's expansion are explored, along with the qualities of its social relations and the character of its ruling class, and, decisively, the question of its adaptability. For if capitalism cannot alter its fundamental ecological course, then the case for radical trans-formation is established.

All of which is, needless to say, a grand challenge. The ecological crisis is intellectually difficult and horrific to contemplate, while its outcome must always remain beyond the realm of positive proof. Furthermore, the line of reasoning pursued here entails extremely difficult and unfamiliar political choices. Even though people may accept it in a cursory way, its awful dimensions make resistance to the practical implications inevitable. The argument developed here would be, for many, akin to learning that a trusted and admired guardian – one, moreover, who retains a great deal of power over life – is in actuality a cold-blooded killer who has to be put down if one is to survive. Not an easy conclusion to draw, and not an easy path to take, however essential it may be. But that is my problem, and if I believed in prayer, I would pray that my powers were adequate to the task.

In Part II, 'The Domination of Nature', we leave the direct prosecution of the case to establish its wider ground. This is necessary for a number of reasons, but chiefly to avoid a narrow economistic interpretation. In the first of these chapters, the fifth overall, I set out to ground the argument more deeply in the philosophy of nature and human nature. This is entailed in the shift from a merely *environmental* approach to one that is genuinely *ecological*, for which purpose it is necessary to talk in terms of human ecosystems and in the human fittedness for ecosystems – that is, human nature. If the goal of our effort is to build a free society in harmony with nature, then we need to appreciate how capital violates both nature at large and human nature – and need to understand as well how we can restore a more integral relation with nature. These ideas are pursued further in Chapter 6, which takes them up in a historical framework and in relation to other varieties of ecophilosophy. We see here that capital stands at the end of a whole set of estrangements from nature, and integrates them into itself. Far from being a merely economic arrangement, then, capital is the culmination of an ancient lesion between humanity and nature, expressed

pathological

in the notion of the 'domination of nature'. It follows that capital is a whole
way of being, and not merely a set of institutions. It is therefore this way
of being that has to be radically transformed if the ecological crisis is to be
overcome – even though its transforming must necessarily pass through a
bringing down of the 'economic capital' and its enforcer, the capitalist state.
We conclude the chapter with some philosophical reflections, including a
compact statement of the role played by the elusive notion of the 'dialectic'.

Then, in Part III, 'Towards Ecosocialism', we turn to the question of
'what is to be done?' Now the argument becomes political, and, because we
are so far removed these days from transforming society, to a blend of
Utopian and critical thinking. We begin with a survey of existing ecopolitics
in Chapter 7, to see what has been done to mend our relation to nature, and
to assay its potential for uprooting capital. One aspect of this critique is
entirely conventional, if generally under-appreciated. We emphasize that
capital stems from the separation of our productive power from the possibilities of its realization. It is, at heart, the imprisonment of labour and the
stunting of human capacities (capacities that need full and free development in an ecologically sound society) Therefore, all existing ecopolitics have
to be judged by the standard of how they succeed in freeing labour, which
is to say our transformative power. The chapter ranges widely, from the
relatively well-established pathways to those relegated to the margins, and it
generally finds the existing strategies wanting. It concludes with a discussion
of an insufficiently appreciated danger: that ecological movements may
become reactionary or even fascistic.

Having surveyed what is, we turn in the last two chapters to what could
be. In the eighth chapter, 'Prefiguration', the general question of what it
takes to break loose from capital is addressed. This requires an excursion
into the Marxist notion of 'use value', as that particular point of the economic system open to ecological transformation; and another excursion
into the tangled history of socialism, as the record of those efforts that tried
– and essentially failed – to liberate labour in the past century. Finally, the
chapter turns to the crucial matter of ecological production as such, using
for this purpose a synthesis with ecofeminism, a doctrine that connects the
liberation of gender to that of nature. We conclude with the observation
that the key points of activity are 'prefigurative', in that they contain within
themselves the germ of transformation; and 'interstitial', in that they are
widely dispersed in capitalist society. In the final chapter, 'Ecosocialism', we

attempt a mapping from the present scattered and enfeebled condition of resistance to the transformation of capitalism itself. The term ecosocialism refers to a society that is recognizably socialist, in that the producers have been reunited with the means of production in a robust efflorescence of democracy; and also recognizably ecological, in that the 'limits to growth' are finally respected, and nature is recognized as having intrinsic value and not simply cared for, and thereby allowed to resume its inherently formative path. This imagining of ecosocialism does not represent a kind of god-like aspiration to tightly predict the future, but is an effort to show that we can, and had better begin to, think in terms of fundamental alternatives to death-dealing capital. To this effect, a number of pertinent questions are addressed, and the whole effort is rounded off with a brief and speculative reflection.

Some last points before taking up the argument. I expect some criticism for not giving sufficent weight to the population question in what follows. At no point, for example, does overpopulation appear among the chief candidates for the mantle of prime or efficient cause of the ecological crisis. This is not, however, because I discount the problem of population, which is most grave, but because I do see it as having a secondary dynamic – not secondary in importance, but in the sense of being determined by other features of the system.[5] I remain a deeply committed adversary to the recurrent neo-Malthusianism that holds that if only the lower classes would stop their wanton breeding, all will be well; and I hold that human beings have ample power to regulate population so long as they have power over the terms of their social existence. To me, giving people that power is the main point, for which purpose we need a world where there are no more lower classes, and where all people are in control of their lives.

The Enemy of Nature need make no apologies for moving within the Marxist tradition, and for adhering to fundamental tenets of socialism such as the necessity of emancipating labour. But its approach is not that of traditional Marxism. What Marx bequeathed was a method and a point of view that require fidelity to the particular forms of a given historical epoch, and the transforming of its own vision as history evolves. Since Marxism emerged a century before the ecological crisis matured, we would expect its received form to be both incomplete and flawed when grappling with a society, such as ours, in advanced ecosystemic decay. Marxism needs, therefore, to become more fully ecological in realizing its potential to speak for nature as well as humanity. In practice, this means replacing *capitalist* with *ecologically sound/socialist* production through a restoration of use-values open to nature's intrinsic value.

I expect, too, that some will find the views of *The Enemy of Nature* too one-sided. It will be said that there is a hatred of capitalism here that leads to minimization of all its splendid achievements and underestimation of its prodigious recuperative powers. Well, it is true that I hate capitalism and would want others to do so as well. Indeed, I hope that this animus has granted me the will to pursue a difficult truth to a transformative end. In any case, if the views expressed here seem harsh and unbalanced, I can say only that there are no end of opportunities to hear hosannas to the greatness of Lord Capital and obtain, as they say, a more nuanced view. Nor is hatred of capital the same, I hasten to add, as hating capitalists, though there are many of these who should be treated as common criminals, and all should be dispossessed of the instrument that corrupts their soul and destroys the natural ground of civilization. This latter group includes myself, along with millions of others who have been tossed by life into the capitalist pot (in my case, for example, by pension funds in the form of tradeable securities; in all cases by holding a bank account or using a credit card). One of the system's marvels is how it makes all feel complicit in its machinations – or rather, tries to and usually succeeds. But it needn't succeed, and one way of preventing it from doing so is to realize that in fighting for an ecologically sane society beyond capital, we are struggling not just to survive, but, more fundamentally, to build a better world and a better life upon it for all creatures.

Notes

1. Meadows et al. 1972.

2. Much of this is taken from Donella Meadows, 'Earth day plus thirty, as seen by the Earth', distributed on the internet, April 2000. Meadows, tragically recently deceased, is also the co-author of Meadows et al. 1992, a follow-up study to *The Limits to Growth* (Meadows et al. 1972), which argued hopefully – but mistakenly – that, of all the major environmental crises, ozone depletion was the only one against which concerted international effort had been successful.

3. Personal communication, Daniel Faber. This is the highest for the ten-year period during which such measurements have been taken (these being, according to Faber, almost certainly too low, as the information is based on voluntary reports by corporations).

4. Here is another straw in the wind. At a meeting in October 2000 of 222 delegates to a conference in Chiapas, Mexico, of indigenous communities of the Americas, the resolution was adopted that as 'neoliberalism was merely the strategy to expand the reach of global capitalism ... the general objective would be [to] 'Achieve the defeat of capitalism in the Americas – especially in its current manifestation: neoliberalism' (ACERCA 2001). Such sophistication and militancy would have scarcely been possible a decade ago.

5. Meadows et al. 1992. The authors – no Marxists – conclude (p. 118) rather grimly: '[there is] ... a self-limiting constraint on population. Population will eventually level off, if industrial output per capita rises high enough. But the model contains no self-limiting constraint on capital. We see little "real-world" evidence that the richest people or nations have lost interest in getting richer. Therefore we have assumed that capital-owners will continue to try to multiply their wealth indefinitely and that consumers will continue to be willing to increase their consumption.'

2 The Ecological Crisis

Something has gone terribly wrong in the relations between humanity and nature. Consider the following article, quoted in its entirety, which appeared in the *Guardian Weekly*[1] during 1999:

> Environmental refugees fleeing from drought, floods, deforestation and de-graded land totalled 25m last year, outnumbering those displaced by war for the first time, according to the Red Cross.
>
> The 1999 World Disasters report, an annual survey of humanitarian trends, said that last year's 'natural disasters' were the worst on record, creating 58% of the world's refugees.
>
> 'Everyone is aware of the environmental problems of global warming and deforestation on one hand and the social problems of increasing poverty and growing shanty towns on the other,' Astrid Heiberg, the president of the international federation, said, 'but when these two factors collide, you have a new scale of catastrophe.'
>
> Last year environmental problems drove 25m people from their land to already vulnerable squatter communities on the edge of fast-growing cities. Dr Heiberg predicts that 'combination of human-driven climate change and rapidly changing social and economic conditions will set off a chain reaction of devastation leading to super-disasters.'
>
> The report looks at the consequences of Hurricane Mitch on Central America, and the 'deadly twins' El Niño and La Niña, which altered sea temperatures in the Pacific and Atlantic, causing droughts and floods on the continents each side of the oceans and believed to be made more extreme by global warming. Last year was the hottest recorded. (1998)
>
> El Niño caused the worst drought in Indonesia for 50 years, setting off a chain reaction of crises, the report says. The rice crop failed, the price of imported rice quadrupled, the currency dropped by 80% and riots erupted.

In the countryside forests burned out of control, covering areas with a toxic layer of smoke.

El Niño is estimated to have cost 21,000 lives in 1998, while the deforestation in China's Yangtze river contributed to flooding that affected the lives of 180m people.

Current trends are putting millions more into the path of potential disaster. One billion people are living in the world's unplanned shanty towns, and 40 of the 50 fastest growing cities are located in earthquake zones. Another 10m live under constant threat of floods.

China, whose reponse to the floods in the Yangtze has been to plant millions of trees, has invested more than $3bn in flood control over the past 40 years and estimates it has saved the economy about $13bn in avoided losses.

Peter Walker, director of disaster policy for the Red Cross, said: 'We have to think internationally the same way as we do domestically. We don't wait until a house catches fire and then raise money for the fire department. We must spent [*sic*] more money before disaster strikes.'

A grim watershed, indeed, that catastrophic effects from environmental sources would grow to exceed those stemming from direct human aggression. But this remarkable occurrence has more to do with bookkeeping than with basic mechanisms. For surely there is not environmental catastrophe in one column and human aggression in another, like the neat work of accountants. Human aggression has always had a lot to do with disruptions in the natural ground of society – consider all the wars driven by depletion of soils – while disruption of the environment is virtually always related to human activity, which as we know is all too often marked by 'aggression'. In fact, the 'environment' itself is marked everywhere by human hands, and what we call nature has a history. Now, however, that history is plainly entering a new phase.

Was Hurricane Mitch an 'act of God', in this time when global warming, finally accepted as the product of human activity, goads storms to new levels of fury? And to what extent were its horrific effects the result of deforestation and the displacement of poor people to unstable hillsides and other places in harm's way? Can an earthquake's destruction be divorced from the fact that 40 of the 50 fastest-growing cities are chaotically built over fault-lines? Were El Niño and La Niña themselves affected by global warming, hence to some degree socially caused? Then there are the effects related to governmental policy and corruption, themselves the outcome of global economic and political circuits. In Indonesia, for example, the burning was 'out of control', in good measure because Suharto, then the dictator of that country and darling of the international business community, had turned over great swatches of forests to his cronies. Finally, is there not something deficient about the response of the authorities? When the Red Cross official calls for the spending of money to stave off disaster, is he being prudent or bureaucratically stupid? Isn't something much more substantial than throwing money at the problems called for? Is not government, as the saying used to go, part of the problem?

The issue is not society and nature, as two independent bodies bouncing off each other. It is the evolution, accelerating with amazing velocity, of an ancient lesion in humanity's relation to nature. We have become witnesses to the inflammation of this long-smouldering pathology – witnesses, victims, and, if we awaken in time, healers.

In the meantime, all sorts of unpleasant surprises result from the ceaseless and unpredictable interaction of destabilized ensembles of nature – let us call them *ecosystems*. Thus the greenhouse effect resulting from accumulation of heat-retaining gases is implicated not only in these storms but also in a renewed proliferation of deadly infectious disease – both the recurrence of long-time killers such as malaria and tuberculosis and the appearance of new and exotic forms such as the Ebola, Hanta and West Nile viruses.[2] Only a generation after medical science was confidently predicting the end of infectious disease, we enter an epoch of pandemics of the scale of the plague-ridden fourteenth century. There are many reasons for this, and among them is global warming, which, by destabilizing climate, leads to increasingly chaotic weather and habitat alteration. This releases the pathogens as well as their vectors from feedback loops of control. The story only begins here: beyond the effects of climate, other processes of habitat deterioration supervene, notably destruction of forests because of logging, the desperate cutting of firewood by destitute peoples, or the shift from a subsistence economy to one based on cattle or export crops. These interact with climate-driven changes in fundamentally incalculable ways, which include the fact that deforestation itself affects climate. Equally important are the direct effects on the hosts of these pathogens, which in the aggregate greatly lower resistance to infection.

The 'nature' that is the object and subject of the ecological crisis includes

the ecosystem known as the human body. At this level, malnutrition, un-
employment, social alienation, systematic poisoning by chemical discharges,
and the subtle effects of radioactive fallout and, indeed, of climatic change
itself – all increase the likelihood that infections will take hold and become
both lethal and pandemic. And so, of course, does the current breakdown
in health care affecting incomprehensibly vast numbers of people – recent
estimates run as high as 800,000,000 – who now essentially lack all medical
resources. In the current order of globalization, the world is subject to
chaotic degrees of circulation of people, signals and substances, while civil
society and community disintegrate across a great range of settings. Lethal
pandemics are the inevitable accompaniment, as AIDS now looms to decim-
ate sub-Saharan Africa, with South Asia and the former Soviet Union
waiting their turn. And what of the still more subtle yet profound effects of
demoralization, as people with no chance of real power over their lives lose
hope in a sea of troubles, or turn to irrational beliefs and self-destructive
practices as an escape from an unbearable and incomprehensible reality?
Should we not think of demoralization as an ecological phenomenon?[3]

These changes ramify throughout the whole of nature. The immense
ecosystem of the oceans comprises innumerable interconnected others
defined by particular depth, or relation to the shore, or currents, or coral
reefs, and so on, as well as by the organisms that live within and between
them. Assessments can be made of the integrity of these sub-systems, as
well as of the oceans as a whole, in relation to ongoing changes in other
aspects – for example, climate. As of the late 1990s, the following obtained:

- The waters of the oceans have warmed on average about 1.8 degrees
  Fahrenheit during the twentieth century. This may not seem like much.
  However, since warmer water holds less oxygen, a small increase in heat
  energy can translate to a major decrease in organic productivity.
- Studies have shown that the Pacific Ocean off California yields declining
  volume of kelp; worse, during the last 40 years, production of zoo-
  plankton has dropped by 40 per cent.
- As a result, many species have moved northward, causing the population
  of pelagic birds to decline by 40 per cent since 1987 (one species, the
  sooty shearwater, has dropped by 90 per cent).
- The set of these changes has brought about a 50 per cent loss of nutrients
  on the deep ocean floor, habitat to an immense number of creatures – an

estimated 10 million species, the great majority unknown to our science.

- Elsewhere, about 10 per cent of the world's corals have died from the warm water, with an additional 20–30 per cent under threat. These are, as the oceanographer James Porter has put it, 'like the canary in the mine. They are telling us that the water where they live is becoming suboptimal for their existence.' In parts of the Indian and Pacific oceans, corals have declined by 80–90 per cent.

- Bacteria and viruses released by sewage have led to a four-fold increase in 160 coral sites along the coast of Florida. About 25 per cent of people who visit Florida beaches now become ill as a result. In addition, as many as 40 per cent of shellfish off the coast of New York have been found to be infected.

- All of this necessarily has a deleterious effect on fish populations, already so deeply compromised by overfishing that 13 of the world's 17 major fisheries are either depleted or in steep decline – and this in turn has major effects on society.[4]

From these countless *environmental* events we derive a crisis of global *ecological* proportions. The environment is by definition a set of things outside us, with no essential structure, while an ecology is a *whole defined by internal relations*. Environments can be listed and numerically evaluated. Ecologies offer no such packaging and the boundaries between them are sites of active transformation, without a fixed line between inside and outside. In particular, the boundary between humanity and nature becomes highly dynamic, and a matter to be understood historically and transformed politically. It is in this spirit that we would approach the question of an ecological crisis.

The ecological crisis is an abstraction from an obdurate set of facts: that 'environmental' troubles are breaking out all over the place, that this is peculiarly linked to the contemporary condition, and that it clearly poses a major threat to the future integrity of society and nature. Logically, one can ascribe this to chance, or believe that the set of troubles is self-limiting and will go away of itself in a little while. But neither of these propositions rests on more than wishful thinking. This leaves a more sombre, but also more rational alternative: that the ecological crisis will not go away of itself, and that it is caused by human activity. From this we may turn to understanding what this activity is as well as whether and under what terms its effects on ecologies may be overcome.

An individual may experience ecological disruption through some local phenomenon: a birth defect, say, or asthma, or a flood, but in no case can any unequivocal extension be made from any of these phenomena either to their immediate cause or to a global process. Occasionally, something egregious comes along – a Love Canal, Chernobyl or Exxon Valdez. But there is no clear path from these infractions to a global crisis, or even to a pattern of malfeasance, since it will always be possible to argue that each instance is exceptional or remediable by some counter-measure.

Ecosystem damage is often difficult to assess, as in phenomena such as global warming or declining sperm counts. At this level, empirical evidence tends to get fuzzy, and we contend with nothing specific or, in some cases, even perceptible. There is general agreement about ozone depletion as an ecosystemic lesion. But reputable scientists have disagreed that global warming is even taking place, or that it is related to the inputs of carbon dioxide or methane, or that it is permanent, or that it is a bad thing. This fraction comprises a dwindling minority of the overall view, and, needless to say, does not correspond to the view argued here. But that is not the point. Science is not a popularity contest, and minorities, even individuals, have been known to prevail in the court of truth. Whatever the motives of the differing sides, they each contend with ultimate unprovability.

How can one make useful comparisons about sperm counts, for example, across great stretches of time, location and ethnic make-up, or where the investigators have never conferred about what they are doing? The same reasoning holds for other kinds of medical–epidemiological data. Yes, asthma rates have gone up in urban areas; yes, mice have got cancer from exposure to the apple fumigant Alar; yes, malaria is on the way back. But what does that prove, beyond the fact that progress has its costs?

The Hooker Chemical Company can be held responsible for Love Canal, and Exxon for the spill of oil from one of its tankers. And in some cases, such as ozone depletion, chlorofluorocarbon production can be held responsible for ecosystemic breakdown. But for the majority of ecosystemic threats, contestation and doubt seem to increase as one approaches a more global level of analysis. How, then, can one assert anything at all about a crisis at the even grander level of an 'ecological crisis' affecting the entire relationship of humanity to nature?

In fact, this level is scarcely addressed, even by the most relentless and uncompromising critics of the system. What seems to happen instead is that the problem is taken to an ecosystemic level such as biodiversity loss or climatic aberration, following which the assertion is made that governments, or 'the people', must bring about basic change. This change is admitted to require 'large-scale', even 'profound' economic adjustments as well as a new 'lifestyle' in which the rich people of the North will have to consume less and the poor people of the South will have to breed less. Various recommendations are made about tax policies, international governance, and the like. Obeisances are paid to the care of the earth, to adopting a more 'holistic' approach, or getting in touch with one's feelings about nature. And then everyone goes home and nature continues being ravaged.

It is as if the elementary fact of extrapolation does not exist. Yes, it could be that El Niño was a fluke, as far removed from human causality as the meteorite whose impact some 70 million years ago brought the Jurassic era to a screeching halt. And yes, it could be that all this is ultimately for the good. But how can it be denied that the ecological crisis has come on with a sickening rapidity by geo-historical standards, or that it is plainly accelerating, thereby placing more and more ecosystems in harm's way, and opening the way for exponentially increasing destabilization? As individuals we may be unable to see this directly, given the scale of change and the fact that, however momentary it may be from a geological standpoint, the crisis only rarely impacts on an individual life in a convincing way, and even then, the impact tends to be glancing, as the sun comes out after the latest horrific storm. But that all this has accelerated so in the last 30 years remains astounding, even as it fails to astound. From the perspective of the universe as a whole, our existence looks like a Roman Candle going off with a 'whoosh', leaving little trace behind.

However, despite the intellectual and emotional difficulties in understanding the global ecological crisis, its existence is actually easier to establish than that of any particular ecosystemic lesion. For we looking not at any given phenomenon, but at a crisis that conditions all phenomena. The empirical test for an individual phenomenon, particularly one at so great a level of abstraction as, say, biodiversity loss, has to be settled by the gathering, analysis and interpretation of an immense number of concrete data. The empirical test for the ecological crisis as a whole, on the other hand, rests on the thoroughly obvious point that problems comprising various environmental injuries are arising not randomly but in a kind of historical crescendo that belongs to the present moment and to it alone. Yes, of course, societies have fouled their nests before, often paying for their actions with extermination.[5] But the evidently *global* character of the crisis before us brings forward radically new factors: the interaction of planetary ecosystems, such as the atmosphere and the oceans; the immense acceleration in species loss, to levels 10,000 times greater than the background; the appearance of new, planetary breakdowns such as the ozone hole, or widespread endocrine destabilization – and, of special importance for our practice, new orders of social integration and disintegration. To repeat, this is an old lesion at a new level, like a smouldering that breaks into open flame, or a precancerous wart that becomes a malignant melanoma, and it requires measures of a radically new sort.

The ecological crisis is therefore not about any given ecosystem damage, such as global warming, species loss, resource depletion, or the widespread intoxication by new chemicals, such as organochlorines, which have been released into the biosphere. It is about the fact that these kinds of things are all happening together – that they all arise at and belong to the same moment in history. There are innumerable experts who play the role of Voltaire's Dr Pangloss and make a handsome living by denying the grim implications of one ecosystemic aspect or another of the crisis. But none of the experts or Panglosses has any answer for the fact of the crisis itself.[6]

On Human Ecology and the Trajectory of the Ecological Crisis

Ecology takes on a human form, since humans are part of nature, and, like all other creatures, require a pattern of relationships to survive and flourish. Each kind of creature has its ecological signature, which for humans is given in the terms of our peculiar species traits of sociality, language, culture, and the like. Society, which results from the expression of these traits – that is, of our *human nature* – is plainly an ecosystem, since it is internally related and has dynamic boundaries with other, natural ecosystems. We shall discuss this more fully in Part II, and here may confine ourselves to broadly considering how it is that society becomes the agent of the ecological crisis.

All of the characteristics of ecosystems, including degrees of destabilization and disintegration, apply to societies. But there is one property that human society uniquely possesses as the species-specific expression of human nature, namely, that the boundary between human and natural ecosystems is the site of the peculiarly human activity known as *production*, the conscious transforming of nature for human purposes. All creatures transform others – that is simply another way of expressing the dynamic relations between ecosystems. But only humans do so consciously, with all that entails. The rest of this study will be in effect a critique of those ways of production and their relations to nature – of the ways we change nature, and the ways nature changes us, and also a bit about the ways nature deals with the effects of our productive activity. From this standpoint, the ecological crisis may be said to be human production gone bad.

Put more formally, the current stage of history can be characterized by *structural forces that systematically degrade and finally exceed the buffering capacity of nature with respect to human production, thereby setting into motion an unpredictable yet interacting and expanding set of ecosystemic breakdowns.* The ecological crisis is what is meant by this phase. In it we observe the desynchronization of lifecycles and the disjointing of species and individuals, resulting in the fragmentation of ecosystems human as well as non-human. For humanity is not just the perpetrator of the crisis: it is its victim as well. And among the signs of our victimization is the incapacity to contend with the crisis, or even to become conscious of it.

Although the essentials of the ecological crisis lie in qualitative relationships, its outcome will turn upon quantity. It does not take the proverbial rocket scientist to tell us that if the load placed by humans upon the earth's buffering capacity keeps growing, then collapse will ensue, with consequences that logically include the possibility of extinction. It is not our province to dissect these buffering mechanisms, or how they are surpassed in the plurality of ecosystemic insults. Nor do I wish to evoke apocalyptic imagery to make my point, or calculate the number of years we have left until doomsday, if only because the scenario of apocalypse, with its sudden and total end accompanied by rapture, retribution, and so on, is not on the cards so much as a kind of steady, deleterious fraying of ecosystem with incalculable after-effects. Our job in any case is to understand the social dynamics of the crisis, and to see whether anything can be done about them. Here it is useful to consider society from a ecosystemic standpoint, and ponder the meaning of findings such as the fact that even as the situation of global ecology has markedly worsened in the past 30 years, so has the level of elite reponsiveness declined.

Since Plato at least, people have been observing the potential for deleterious environmental effects, and since the publication of George Perkins Marsh's *Man and Nature* in 1864, the possibility of systemic ecological damage has been raised. Marsh, however, was a visionary, and it took another century for the grim possibility of global ecosystemic decay to enter the general consciousness and become a concern of elites. In 1970, the notion of the 'limits to growth' entered the collective vocabulary, to be joined as time went on by other buzzwords such as 'sustainability' and 'throughput'.[7]

For a time it seemed as if humanity had awakened to its own harmfulness. But then something strange happened. Even as the vocabulary of ecological concern proliferated, along with a large bureaucratic apparatus, non-governmental as well as governmental, for putting it into effect, a shift occurred and the notion of 'limits to growth' became passé. Where once not so very long ago there was substantial concern that some combination of rising population and industrial expansion would overwhelm the earth with catastrophic consequences for civilization, today thoughts of the kind are distinctly unfashionable, even if not entirely extinguished.

What is odd is that, as we have already seen, 'growth', whether of population or industrial output, certainly did not slacken in this period. The latter is especially troubling, inasmuch as population, however unacceptably large it may be, shows signs of levelling across most of the world (even reaching zero or slightly negative levels in Japan and some Western European countries, and rather precipitous declines in the former Soviet bloc). Nothing of the sort can be said about the other kind of growth, that pertaining to industrial output or production in general, however this may be measured.[8] According to the Worldwatch Institute, a mainstream organization charged with monitoring the world's ecology, the global economy increased from $2.3 trillion in 1900, to $20 trillion in 1990 and an astounding $39 trillion in 1998. To quote, the 'growth in economic output in just three years – from 1995 to 1998 – exceeded that during the 10,000 years from the beginning of agriculture until 1990. And growth of the global economy in 1997 alone easily exceeded that during the seventeenth century.'[9] This is consistent with the fact that world trade has increased by a factor of 15 over the past four decades, all of which lends support to the prediction, made in 1997, that gross world product will *double* within the next 20 years, that is, to some $80 trillion dollars.[10]

The Malthusian principle that population will increase exponentially – a crude reduction of conscious creatures to machines obeying the rules of elementary algebra – has now been empirically as well as theoretically demolished. If there is to be a fatally destabilizing exponential increase of load, it will come in the economic sphere. This is certified by the figures just given, and, more significantly, by the value accorded them in established channels of opinion. We can easily imagine the horror and outrage with which an announcement that population would double in the next 20 years would be greeted. A similar claim made for economic activity, however, not only evades criticism but is greeted as though a sign of the Second Coming. Predictions of growth may or may not turn out to be on schedule. In fact, they got slowed a bit by the Asian financial meltdowns that began even as they were announced, and all the vagaries of the global economy will play a role in their realization. What matters, however, is that the world is run by those who see limits to growth as anathema. —Curse

The scenario of ecological collapse holds, in essence, that the cumulative effects of growth eventually overwhelm the integrity of ecosystems on a world scale, leading to a cascading series of shocks. Just how the blows will fall is impossible to tell with any precision, although a number of useful computer models have been assembled.[11] In general terms, we would anticipate interacting calamities that invade and rupture the core material substrata of civilization – food, water, air, habitat, bodily health. Already each of these physical substrata is under stress, and the logic of the crisis dictates that these stresses will increase. Other shocks and perturbations are likely to ensue as resource depletion supervenes – for example, in the supply of petroleum, which is expected to begin levelling off and then decline after the next ten years.[12] Or some unforeseen economic shock will topple the balance: perhaps climatic catastrophes will trigger a collapse of the $2 trillion global insurance industry, with, as Jeremy Leggett has noted, 'knock-on economic consequences which are completely ignored in most analyses of climate change'.[13] Perhaps famines will incite wars in which rogue nuclear powers will launch their reign of terror. Perhaps a similar fate will come through the eruption of as yet unforeseen global pandemics, such as the return of smallpox, currently considered to be within the range of possibilities open to terrorist groups. Or perhaps a sudden break-up of the Antarctic ice shelf will cause seas to suddenly rise by several metres, displacing hundreds of millions and precipitating yet more violent climatic changes. Or perhaps nothing so dramatic will take place, but only a slow and steady deterioration in ecosystems, associated with a rise in authoritarianism. The apocalyptic scenarios now so commonly making the rounds of films, best-selling novels, comic books, computer games and television are not so much harbingers of the future as inchoate renderings of the present ecological crisis. With terror in the air, these mass fantasies can become the logos of a new order of fascism – a fascism that, in the name of making the planet habitable, only aggravates the crisis as it further disintegrates human ecologies.

Or maybe things will work out and we will all muddle through somehow. The notion of limits to growth may have been shelved, but the system has not been sleeping. A vast complex of recuperative measures has been installed in its place, remedies that seek to restore ecological balance without threatening the main economic engines. Given the skill and resources devoted to the project, there is bound to be some good news to report. What is at issue, however, is adequacy: whether all the pollution controls, efficiencies, trading of credits, resource substitutions, information-rich commodities, engineered biological products, 'green business' and the like can compensate for retaining a system whose very heartbeat is growth without boundaries. Remember, the point of all these counter-measures is not just to protect against ecological breakdown, but to bring on line new sources of growth. This raises the spectre of a world like a gigantic Potemkin village, where a green and orderly façade conceals and reassures, while accelerated breakdown takes place behind its walls.

All this brings us to the larger question of just what is growing in the regime of 'growth'. We can see right away that the answer engages a number of levels. From the standpoint of ecosystems, the concrete agents of breakdown are the material forces thrown into nature by our industrial apparatus, and this is ultimately a question of molecules and energy flows, whether these be organochlorines, carbon dioxide or the blade of a chainsaw. But although this level grows, it is as a function of another kind of growth. Here we find the true god of society, and the actual subject of growth that its rulers will not compromise. At this level, what grows is the imaginary and purely human entity of money – not money in itself, but money in motion: Capital. The real issue of the ecological crisis resides in this mysterious entity and the social forces established for its nurture and reproduction. We have to ask whether we can overcome the ecological crisis without overcoming Capital. If the answer is no, then the map of the future needs to be redrawn.

Notes

1. P. Brown 1999.

2. Epstein 2000. Epstein points out that 'several climate models predict that as the atmosphere and oceans heat up, El Niños themselves will become more common and severe'.

3. 'All ecological disruptions ... tip the balance between people and microbes in favor of microbes.' Platt 1996. See also Mihill 1996. The situation particularly affects children, and itself is the result of a host of interrelated problems, including a precipitous decline of aid from rich countries to the poor. Sixteen African countries, along with Bangladesh, Nepal, India, Vietnam and Pakistan, spent less than $12 per person per year on health care in the late 1990s. Congo, in the grip of intractable civil war, spent 40 cents, while Tanzania spent 70 cents (as against $105.30 per person per year on its military).

4. Unless otherwise stated, the information from this section is drawn from Montague 1999.

5. Ponting 1991 provides a useful summary.

6. An example of neo-Panglossism, extending to denial of the crisis itself, is a column in the *Wall Street Journal* by Michael Fumento (Fumento 1999), a senior fellow at the Hudson Institute. The title of this piece sets the tone: 'With Frog Scare Debunked, It Isn't Easy Being Green'. This refers to new findings of what had been a puzzling phenomenon: the disappearance of many frogs, and the appearance of grotesque birth defects in many others. This is variously hypothesized as being due to pesticides or ozone depletion, and new findings suggest that the culprits are 'tiny parasites made in the factories of Mother Nature Inc.' From this (and similarly adduced good news regarding child health, along with denials of global warming, and so on), Fumento argues that the ecological crisis is not really happening except in the heated and opportunistic brains of environmentalists. Fumento seems to think that what makes a problem 'environmental' is the identification of isolated pollutants as causes rather than looking at disintegrated patterns and their mediated effects. At the ecosystemic level, Fumento fails to realize that parasites are most definitely ecologically dependent creatures, and fails to ask whether the appearance of these parasites may be related to ecological destabilization (as is very much the case with the emergence of other diseases). The grotesque metaphor of Mother Nature's factories may help us understand why this level of thinking doesn't occur to him, as a factory is set up to produce singular commodities and to minimize field effects. Similarly, Fumento prates on about the good news concerning child health, specifically rules out air pollution as a cause of childhood asthma, then smugly walks away from the problem as though the whole disease were a figment of the imagination (or perhaps produced also by 'parasites', and thereby moving out of the environmental frame of reference). That asthma rates have doubled in the last 20 years, and that, in a study reported at the same time in the *New York Times*, children in poor and minority communities in New York City are hospitalized 20 times as often as those from affluent areas, would be inconsequential to him. More generally,

Fumento is led to the ridiculous position of blaming Greens and environmentalists for making up the innumerable manifestations of ecodestabilization, as though the myriad stories about ecological harm were no more than a Green plot to throw monkey-wrenches into the machinery of progress. As for global warming, in a 1991 study, Wilfred Beckermann (Beckermann 1991: 73) concluded that, although 'every aspect of the problem that one peers into only reveals a whole new mass of uncertainties', nevertheless the evidence firmly suggests that the damage from global climate change 'is nothing like as great as it is widely believed and certainly not the inevitable global catastrophic scenario hawked around by most environmental movements, politicians trying to get some mileage out of the environmental bandwagon, or sections of the media that love scare stories of any kind.' The big answer, as far as he is concerned, is to remove 'existing market imperfections' that hamper solutions, 'and governments should not let ecological horror stories frighten them into making any moves [to cut greenhouse gas emissions]' (ibid.: 83). Among Beckermann's practical recommendations: to the people of Bangladesh, one of the places slated to be inundated by rising seas, build dykes like the Dutch, or if all else fails, emigrate. This is an interesting suggestion given the present and likely future global attitude toward mass immigration. One wonders if he would welcome hordes of displaced Bangladeshis to Oxford, where he teaches.

Ten years on, a representative of the Scottish insurance industry told the Hague Conference, whose mission was to ratify the Kyoto protocols of 1997 (and that, as we know, failed to do so), that at the present rate, increasing damages from global warming would bankrupt the world economic system by 2065; while in January 2001, the Intergovernmental Panel on Climate Change 'officially' put an end to the debate in citing around 3,000 scientific studies to conclude that firm evidence of change is already evident in some 420 distinct ecosystems, and the future portends the worst-case scenario of 'ecological horror stories', with temperature rises of as much as 10 degrees F by the end of the century.

7. Marsh 1965, about which Andrew Goudie writes that it was 'probably the most important landmark in the history of the study of the role of humans in changing the face of the earth'. (Goudie 1991: 3). See also Meadows et al. 1972. Another landmark study of the next decade was the Brundtland Report (Brundtland 1987).

8. For present purposes, we may regard measures in monetary units, like gross national (or world) product as equivalent to, and moving in tandem with, measures of a directly physical kind, such as resource depletion. There are major problems with this, including the adequacy of GNP as an indicator of economic well-being, and also its equivalency with ecological processes. Thus spending $100 on a psychoanalytic interview and buying $100 worth of herbicide for one's lawn are not exactly the same ecologically, although both increase GNP by the same amount. In an ecologically sane society, as many have pointed out, indices such as GNP will no longer guide policy. For now, however, it is a useful indicator of the problem. See Chapter 7 for further discussion.

9. Brown 1999: 10. See also Brown et al. 1991: 23.

10. From the authoritative voice of Renato Ruggiero, then director of the World Trade Organization, quoted 23 April 1997 in the *Wall Street Journal*. See next chapter for further discussion.

11. As in Meadows et al. 1992.

12. Less in absolute terms than in the cost of extraction. No effort need be made here to evaluate the precise contours of this looming crisis – or that in other essential resources, such as topsoil. The situation is too complex and unpredictable for that. And

it moves in multiple directions. As petroleum is the source of most of the greenhouse gases, it might be hypothesized that its decline as a resource would place less of a load on the ecosphere and perhaps open the way for new and ecological energy replacements. The question, though, is whether the currently installed market system can deal rationally with these and other stresses.

13. Quoted in Goldsmith and Henderson 1999: 99.

3 Capital

A Case Study

There is a substance called methyl isocyanate (MIC), which does not exist in nature but was introduced into the ecosphere by industry in the last century. A simple but very potent molecule (CH_3NCO), MIC is widely used in the manufacture of pesticides and herbicides because of its reactivity and deadly effects on living organisms. According to the website of the US Environmental Protection Agency:

> MIC … is an ester of isocyanic acid (HNCO). The parent isocyanic acid is a weak acid and exists in equilibrium with cyanic (HCNO) acid [the differences between the two HNCO's being in the spatial configuration of the atoms]. MIC's boiling point is yet to be clearly established. It is a highly volatile and inflammable gas; its vapours are denser than air; it is stable under dry and neutral conditions at room temperature but can violently react in the presence of acids, alkali, and the like. The carbon centre in the isocyanate group is electron deficient (electrophilic) and therefore will react with electron-rich nucleophiles, e.g.: water, alcohol, phenol, alkali, and the like.

Being denser than air, MIC vapour does not dissipate but settles on whatever is nearby. If exposed to water-bearing tissues, it reacts violently, leading to changes that cannot be contained by the normal protective devices of the affected organism. The amount of energy released by the ensuing reaction swiftly exceeds the heat-buffering capabilities of the body. As a result, many molecules of service to the organism are degraded and/or thrown into disarray, while others that are toxic are formed. Put simply, the body suffers severe burns, especially of exposed tissues rich in water, such as lungs and eyes. Chest pain, breathlessness and severe asthma result *capitalism is taken for granted, "natural" in USA*

Orwell - unconscienly obedient

power of social constructionalism

immediately. If the exposure is high, blindness, severe bacterial and eosino-philic pneumonia, or laryngeal oedema and cardiac arrest follow.

What has been said so far would explain at the physiological level why a person who inhaled MIC, say, as she slept, could become dangerously ill. Within this framework, we can say that MIC 'causes' the illness and death. Needless to say, such an explanation would tell us nothing about another set of questions, namely, why was the sleeper in such proximity to MIC, and more, what was methyl isocyanate doing in the environment in the first place, at so close a distance that it interacted with bodies? To repeat, MIC does not exist in nature; and were it by chance to issue from some natural source such as a volcano, its fabulous reactivity would ensure it a very transient existence. How, then, does MIC happen to be present so that bodies are affected by its violent chemical proclivities? In other words, MIC can cause the illness, but not itself. There needs be a cause at a higher level of generality that brings MIC into existence and deploys it in certain ways. This property of being able to set other causes into motion is what we mean by the 'efficiency' of a cause.

What 'causes' MIC is the fact of being *produced*, through the conscious alteration of nature to serve human ends – in this case, industrial ones relevant to the development of agriculture. Industry, however, does far more than produce large amounts of strange substances: it also alters the human ecology, putting some people in its way, and serving others. Chemical science will be necessary to understand how MIC affects living tissue. Industrial production, however, understands science and nature in order to bring substances such as MIC into the world, and to gather them for its uses – in this case, the manufacture of pesticides for the purposes of modern agriculture. To understand the full event, then, and not just the pathological effects on the organism, requires a grasp of the history and social relations of production, of its industrial turn, of the peculiarities of pesticide manu-facture – and in this instance, of the reasons why so deadly a substance escaped sequestration and found its way into human bodies, and if the poisoning took place in many lungs all at once, why they all happened to be there together to receive MIC's deadly embrace.

The reader will have doubtless gathered by now that I am referring to a very specific eco-catastrophic event: the release, on 4 December 1984, of 46.3 tons of methyl isocyanate from the factory run by the Union Carbide corporation, an American transnational with a pesticide manufacturing

less enforcement of regulations
env. regulations
cheap labor
lower costs

facility in Bhopal, India. The gas escaped around midnight, and so it found the inhabitants of Bhopal, great numbers of whom lived close to the factory, sleeping. It is impossible to convey in words the suffering this caused. But some results can be enumerated: an estimated 8,000 people died on the spot and as many afterwards, with over 500,000 injured, some 50,000 to 70,000 of those injuries permanent.[1] People were still dying, 15 years later, at a rate of 10–15 a month, and the ruins of the factory still deface the city and leach toxic materials into the environment.

The worst industrial accident in history, Bhopal has become synonymous for the hazards posed to human beings by the industrial process, and an emblem for the ecological crisis itself. To understand the cause of Bhopal may give a window on to the cause of the crisis, not in the sense that this is to be composed of horrendous accidents such as this, but because in Bhopal's magnitude all the elements of the crisis as a whole are concentrated.

To comprehend Bhopal, however, we need to expand our thinking from the physiological dimension to comprehend the role played by human agency, along with its ideological implications. Understanding this event, where not one but thousands of lives were mutilated, involves the judgement of competing claims and differing views of reality. Methyl isocyanate, as the active cause of bodily damage, is a mute killer without motive or interest in the outcome of its chemistry. When, however, we attempt to understand the causes of the accident at Bhopal, we need to think beyond the molecular level. For example, the element of *money* now enters the picture. It is not just the vast amounts at stake – some $3 billion in damages originally asked by the Indian government, with $470 million finally agreed to by Carbide (plus $50 million in legal fees, and $20 million offered for construction of a local hospital[2]) – but money's full power in human existence: in short, a whole social order is entailed, of power, and meaning, and the relationships between the actors of society. And now, too, we look for a kind of causation that would best comprehend these specifically human–ecological issues.

But let us be concrete, and consider what happened at Bhopal that deadly night in 1984. Essentially, the questions come down to this: what was MIC doing in Bhopal in the first place? Why was it released in such a manner? Why were the people so exposed, and why so shabbily treated? And as for the responsible agents, what were the driving forces acting on them?

To the first question the answer is that Union Carbide put it there for its purposes, that is, the corporation caused the factory to be built where and when it pleased. In a literal sense, this is an absurd statement. Union Carbide is not a person who can put anything anywhere; and the actual people who immediately caused the MIC plant to arise in Bhopal were a great mass of labourers, architects, suppliers, and so on, most of whom had no direct relation to the company but were hired by subcontractors. Yet we cannot claim that these workers built the factory except as the necessary but partial final human instrument, just as the tools in their hands were necessary but partial technological instruments. Therefore the answer to the question of what caused a factory, or any other social product, to be built would be: that which effectively organizes the social labour that went into it. And, since labour is the human faculty of making events happen, said cause, which organizes all the others, becomes efficient.

In a different kind of society, where workers controlled their productive life activity, or where, as in the original, tribal society, the whole community did the same, we would be entitled to end our account of what caused the factory to arise with citation of the people who actually constructed it. But in our kind of society that statement would be false, since under the regime of capital workers do not determine their own activity. For an understanding, therefore, of the social organization of a vast number of individual activities we would have to turn to that which commands and controls them all in production, and in this case such an agent would have to be the Union Carbide corporation, despite the fact that it is headquartered thousands of miles away and served to express the interests of individuals who need never have set foot inside India, much less Bhopal.

We may say, then, that the workers, and so on, were the instrumental causes of the factory at Bhopal, while the Union Carbide corporation was the efficient cause. That is, Carbide was the agent capable of organizing and fruitfully combining all the factors required for the production of the factory, and, once it had been built, for the manufacture, distribution and sale of the products, including MIC as an intermediary product. In any complex phenomenon, many causal processes are at work. But insofar as the phenomenon functions as a whole, we may identify an overarching, integrating kind of cause that sets the instrumental causes into motion, regulates them, and directs them toward an end – and the alteration of which would be necessary to change the phenonemon as a whole. Such is what is meant by the efficient cause.[3]

Each cause is specific for the level of effect it sets into motion. Methyl isocyanate is the efficient cause of the bodily devastation which ensues upon its inhalation, just as Union Carbide was of the factory at Bhopal. But what drives Carbide? And what of the incident of December 1984 and its social sequelae? What caused that, and how does this relate to the question of an 'efficient cause'? Here is where conflicting views of reality enter most forcefully, because so much is at stake. Carbide has not denied that Bhopal is the site of its factory or that MIC is its product – in fact it is quite proud of the fact and the role it has played in the so-called Green Revolution, which has augmented food production in nations of the South. As the company laid out in its website, 'Ironically, the plant at Bhopal had its origin in a humane goal: supplying pesticides to protect Indian agricultural production', and more generally, to enhance the '"Indianization" of industry in that country' through its 'willingness to offer expertise, readiness to comply with Indian laws, and acceptance of a gradual approach to developing Indian consumer markets. Union Carbide's investment had gained us widespread good will – or so we thought.' Insisting on the integrity of its safety standards and quality controls ('a deeply ingrained commitment … [with] stringent internal standards dating back to the 1930s'), the company is deeply distressed by having been 'recast … as an archetypal multinational villain, exploiting India's people and resources', a 'caricature [no doubt] designed to gain access to Union Carbide's financial resources'. As for the tragic incident, with respect to which 'from the first day, we had been moved by compassion and sympathy', the company had done its own investigation proving that the cause of the disaster 'was undeniably sabotage. The evidence showed that an employee at the Bhopal plant had deliberately introduced water into a methyl isocyanate storage tank. The result was the cloud of poisonous gas.' Alas, this truth has not caught on, evidently due to the Indian government's 'apparent indifference to the plight of the Bhopal victims'.

It is a coherent explanation: the disaster at Bhopal was not Union Carbide's fault, but that of a disgruntled employee, compounded by the callousness and fecklessness of the Indian government. In this universe of meaning, configured by the ever-present spectre of legal action and major financial consequences (remember the $50 million spent by the corporation to defend itself), causality equals *blame*, to be determined legally. A similar discourse prevails throughout the ecological crisis, which tends to get reduced to a series of individual acts for which blame – and financial allocations on the basis of blame – become the relevant criteria.

The discourse of blame, or fault, or legal responsibility, is essential when it comes to parcelling out a degree of justice and restitution for victims. Nor, in this instance, is it difficult to ascertain, given the fact that patient investigation has disclosed a mountain of evidence relevant to understanding the fatal night. Let me summarize, to indicate the particular dissection of this one horrific eco-disaster, and to point a way toward a wider understanding:

- Carbide never named the saboteur, nor submitted its claims to a court of law under judicial rules of evidence. It rather deduced his agency from an analysis of the structure of its plant and let the matter rest at that.[4]
- The company failed to notify the authorities of the large amounts of MIC stored at the plant. More, they had designed the plant in a way that made accidents more or less inevitable – for instance, by using carbon steel valves that corroded when exposed to acid.
- Prior to 1978, Carbide produced its pesticide Sevin without directly using MIC. It switched to the use of the deadly intermediate in order to produce more cheaply, and began manufacturing it in Bhopal in 1980. In fact, the German corporation Bayer made Sevin without MIC, in a safer – but more expensive – way.
- Local authorities urged the plant to be built in another part of Bhopal, in an industrial zone out of range of the population. Carbide refused, saying this was too expensive.
- The plant was losing money, because the demand for pesticides was down, and hence chronically overproduced MIC, which Carbide couldn't unload.
- This led to an effort to cut costs, beginning in 1982. To quote Kurzman (1987: 25), 'such cuts ... meant less stringent quality control and thus looser safety rules. A pipe leaked? Don't replace it, employees said they were told. Just patch it up. MIC workers needed more training? They could do with less [including using instruction manuals in English, which few could read]. Promotions were halted, seriously affecting employee morale and driving some of the most skilled to seek work elsewhere.' By late 1984, only six operators, rather than the original twelve, were working with MIC. The numbers of supervisory personnel also had been halved,

and there was no maintenance supervisor on the night shift. Thus indicator readings were checked every two hours rather than hourly, as required.

- In late 1981, inhalation accidents began appearing at the plant. Experts from the USA appeared and warned of a 'runaway reaction' inside an MIC storage tank. This followed upon other warnings from 1979 and 1980. Other warnings from the Indian authorities went unheeded. In October 1982 a leak of MIC caused five workers to be hospitalized.

- The local authorities had no instruments to monitor air pollution near the plant.

- When the workers at the plant, through their union, protested about the safety hazards, they were ignored. One worker who went on a 15-day hunger strike was fired.

- Although workers originally wore safety equipment, the growing slackness caused this to be jettisoned. More than 70 per cent of workers had their pay docked for refusing to deviate from the prescribed safety routines. All the while, pressure to keep making MIC as swiftly and cheaply as possible was sustained.

- The night of the accident, a leaking carbon-steel valve was discovered, which allowed water to slip into the MIC tanks. This was not repaired, as it would have taken too much time – in other words, would have been expensive.

- In addition, the alarm on the tank had not worked for four years, and there was only one manual back-up system instead of the four-stage system used in the USA. The flare tower that burned escaping gas had been out of service for more than five months, as had the vent gas scrubber. The refrigeration system installed to inhibit the volatilization of MIC was also idle, to save power costs. Nor was the steam boiler designed to help clean the pipes in active operation, for the same reason. Virtually every relevant safety instrument, from shutdown devices to monitoring tools to temperature gauges, were either in short supply, malfunctioning or designed improperly. The maintenance temperature of the MIC was kept at 20 degrees Celsius, although the manual called for a temperature of 4.5 degrees (this lower figure, needless to say, being much cooler than the average temperature of Bhopal, hence more expensive to maintain). In addition, 'Carbide's Bhopal plant was designed in such a way that, after the deadly gas leak began, the main safety system – water sprays intended to "knock down" such a leak – could not spray water high enough to reach the escaping stream of gas. In sum, the plant's safety systems had been designed negligently. Internal documents show that the company knew this prior to the disaster, but did nothing about it.'[5]

- Finally, the tank that exploded had been malfunctioning for a week. Instead of dealing with it, the plant authorities used other tanks and let this one sit, and, in effect, stew. One outcome of 'stewing', as any cook knows, is the build-up of pressure and temperature, both of which can trigger further reactions in suitable substances.

So there is no question as to who was to *blame* for the horror at Bhopal. Despite the crocodile tears and bleating protestions, Union Carbide stands revealed as precisely the 'archetypal multinational villain' it tries to deny being. Indeed, the only question remaining at this level is why the firm was not held fully accountable for its criminal negligence. However, the issue of blame, while necessary, is by no means sufficient to grasp the meaning of Bhopal, nor does it clear up the question of causation.

MIC can be held to be the efficient cause of bodily harm, as it is the destabilizing force tearing up the delicate balance of a living ecosystem. Carbide is similarly the efficient cause of the building of the factory at Bhopal. However, when it comes down to this incident, we see that Carbide is itself subjected to other forces, and that the notion of efficient causation requires that these forces be given their due. There is no mystery here: at virtually every point listed above we find that Carbide did this or that to *lower its costs;* further, that the 'this and that' had the effect of summating the risks that the monstrously dangerous MIC (itself chosen as a product in order to lower costs) would escape; and, further, that Carbide's blameworthiness consisted precisely in the callous and self-serving way in which it was prepared to put Bhopal in harm's way in order to lower costs. Its evasion of legal responsibility needs to be understood within the universe of meanings that cluster about this prime necessity, from particular legal and public relations manoeuvres to the whole international setup that makes an ancient and proud country such as India so unable to stand up for the rights of its own people.

The efficient cause here, then, would have to comprise not just the particular greed of this corporation, but the system imposing upon it the never-ending pressure to cut costs – or, from the other side, to *make profits.*

Carbide says it was in India to make pesticides. But it makes pesticides in order to make money. Being a quintessential capitalist corporation of the modern type, Union Carbide has to make money – and has to keep making it faster and faster – in order to survive in the world configured by its master, capital.

An 'accident' is merely the statistically unpredictable end of a chain of circumstances. Therefore accidents are continuous with a range of less spectacular but equivalently disruptive destabilizations. Where a sufficient number of 'cost-cuttings-in-the-name-of profit' occur, there is an accident waiting to happen. At times, this may be facilitated or triggered by human error – possibly itself a product of the same complex (an under-trained, demoralized, alienated staff, for example). However, the 'human factor' fades as an independent cause to the extent people are shaped and distorted by the profit complex. If we take Carbide's own explanation to be true for present purposes, as phoney as it actually is: suppose it was more than mere error that destroyed the plant, but a saboteur who maliciously set the gas loose that night. What shaped him, then? Was it inscrutable evil – or the product of a chain of determinants within the force field of profit-seeking? Was he one of the workers who had been 'disciplined' for refusing to cut corners, or fired for going on strike – or was he simply brutalized by a concatenation of causal factors descending upon him from a hellish human ecology? Was he psychotic – and if so, was this some kind of genetic programming, or did it, too, descend from the mass of alienations that comprised his life world, alienations in whose composition the dominant social system will be found to occupy a place at the end of every line?

It is not that other factors are missing from the network of causal processes that summate to cause an accident, or beyond that, the ecological crisis itself. On the contrary, they must be present, inasmuch as complex events are overdetermined. But they are present as scattered individualities, while through and around them, a great force field shapes and combines them into the effective events that move the world. The more globally and in terms of the whole we regard these things, the less we think in terms of individual blame or look for the 'accidents' that disrupt what is otherwise to be construed as a rational process. Now we inquire whether the process is rational in the first place, and whether or not, in this light, 'accidents are waiting to happen'. We also come to ask the larger question of whether the *normal* and non-accidental functioning of the system is in itself ecodestructive

– in which case it is the system that continually generates insults to ecologies of one kind or another and has to be transformed. An attention limited to the particular contours of the individual event loses track of that larger pattern, of the merits of pesticides themselves, and more generally, the Green Revolution of which they comprise an essential part,[6] along with the never-ending ordeal to which the nations of the South, such as India, are subjected in the world system.

Then there was the payoff. On the very day that the Indian government backed away and agreed not to prosecute Carbide any further, as if by a miracle the company's stock went up by $2 a share on the New York stock exchange. This seemingly small figure takes its significance from the fact that the settlement of $470 million cost Carbide's shareholders only $0.43 a share. Therefore those who held Carbide stocks were, so to speak, richer by $1.57 a share after the company 'suffered' the consequences of causing a nightmare to descend upon the people of Bhopal.

But why did the price of Carbide stock go up? The answer is brutally revealing: because the company proved – in this first large-scale industrial accident case affecting a transnational corporation operating in the so called 'Third World,' or South – that it *could get away with murder*, now and in the future. Wall Street knew then that business could go forward, and that the orderly extraction of profits from the South had become more secure.

Wall Street – to be more exact 'finance capital' – is the command and control centre of the system. The little numbers that flicker by on its tapes are common reductions of the potential for capital expansion as deployed over the manifold energic points of the dominant order. In this way, the individual factories and the managerial decisions affecting them are made in the light of a larger and more comprehensive entity, a gigantic force field that polarizes every event within its range of influence, even as it continually seeks to expand that range. This is how the rules of the game are played out. It also follow that the individual motives of Carbide's executives are meaningless except as public relations material. Ward Morehouse has written in regard to this event: 'Had [Carbide's management] been genuinely forthcoming and made truly disinterested offers of help on a scale appropriate to the magnitude of the disaster, they would almost certainly have been confronted with suits by shareholders seeking to hold the management accountable for mishandling company funds.'[7]

Thus it was capital that constrained Carbide. But there is another side, which makes this an 'if pigs had wings they would fly' type of argument. People who are genuinely forthcoming and disinterestedly helpful do not become managers of large capitalist firms. The tender-hearted are pushed off far down the ladder on which one ascends to such positions of power. For capital shapes as well as selects the kinds of people who create these events.

The story of Bhopal and its corporate miscreant continues. Carbide got out of the pesticide business, but on 7 February 2001 merged with the Dow Chemical company, which does make pesticides – and did make Agent Orange for use during the Vietnam war. The new chemical colossus operates in 168 countries and pulls in more than US$24 billion in revenue. The president and chief executive of Dow stated that the merger should save at least US$500 million annually, though regrettably 2,000 jobs would be lost as well. None of the men at individual fault for Bhopal has ever been brought to justice, nor, I think, will they be in their lifetime.

The Mystery of Growth Revealed

The 'giant force field' is a metaphor for capital, that ubiquitous, all-powerful and greatly misunderstood dynamo that drives our society. The established view sees capital as a rational factor of investment, a way of using money to fruitfully bring together the various features of economic activity. For Karl Marx, capital was a 'werewolf' and a 'vampire', ravenously consuming labour and mutilating the labourer. Both notions are true, and the second one, applied to nature as well as labour, accounts for the ecological crisis in all essential features. From the standpoint of the ecological crisis, corporations such as Union Carbide are the soldiers of capital, and institutions at a higher level in the system, like stock markets, the IMF and the Federal Reserve Bank, the Department of the Treasury, and so on, its general staff. Once these relationships are appreciated, Bhopal is seen in clearer perspective – as an individual accident the repetition of which might be avoided if industry is careful enough, and, more essentially, as the manifestation of anti-ecological tendencies inherent to capital, which will have their day one way or another so long as capital comes to organize social production. These latter are twofold:

self defeating

1. *Capital tends to degrade the conditions of its own production.*
2. *Capital must expand without end in order to exist.*

Grow or die

The combination makes an ever-growing ecological crisis an iron necessity so long as capital rules, no matter what measures are taken to tidy up one corner or another.   parasitic

We need to examine why we talk of capital as though it has a life of its own, which rapidly surpasses its rational function and consumes ecosystems in order to grow cancerously. Capital is not in itself a living organism, needless to say. It is rather a kind of relationship like that set up by a cancer-causing virus that invades living human beings, forces them to violate ecological integrity, sets up self-replicating structures and polarizes the giant force field. It is humans living as capital, people who become capital's *personifications*, who destroy ecosystems.

The Faustian bargain that gave rise to this way of being arose through the discovery that fabulous wealth could be achieved by making money first of all, and things through the making of money. Those who do not know yet that capitalist production is for profit and not use can learn it right away from watching Wall Street discipline corporations that fail to measure up to standards of profitability. Capitalists celebrate the restless dynamism that these standards enforce, with its drive for innovation, efficiency and new markets. They fail to recognize – because a kind of failure of recognition is built into their being – that what looks like resourcefulness and resilience from one side becomes on the other an addiction and a treadmill to oblivion.

Commodities appeared at the dawn of economic activity, and commodity production became generalized with the advent of capital. The germ of capital is inserted into each commodity, and can be released only through exchange, and with this, the conversion of what is desirable into money. To employ a formalism employed by Marx, which we shall find helpful to express our ideas as we proceed, every commodity is a conjunction of a 'use-value' and an 'exchange-value'.[8] Use-value signifies the commodity's place in the ever-developing manifold of human needs and wants, while exchange-value represents its 'commodity-being', that is, its exchangeability, an abstraction that can be expressed only in quantitative terms, and as money. Broadly speaking, capital represents that regime in which exchange-value predominates over use-value in the production of commodities – and the problem with capital is that, once installed, this process becomes self-perpetuating and expanding.

air –
Low exchange value

pet-
Rock

If production be for profit – that is, for the expansion of the money-value invested in it – then prices must be kept as high as possible and costs as low as possible. As prices will tend to be held down by the competition endemic to the system, in practice, cutting costs becomes a paramount concern of capitalists. But costs of what? Clearly, of what enters into the production of commodities. Much of this can be expressed in terms of other commodities – for example, fuel, machinery, building materials, and so on, and, crucially, the labour-power sold by workers for wages at the heart of the capitalist system. However, if the same analysis is done upon the latter, at some point we arrive at entities that are not produced as commodities, yet are treated as such in the great market that defines capitalism. These are the above-mentioned 'conditions of production', and they include publicly produced facilities, i.e., *infrastructure*, the *workers* themselves, and, last but certainly not least, *nature* – even if this nature already expresses, as it almost always does, the hand of prior human activity.

The process is a manifestation of the ascendancy of exchange-value over use-value, and entails a twofold degradation. In the first place, we have the commodification of nature, which includes human beings, and their bodies. However, nature, as we shall examine further in Part II, simply does not work in this way. No matter what capital's ideologues say, the actual laws of nature never include monetization; they exist, rather, in the context of ecosystems whose internal relations are violated by conversion to the money-form. Thus the ceaseless rendering into commodities, with its monetization and exchange, breaks down the specificity and intricacy of ecosystems. To this is added the devaluation, or basic lack of caring, which attends what is left over and unprofitable. Here arise the so-called 'externalities' that become the repositories of pollution. To the extent to which the capital relation, with its unrelenting competitive drive to realize profit, prevails, it is a certainty that the conditions of production at some point or other will be degraded, which is to say that natural ecosystems will be destabilized and broken apart. As James O'Connor has demonstrated in his pioneering studies of this phenomenon, this degradation will have a contradictory effect on profitability itself (the 'Second Contradiction of Capital'), either directly, by so fouling the natural ground of production that it breaks down, or indirectly, as in the case that regulatory measures, being forced to pay for the health care of workers, and so on, re-internalizes the costs that had been expelled into the environment.[9] In a case such as Bhopal, numerous insults of this kind interacted and became the matrix of a ghastly 'accident'. For Bhopal, degradation was concentrated in one setting, while the ecological

Exploation

crisis as a whole may be regarded as its occurrence in a less concentrated but vastly more extended field, so that the disaster is now played out more slowly and on a planetary scale.

It will surely be rejoined to this that a great many countervailing techniques are continually introduced to blunt or even profit from the degradation of conditions of production – for example, pollution-control devices, making commodities of pollutants, and so on. To some degree these are bound to be effective. Indeed, if the overall system were in equilibrium, then the effects of the Second Contradiction could be contained, and we would not be able to extrapolate from it to the ecological crisis. But this brings us to the other great problem with capital, namely, that confinement of any sort is anathema to it.

Accumulation

In this respect, Marx wrote in his *Grundrisse*:

> However, as representative of the general form of wealth – money – capital is the endless and limitless drive to go beyond its limiting barrier. Every boundary is and has to be a barrier for it. Else it would cease to be capital – money as self-reproductive. If ever it perceived a certain boundary not as a barrier, but became comfortable within it as a boundary, it would have declined from exchange value to use value, from the general form of wealth to the specific, substantial mode of the same. Capital as such creates a specific surplus value because it cannot create an infinite one all at once; but it is the constant movement to create more of the same. The quantitative boundary of the surplus value appears to it as a mere natural barrier, as a necessity which it constantly tries to violate and beyond which it constantly seeks to go.[10]

The depth of Marx's insight should be appreciated: capital is quantitative in its core, and imposes the regime of quantity upon the world: this is a 'necessity' for capital. But capital is equivalently *intolerant* of necessity; it constantly seeks to go beyond the limits that it itself has imposed, and so can neither rest nor find equilibrium: it is irremediably self-contradictory. Every quantitative increase becomes a new boundary, which is immediately transformed into a new barrier. The boundary/barrier ensemble then becomes the site of new value and the potential for new capital formation,

Holdss
– Not is dead –

which then becomes another boundary/barrier, and so forth and on into infinity – at least in the logical schemata of capital. Small wonder that the society formed on the basis of producing for the sake of capital before all else is restlessly dynamic, that it introduces new forms of wealth, and continually makes the past forms obsolete, that it is obsessed with change and acquisition – and that it is a disaster for ecologies.

Since each boundary/barrier is a site for commodity formation, this becomes the prescription for the 'generalized commodity production' that is one of capital's hallmarks. Needless to say, the process does not occur neatly, as though capitalists sat around and selected their spots for new commodities. To some degree, of course, they do – imagine network executives trying to develop new sitcoms, or the auto manufacturers a new line of four-wheel drives. But the more interesting examples are those where the unplanned and more or less spontaneous actions of the system create novel conjunctures, which are then seized upon as new places for profitable activity. The prospects, dear to capitalists, of making businesses out of trading pollution credits or the pharmaceutical industry's search for new antibiotics to meet the new diseases unleashed by ecological destabilization itself are examples of this kind. The constant creation of anxieties and needs by the restless movement of the system is constantly funnelled into the circuits of new commodity activity. Does capitalism create an isolated, anxiety-ridden self whose survival requires being placed upon a market? Well, then, capital will also step in to create commodities to service this tensely narcissistic state of being – articles of fashion and image, with technologies to service these and a cultural apparatus to go along – in the case of fashion, say, a whole range of magazines, photographic studios, advertising agencies, public relations firms, psychotherapies, etc, etc.

Capital's regime of profitability is one of permanent instability and restlessness. Even in the ruling class, no one 'rules' without perpetually proving himself, and the CEO must not only produce profit but more importantly, increase the rate of profit, or be swiftly tossed aside. One cannot rest content with the given, but must constantly try to expand it. Growth is simply equated with survival as a capitalist, for anyone who fails to grow will simply disappear, his assets acquired by another. No matter how much one has, one never really has anything: everything must be proved to exist anew the next day. Hence that well-known trait of the bourgeoisie: no matter how rich they become, they always need to become richer. All the fabulous 'growth' of the last decade has not, by one iota, reduced the drive to accumulate still more, nor can it ever so long as capital reigns. The sense of having and possessing dominates all others, precisely because its reality can never be secured. Strictly speaking, individuals can step off this wheel – make their fortune and retire to raise polo ponies or cabbages. But they cease thereby being *personifications* of capital, and others immediately step forward to take their role.

Money – the form of capitalist value – abstracts and dissolves all relationships, replacing them with the cash nexus. This sets going the ruthless competitiveness inherent to capital, since if money is the only true bond, then there are no true bonds at all, and universal envy, suspicion and mistrust reign. The 'system works', for the competition so induced becomes the motor forcing eternal growth as the price of survival. And because money can effortlessly expand even as its material substrate is bound by the laws of nature, the great pools of capital emerging from the ceaseless transactions provide the benchmark of growth, and as they gather, press yet further for expansion. The pressure of capitalist growth is therefore *exponential*, that is, it becomes proportional to the total magnitude of the accumulated capital pressing for discharge. As Marx put it in another passage from the same work:

> The barrier appears as an accident which has to be conquered. This is apparent on even the most superficial inspection. If capital increases from 100 to 1,000, then 1,000 is now the point of departure, from which the increase has to begin; the tenfold multiplication; profit and interest themselves become capital in turn. *What appeared as surplus value now appears as simple presupposition, etc,* as included in *its simple composition.*[11]

If we unpack this highly compressed passage (the *Grundrisse* was written as a notebook for Marx's own study, and not for an outside reader), Marx is saying that in the regime of capital any original profit is only a starting point. If the same process be carried forward through a second cycle, the same expansionary force will be observed, operating however from the higher level. If 10 of some monetary unit goes to 100 the first time around, there will be a tendency for it to go to 1,000 the second time around. Therefore capitalist production is not only expansionary (since money has to be thrown into circulation for it to become capital, and a surplus value needs to be gained), but exponentially so. As Marx commented in *Capital*:

The repetition or renewal of the act of selling in order to buy [i.e., C–M–C'] finds its measure and its goal ... in a final purpose which lies outside it, namely consumption, the satisfaction of definite needs. But in buying in order to sell [i.e., M–C–M'][12] on the contrary, the end and the beginning are the same, money or exchange-value, and this very fact makes the movement an endless one.

For more money is just money with a larger number written upon it, and so

At the end of the movement, money emerges once again as the starting point. Therefore the final result of each separate cycle, in which a purchase and consequent sale are completed, forms of itself the starting point for a new cycle. The simple circulation of commodities – selling in order to buy – is a means to a goal which lies outside circulation, namely the appropriation of use-values, the satisfaction of needs. As against this, the circulation of money as capital is an end in itself, for the valorization of value only takes place within this constantly renewed movement. The movement of capital is therefore limitless.[13]

Capital's disregard for boundaries except as barriers to be surpassed arises from this fundamental property. Every boundary in the real world is useless to capital unless it can be monetized and placed into an M–C–M' circuit, at the end of which another circuit must begin. Any delay or retardation in the flow is registered as a mortal threat. If a boundary, or a feedback process, or an ecological warning signal is produced by one investment cycle, this becomes the starting point for another. It is even a bit misleading to talk of boundaries as merely barriers. They are, inasmuch as capital needs to keep in motion and so must refuse all boundedness. But the barrier–boundary is also the point of investment, commodification and exchange. Therefore capital needs and seeks barrier–boundaries as sites of growth. It is like the oyster's building of a pearl about a grain of sand, but where the life-activity of molluscs and other creatures who live in ecosystems is defined by exquisite internal regulation, capital's growing is like a reckless addiction, which tends to possess individuals in direct proportion to their position in the capitalist command structure. Of course, a degree of prudent calculation is *de rigueur* as well. But this is not internal to the process of accumulation; it is rather applied from without, as a way of enabling the passion. Thus all reforms are installed to permit growth to proceed unchecked.

In case anyone should doubt this enthralment, consider the following, drawn from the early part of 1997, a moment of heady expansion for the world-system. This news was greeted as though a sign of the Second Coming. In a major article in the *Wall Street Journal* of 13 March 1997, the author G. Pascal Zachary sampled the opinion of experts from the highest levels of the economic system, and found them unanimous in declaring permanent victory for capital on a global scale (the only exception was the doubting George Soros, who thought the boom 'may last a century'). 'The positive side is spectacular,' said Harvard economist Jeffrey Sachs; while Domingo Cavallo, architect of Argentina's neoliberal restructuring, added that 'We've entered a golden age.' The phrase, 'golden age' also expressed the sentiments of the new UN Secretary-General Kofi Annan;[14] while Joseph Stiglitz, the World Bank's chief economist, added that with a 'reproducible' world growth rate of 4 per cent predicted over the next twenty years, 'economic growth will reach historic levels that will, in turn, open up a new frontier for industrialized countries'.

In the same newspaper of 28 April, Renato Ruggiero, then director of the World Trade Organization, gave his perspective on the good news. World trade is what has brought us this blessing, increasing by a factor of 15 in the last four decades. Simple algebra gives a clearer notion of the wonder of 4 per cent growth over two decades, by translating it into a *doubling* of the production of goods and services. Around 2020, then, roughly two of everything now produced will be produced: twice as many cars, twice as many jet planes, twice as much insecticide, twice as much material wealth in China and India. All this, according to the WTO leader, because of trade (the 'open economies' grew annually on the average of 4.5 per cent between 1970 and 1989; the 'closed' ones only by 0.7 per cent – and now there are scarcely any closed economies remaining) and open markets for capital; and it makes the US multinational corporations 'almost giddy'. Boeing, for example, looked forward to $1.1 trillion being spent to double the size of the jet fleet in the next 20 years, three-quarters of this coming from abroad. Four times as many escalators were being built in China as in the USA; meanwhile the world was experiencing such an expansion of consumerism that, to take but one example, Citicorp, starting from scratch in 1990, had seven million credit cardholders in Asia and two million in

Latin America by 1997. 'The potential exists for positive surprises that would drive growth even faster, such as massive sales of government assets. "On privatization, we've just scratched the surface," said Shaukat Aziz, Citicorp's chief planning officer.'[15]

Recall: in 1970, only three decades in the span of time, but an eternity so far as capital is concerned, the notion of 'limits to growth' seized the world elites, or at least the significant fraction of them who put forth the report of the same name under the authorship of the 'Club of Rome'. In little more than a generation, then, the notion of containing 'growth', which is to say, reining in capital, had been effectively driven from the collective mind of the ruling class.

The last few years have been distinctly less exhilarating from the standpoint of 'growth'; indeed, as this is being written, the economy is in the grip of a long-postponed downturn. Nevertheless, however the concrete specifics constantly change, the essential mentality and dynamics remain the same, through rich times and poor.

With respect to global warming, arguably the supreme instance of the ecological crisis, we now find a gathering realization of just how deadly the prospects are. But the chaotic world-system keeps the response lagging far behind the pace of events. Consider only the frequency and impact of violent storms. These are the equivalent, on the climatic level, of methyl isocyanate, on the physiological level, tearing through a body. Each represents the intrusion of wild energy uncontainable by ecosystemic buffering, with chaotic and devastating results. In the last few years, we have seen Hurricane Mitch, which laid waste to Honduras and Nicaragua, along with other devastating storms, all leading to deaths in the tens of thousands, which struck China, India, Mozambique and Venezuela. In the latter instance, the killer became rain-induced landslides sweeping down on shanty-towns on the lee side of a mountain next to Caracas, burying or sweeping out to sea some 20,000 poor folk who would never have been living there in a just or sane society. Each of these catastrophes, observe, is of the scale of a Bhopal, yet none is considered an event for which the industrial system is to be held responsible, because there is no accident to focus on, no Union Carbide to blame, only the dispersal of an uncountable number of ecosystemic insults, and the unpredictable yet inevitable reckoning.

We know with great precision what MIC does and how it got to where it could wreak havoc at Bhopal, whereas the evidence of storms is subject to much uncertainty. But there is something called the 'precautionary principle', according to which society is obliged to err on the side of caution where significant evidence exists of an ecologically disruptive relationship without a final proof (which, given the nature of such events, may never transpire). It is clear that sufficient evidence exists as to the presence of greater quantities of trapped solar energy, and the mounting frequency of devastating storms.[16] After all, what are storms but the coming down of energy beyond the capacity of the atmosphere to bind? Yet in proportion to the menace, the world-system's response is as negligent as was Carbide's at Bhopal.[17]

The explanation lies within the logic of accumulation. It is not just the obvious fact that any serious grappling with greenhouse gas production will spell trouble for profit in the short and medium run that comprises the horizon of capital's vision. No, there is another motive right here in the present. And that is a realization that global warming, here and now, is *good for business*. In France, for example, the terrible storms of 1999 not only turned out to have little macro-economic impact; they are said to be, according to Denis Kessler, president of the French Insurance Companies' Federation, 'a rather good thing for GDP'. This is because the damages caused by such events for a highly developed country are relatively low – no shanty-towns in France, plenty of emergency equipment, and so on– and exceeded in monetary value by the funds spent on repairs, which tends to renovate damaged property in a more modern manner. As the author of the article, Hervé Kempf, comments:

> It looks as though the world's economic decision-makers have decided to do nothing about climate change on the basis that if no change happens, we shall take advantage of a form of growth that continues to intensify the greenhouse effect; and if it does happen, we shall be able to protect ourselves from it – and it may even have a favourable effect on the global economy.[18]

The 'we' here refers not to humanity as a whole, but to the inhabitants of the 'developed' nations – to be more exact, their privileged classes. As for the others, well, let them eat mud. Like the untold numbers of birds and other animals wasted by these storms, the fate of the poor is irrelevant to the great march of accumulation, and so becomes a non-issue. Thus Kempf comments: 'Venezuela's flood victims counted for little economically in so far as the country's oil output remained unaffected.' Consequently their fate, like that of billions of others, is discounted.

Such thinking is both a manifestation of the ever-widening gap between the world's rich and poor, and a cause of that gap's widening. It is also a prime example of the kind of reasoning specific to capital, which employs purely quantitative indices such as gross domestic product (GDP) because they are convenient indices of accumulation. Scarcely a critic of the ecological crisis has refrained from commenting upon the stupid brutality of this number, which reduces the living and the dead alike to the common denominator of what can be extracted from their commodification. It is necessary, though, to see thinking in terms of GDP as no mere error, but the actual logic of the reigning power; and all cries for revising it to reflect human and ecological judgements are simply risible so long as that power remains in place.

But it still is an error, and a huge, future-threatening one. In the reduction of the world to value, and the economy to GDP, there occurs both an abstraction and a narrowing. All things seen through the lens of capital become commodities whose concrete sensuous ecological links are now merely quantities. Hence they drift apart and are separated. The bourgeois calculator of global warming reduces the subject to a series of storms and their effect on profits. 'Aha!' he says, 'we're still making money,' then closes his books and narrows his vision, until he sees the world, in Blake's term, 'thro' narrow chinks' in a prison-house of the mind, and forgets that global warming is a process at the level of the whole, all ecosystems engaged and mutually interacting. While he counts his money and contentedly spews forth his greenhouse gas, events elsewhere take their course. Capital wants boundaries dissolved strictly according to its logic of endless accumulation, but there are other boundaries whose dissolution is not at all to its taste. The polar ice cap melts, and oceanic currents are transformed. And then, like a colossal Bhopal, all these little negligences may come together some day into a very nasty surprise. Perhaps one day, the French bourgeoisie may wake up to find that the Gulf Stream no longer flows by their fair country, but dissipates its warmth into an undifferentiated sea. And what will that do to the GDP?

We have paraphrased the queen with our 'let them eat mud', and may conclude this passage with the prescient words of the king, to be interpreted literally as well as metaphorically: 'Après moi, le deluge.'

Notes

1. Estimated deaths range from 2,000 to 20,000. This figure is drawn from Kurzman 1987: 130–3. For further summaries of evidence, see Montague 1996; also the website www.corporatewatch.org/bhopal/.

2. Montague: 'After all the lawyers and Indian government officials had taken their fees and bribes, the average claimant received about $300, which, for most victims, was not enough to pay their medical bills.'

3. The notion derives from Aristotle's *Metaphysics*, where the efficient cause is one of four elemental causes, the others being the formal essence (in Plato's meaning) of a thing, the ultimate material nature of that thing, and, third, the final cause, or goal, toward which a thing is headed. The efficient cause is, by contrast, the source of a thing's motion, which may or may not be external to the thing in question. Much of this exceedingly difficult text (actually a series of lecture notes) is given over to critique of Plato and other philosophers for not taking the efficient cause into account. Aristotle 1947: 238–96.

4. This passage, and most of the evidence in this section, are drawn from Kurzman 1987. However, the next item is taken from testimony given at the end of 1999, in the ongoing civil action suits in India. Kurzman, it may be added, approached his work as a journalist with no axe to grind, as revealed in a number of sympathetic passages about Carbide's executive leadership.

5. Montague 1996, citing Lepkowski 1994.

6. Shiva 1991. A great many people now reject the world view of Carbide as to the merits of this transformation, which among other things has driven many rural Indians to choose pesticides as a means of suicide.

7. Morehouse 1993: 487, quoted in Montague 1996.

8. These terms appear on the first page of Volume One of Marx's *Capital*, an indication of how important he thought them.

9. Drawn together in O'Connor 1998. The 'First Contradiction' is that of the classical 'realization crisis', where cutting worker's wages makes it more difficult to purchase the commodities they produce.

10. Marx 1973: 334. Martin Nicolaus, translator and editor, draws a connection between this passage and Hegel's *Science of Logic* (Hegel 1969).

11. Marx 1973: 335, italics in original.

12. In the first cycle, the simple circulation of commodities, C is a commodity sold for a given sum of money, M, which is then exchanged for another commodity of equivalent value, C'. In the second cycle, which is of capital, a sum of money, M, is advanced into circulation to pay for a commodity, C, which is then sold for a different sum of money, M'. If M' is greater than M, the prime desideratum of the capitalist, we have M'–M, or ΔM, as the 'surplus value'. Marx uses the term 'value' as synonymous with exchange-value.

13. Marx 1967a: 252–3.

14. In an end-of-the-millennium survey by the BBC of who was the greatest man of the last 1,000 years, the secretary-general offered Adam Smith as his first choice. Can we imagine Dag Hammarskjöld or U Thant doing the same? Annan was instead rewarded for his unquestioning loyalty to transnational capital.

15. Zachary 1997; Ruggiero 1997. See Chapter 8 for more on Stiglitz, who has been cast as a kind of hero because he was sacked for dissenting from World Bank policies. Admirable this may have been, yet here he reveals a characteristically insane blindness to the implications of growth.

16. According to the National Oceanic and Atmospheric Administration, the ten most costly disasters in the history of the USA, including four hurricanes, have all happened in the 1990s. Taub 2000: D10.

17. The news that the North Pole had turned to water in August 2000 – for the first time in *50 million years* – was greeted with yawns and derision by ruling elites. An op-ed in the *Wall Street Journal* opined 'So what?' in its headline, pretty much representative. We cannot pursue this question here, but there is ample reason to believe that the Kyoto Protocols themselves fall far short of what is needed to contain global warming.

18. Kempf 2000: 30.

4 Capitalism

Capital's responsibility for the ecological crisis can be shown empirically, by tracking down ecosystemic breakdowns to the actions of corporations and/ or governmental agencies under the influence of capital's force field. Or it can be deduced from the combined tendencies to degrade conditions of production (the Second Contradiction), on the one hand, and, on the other, the cancerous imperative to expand. Although the Second Contradiction may be offset in individual circumstances by recycling, pollution control, the trading of credits and the like, the imperative to expand continually erodes the edges of ecologies along an ever-lengthening perimeter, over-coming or displacing recuperative efforts and accelerating a cascade of destabilization. On occasion, the force of capital expansion can be seen directly – as when President George W. Bush abruptly reversed his pledge to trim emissions of CO_2 in March 2001, the day after the stock market went into free-fall and in the context of a gathering crisis of accumulation. More broadly, it operates through a host of intermediaries embedded within the gigantic machine for accumulation that is capitalist society.

We need to take a closer look at how this society works on the ground. Too much is at stake to close the argument with a demonstration of abstract laws. Capital is no automatic mechanism, and the laws it obeys, being mediated by consciousness, are no more than tendencies. When we say 'capital does this' or that, we mean that certain human actions are carried out under the auspices of capital. We need to learn, then, as much as we can about just what these actions are and how they can be changed.

Capital originates with the exploitation of labour, and takes shape as this is subjected to the peculiar forces of money. Its nucleus is the abstraction of human transformative power into labour-power for sale on the market. The nascent capitalist economy was fostered by the feudal state, then took over that state (often through revolution), centring it about capital accumulation.

With this, the capitalist mode of production was installed as such – after which capital began to convert society into its image and created the conditions for the ecological crisis. The giant corporations we rightly identify as ecological destroyers are not the whole of capital, but only its prime economic instruments. Capital acts through the corporation, therefore, but also across society and within the human spirit.

Broadly speaking, this has taken place in three dimensions – existentially, temporally and institutionally. In other words, people increasingly live their lives under the terms of capital; as they do so, the temporal pace of their life accelerates; finally, they live in a world where institutions are in place to secure this across an ever-expanding terrain: the world of *globalization*. In this way a society, and a whole way of being, are created hostile to the integrity of ecosystems.

The Penetration of Life-worlds

The capitalist world is a colossal apparatus of production, distribution and sales, perfused with commodities. The average Wal-Mart stocks 100,000 separate items (with 600,000 available through its website) and, as a drive through America bitterly confirms, Wal-Marts – some 2,500 as of early 2000, with 100 million shoppers a week – spring up everywhere along the roadsides like gigantic toadstools, destroying the integrity of towns and feeding from their decay.[1] There is much more to this than the peddling of mere objects. As capital penetrates society, and as a condition for capital to penetrate society, the entire structure of life is altered.

Each creature inhabits a 'life-world,' that portion of the universe that is dwelt in, or experienced.[2] The life-world is, so to speak, what an ecosystem looks like from the standpoint of individual beings within it. The use-values that represent the utility of commodities are therefore inserted into life-worlds, the point of insertion being registered subjectively as a want or desire, and objectively as a set of needs. As capital penetrates life-worlds, it alters them in ways that foster its accumulation, chiefly by introducing a sense of dissatisfaction or lack – so that it can truly be said that happiness is forbidden under capitalism, being replaced by sensation and craving. In this way, children develop such a craving for caffeine-laced, sugar-loaded or artificially sweetened soft drinks that it may be said that they positively *need* them (in that their behaviour disintegrates without such intake); or grown-ups develop a similar need for giant sports-utility vehicles, or find gas-driven leaf-blowers indispensible for the conduct of life, or are shaped to take life passively from the TV screen, or see the shopping malls and their endless parking lots as the 'natural' setting of society.

Note a twofold alteration. The commodities so introduced, say, the four-wheel drives, are both ecodestructive and profitable; and the people who use and desire them are, because of their changed needs, themselves changed in an 'anti-ecological' direction, that is, they become complicit in the ecological crisis and unable to take action against it. In contrast to an 'environmental' point of view, directed to what is located outside us, the ecological perspective includes not just external nature, but society as well, and especially all aspects of life that have a 'nature-like' component, such as tradition, or community, or, most generally, the past. All these are to be torn up so that accumulation can proceed. Hence capital's relentlessly forward-looking attitude, and its iron lock on the logic of modernity.

I first became aware of this process before I had any coherent realization of what capital meant, during a tropical medicine elective taken in 1961 in the country of Suriname, freshly broken from Dutch colonialism yet very much still in the Western orbit.[3] The experience entailed a range of exposures: to the capital city, Paramaribo, to smaller outlying towns, and finally into the great equatorial rain forest for a three-week trip by dugout canoe escorted by native guides. I had the chance to see at first hand the tribal way of life in an as yet relatively preserved rainforest ecosystem, and also something of Third World urbanization. The reader will not be surprised to learn of my preference for the former and repulsion from the latter. I had become subject to an old Western desire: what Melville or Humboldt must have felt when they encountered lands such as these. I travelled enthralled by the natural grandeur, and equally by the vibrant, dignified cultures I encountered along the river bank, the villages bright and clean, and brilliantly decorated with indigenous art. All of life was ceremonial, suffused with music and dance, festive and, so it seemed, whole. One could have called the riverine village an integral human ecosystem were the term in circulation in 1961. By comparison, the dusty and dreary town, under sway of the aluminum company, with barracks for homes, and the White Man's culture at every turn, was as alienating a spot as I had ever seen. It was appalling in itself, and especially appalling was the evident attraction of this dependent culture to the youth of the villages along the river. Although by our terms they had little, there was no sign of malnutrition or poverty as such in the village, yet the youth would leave as soon as they could. The lure of cash for work, the lure of Coca-Cola, the lure of the city beyond the small town – all this proved compelling.

My stay was too brief, and my powers of observation too weak, for more than speculation as to what destabilized the indigenous people of Suriname in 1961. Typically, what breaks up the life-world of tribal society is some encroachment upon the land. With the productive foundation of society interrupted, a complex and disintegrative chain of events is set in motion. As the 'old ways' no longer make sense, a kind of desire is set loose, and as this is now relatively shapeless and boundless, the virus of capital, with its promise of limitless wealth, is able to take hold. This is always accompanied by the mass-cultural invasion that encodes capital's logos in the form of commodities. Once 'Coca-Cola, the real thing' replaces traditional reality, the internal colonization that perfects the takeover of peripheral societies is well under way.

Expanding capitalism, like the expanding Catholicism of an earlier conquest, does not so much impose its ways *tout court* as meet the colonized life-worlds halfway. The actual result, then, is generally syncretic, with a considerable persistence of indigenous forms. Aficionados of the postmodern are generally pleased with this, seeing it as an affirmation of 'resistance', 'diversity', and the like. But they can be no more pleased than capital, which celebrates diversity as a source of new use-values.

The McDonald's corporation, with some 26,996 outlets in 119 countries as of the year 2000, offers a particularly robust example of capital's global penetration.[4] Since 1955, McDonald's has pioneered the industrialization of eating through conversion of the immemorially ritualized event of the meal into 'fast food'. As above, the old ways fail to make sense, and again, new and syncretic desires, needs and commodities are inserted. Rather than simply push beefburgers to its growing clientele in Asia and Latin America, McDonald's offers them Vegetable McNuggets in India, Teriyaki Burgers in Japan, McHuevos in Uruguay, and so on, fraying the indigenous cultural forms and weakening resistance to the culture of beef. Every trick of the trade is pressed into action – clowns, children's games, playgrounds, an advertising budget second to none. Capital gets its commodities, and the people get a pseudo-community to break up life-worlds and further cultivate new desires and needs.

Capital's invasion takes place across an ecosystemic manifold encompassing both culture and nature, with points of commodity formation arising everywhere. From this standpoint it is artificial to distinguish the symbolic and material aspects of events – although it should be observed that the industrialization of eating has definite somatic effects on a society. The magnitude of McDonald's activities in Hong Kong is suggested by the fact that 25 of its top 50 outlets in the world were located there by 1997, and that in the 20 years since it and its fellow fast food emporiums took hold, the average weight of a local teenager has risen 13 per cent, and the age of girls at menarche has dropped to 12, compared to 17 in mainland China. Hong Kong now has the second highest childhood cholesterol levels in the world, after Finland. Meanwhile, in the 28 years since McDonald's entered Japan, its 2,000 outlets (as of 1997) controlled 60 per cent of the hamburger market and the per capita fat intake tripled.[5] These effects parallel those in America and across the world, which has seen an unprecedented increase in both obesity and hunger, to the point where the numbers of overweight and starving people are roughly equivalent.[6] This is, to repeat, the *normal* working of the system, highly praised and emulated, and not the result of accidents such as Bhopal. Such figures do not enter the ordinary 'environmental' appraisals, but they are as much part of the ecological crisis as pollution with dioxin (whose bodily accumulation, it may be added, is a direct function of how much fat is in the diet).

A similar splitting is played out in the sphere of gender. As ecosystems are broken up and rearranged under capitalism, a fraction of women in metropolitan regions attain considerable autonomy and opportunity, while conditions for the world's majority sharply deteriorate. This is evident in the high percentage of women in sweatshops around the world (where fine motor skills and patriarchally imposed docility are valued); the burgeoning sex trade industries, where numberless women have now, in the era of free trade, become actual slaves (as have innumerable others in the sweatshops); as well as the general rise of rape and spousal abuse as concomitants of a disintegrating social order, so far gone that a recent UNICEF report indicates that nearly half the world's women come under attack by those closest to them.[7]

As capital penetrates, its disintegrating effects on ecologies are shown most dramatically at boundaries. That is why instruments like the North American Free Trade Agreement (NAFTA) have been such disasters for the border towns along the US–Mexican border. The environmental pollution has been well documented,[8] but that affecting human ecosystems, especially those incorporating gender, are less well known, and can be illustrated by an example from one of the largest cities along the border.

The city of Juárez, Mexico, across from El Paso, seems simply tossed over the desert. There shouldn't be concentrations of people in these places, and there wouldn't be, were they not so close to the largest markets on earth. But the people arrive, wave after wave from the south, living in shanty-towns or *colonias*, and seeking a living in the *maquiladoras*, or assembly factories, set up to take advantage of the opportunities provided by NAFTA. Many of the workers are young, 17 and under, and most are women – some 60 per cent of the 170,000 *maquiladora* workers in Juárez, who earn $20–25 for a six-day week where the cost of living is at least 90 per cent that of the USA, and the turnover rate is over 100 per cent a year.

A fair guess says 2 million people inhabit Juárez, great numbers subsisting in cardboard or corrugated metal shacks, on the 1,100 miles of dirt road within the city, with hijacked electricity, water bought from trucks (the city is scheduled to run out of water in about five years) and no sewers – often within feet of the other country from which the managers of their *maquiladoras* drive over in their Lexuses each morning. Frederick Engels, whose documentation of the working class of Manchester, England, in 1844, created the first awareness of proletarian life under industrial capitalism, would recognize the poverty of Juárez, for all its differences in terrain, weather and culture. However, Engels would almost certainly be startled by the degree of the rootlessness of the city – even though rootlessness was also a feature of the Manchester workers – as well as by its violence, although violence, too, was certainly a feature of mid-nineteenth-century Manchester, as it would be in any rapidly transforming society.

But Juárez is something else. In the words of a local vendor, 'Even the devil is scared of living here.' As Charles Bowden puts it in his powerful witness to hell on the border:

> Juárez is different [from other, equivalently impoverished places] in a way that tables of wages and economic studies cannot capture: in Juárez you cannot sustain hope … We tell ourselves that there are gangs and murders in American [*sic*] cities. This is true, but it does not deal with the reality of Juárez. We are not talking about darkness on the edge of town or a bad neighborhood. We are talking about an entire city woven out of violence.[9]

The fabric is made from certain elements unknown to nineteenth-century capitalist society: decay of religion, narco-trafficking, promiscuously available assault weapons, gangs (an estimated 250 in Juárez) who are a law unto themselves, and, in the case of places such as Juárez, the breaking up of moral systems that comes from having a superpower suck a society's blood with instruments such as NAFTA and the *maquiladora*. There is a nihilism that brings out the predatory remorseless killing potential in human beings bred in conditions of extreme alienation.

Just as the population of Juárez is unknown, so is the murder rate, although it is generally agreed to have at least doubled since the pre-NAFTA year of 1991. Hundreds of people simply disappear each year, but since many are just passing through and known to no one, their fate cannot be determined. Scores of others just show up as unidentifiable, badly decomposed corpses in dumpsters, or strewn about the desert. The majority of the corpses are of adolescent girls showing signs of rape and sexual mutilation. A mass sex murderer is sought – periodically, some gang or gangster is fingered and arrested – and then the finding of corpses resumes.

Debbie Nathan has identified a pattern to the killings. The wages paid by *maquiladoras* provide more than subsistence; they are also solvents through which traditional bonds of family and community break up. When these bonds patriarchally repress women, working away from home in a factory can be experienced as liberating. It is like the opera *Carmen*, a male fantasy of the workplace sexpot, here readily seized upon by powerless young women. The teenage *maquiladora* workers have been raised on a cultural diet of *telenovelas* and *fotonovelas*, endless variations on the theme of the poor but worthy girl found by a rich older man, who, after the necessary travail, wins him. In the *maquiladoras*, the elements of this narrative are laid out and fully eroticized. Often dressed to the nines under their chaste smocks, female workers vie for the attentions of the male supervisors, who flirt with them, ask them for dates and set going a dense network of intrigue. The process is continued into beauty contests and swimsuit competitions that transform the dreary workplace into a fairyland of romantic fulfilment.

The fantasy extends into the hours after work. In the sexually charged nightclubs to which would-be Carmens repair after dark, opportunities abound for selling the only thing of value they possess besides labour-power. Formal and informal prostitution flourishes alongside, or in place of, factory employment. To further sweeten the pot, the clubs advertise contests such as 'Most Daring Bra', or 'Wet String Bikini', with prizes that generally exceed a week's salary. In these ways, hapless women may join up with their executioners, themselves suitably positioned by the macho barbarism set going in places like Juárez, whose murder rate becomes a grim index of capitalist nihilism.[10]

Speed-up, or the Ever-decreasing Circulation Time of Capital

The relentless expansion of capital occurs primarily in terms of *time*, whose equivalence to money is much more than metaphoric. This is shown vividly in the case of 'fast-food', whose penetration we have already observed. It stands to reason that the 'fast' in this food applies to the production process, as we see from a recent lead article in the *Wall Street Journal*:

> 'HimayItakeyourorderplease?' says the drive-through-greeter at Wendy's Old-Fashioned [*sic*] Hamburgers. This greeting takes only one second – a triumphant two seconds faster than is suggested in Wendy's guidelines – and the speed of it was clocked by a high-tech timer installed this January. In just three months, the timer – which measures nearly every aspect of drive-through performance – helped knock eight seconds off the average takeout delivery time at this restaurant. But manager Ryan Tomney wants more. 'Every second,' he says, 'is business lost.'

Wendy's, whose ads promote the avuncular image of Dave Thomas as the kindly, slow-moving and somewhat befuddled boss, is the fastest of the fast-food chains ('Most chains would sell their first-born to get that speed,' says a researcher). Its success translates into augmented profit in a time when the spatial expansion of these emporia is running out of room: for every six seconds saved at the drive-through, sales increase by 1 per cent. The enhanced profitability means an emphasis on drive-through windows (growing three times as rapidly as on-premise sales), which in turn reinforces the culture of automobilia (see below) while fostering waste of all sorts. Then there are the effects on those incidentals, human beings:

> The attempt to turn drive through into a science inevitably encounters two wild-cards: employees and customers. Management at big chains insist that employees like the timer because it turns their work into a game – can I make 300 consecutive sandwiches in less than seven seconds each? But working in the new world of sensors and alarms isn't always fun.

Indeed. Mr Tomney wants to get the order-fulfilment time down to 90 seconds from the current industry-leading 150 seconds. 'The new timer will help. It emits a series of loud beeps every time an order isn't filled within 125 seconds.' This does tend to take away some of the fun of working for fast food (an industry that averages as much as 200 per cent turnover annually).

> Certainly, the seven drive-through employees demonstrate incredible concentration and effort during a recent lunch hour. The griller keeps 25 square burgers sizzling on the grill ('Not enough,' Mr Tomney says) and, within five seconds of a customer's order, places one on a bun. Once the meat hits the bun, the griller hands off to the sandwich makers, who have no more than seven seconds to complete each customized creation.
>
> Watching the operation, Mr. Tomney looks for ways to save time. The bun grabber retrieves buns from the warmer the instant she hears a customer order through her headset. But watching her wait for a customer order, Mr Tomney [notices something]. Her hands aren't positioned.
>
> 'Two hands on the bun-warmer door as the order is being placed, just like you're taking the frisk position,' her manager demonstrates, hands against the wall, legs slightly spread. [11]

A nicely chosen image, one must admit, for this vignette of today's go-go society.

The rapid growth of capital is paralleled by the rapid rate of technological change, from the mechanical technologies of the early industrial period to the electronic technologies (like the above timer) of the ill-termed 'information age', on to the biotechnologies and nano-technologies of the century now under way.[12] The commodities of this world are to capital only deposits of value, which will not be freed unless those goods are circulated, exchanged for money, and consumed, i.e., realized. For capital to 'grow', then, its realization must speed up; this routinely means a diminution of its circulation time, from the original investment at the point of production, to the speed-up – i.e., 'productivity' – of workers, to its release for the next cycle at the point of consumption.

The significance of time for capital is closely tied to its rupture from nature. Exchange-value and money have no natural ground; they can be only the abstraction of what enables one thing to be made equivalent to another. Applied to labour, this means that there is only one standard by means of which different human labours can be compared in monetary terms, namely, the time expended in production. Between this function and the equally important one of regulating its complex, technically coordinated productive apparatus, capitalism becomes the time-obsessed society. It could never have come to exist without profound shifts in temporality, from a world regulated by the complex and interrelated temporalities of ecosystems to one in which a single, uniform and linear standard is imposed upon reality and comes to rule it.[13] The desynchronization between natural time and workplace time devolves, therefore, into a disarticulation of human being and nature. We would say that capital *binds time*, yoking linear temporality and social control into a regime supervised by clocks and their personifications such as Wendy's Mr Tomney.[14] As Marx put it in a poignant lament:

> If the mere quantity of labour functions as a measure of value regardless of quality … It presupposes that labour has become equalized by the subordination of man to the machine or by the extreme division of labour; that men are effaced by their labour; that the pendulum of the clock has become as accurate a measure of the relative activity of two workers as it is of the speed of two locomotives. Therefore we should not say that one man's hour is worth another man's hour, but rather that one man during an hour is worth just as much as another man during an hour. Time is everything, man is nothing; he is at the most, time's carcase [*sic*]. Quality no longer matters. Quantity alone decides everything; hour for hour, day for day.[15]

Bound time signifies life lived compulsively, estranged from natural cycles and indifferent to ecosystems under assault. Its acceleration is played out across many frontiers:

Intensification of the sales-mentality, as everything, including the self, is reduced to commodity-form. Along with this, contempt for truth spreads throughout society. Lying is embedded in the pressure toward profitability, which depends upon persuading someone to buy something they don't really need at a price most advantageous to the seller. I recall once idly watching C-Span during the course of a Congressional hearing on some issue between telephone and cable-TV companies. One of the testifiers was asked what he did during the work day. The reasons for this question escape me, but the candour of his answer was unforgettable: 'Oh, the same thing we always do,' was the reply, 'just hustling customers.' No one took any notice; why should they? The man was only expressing the logic of the system. Within capital's order, where advertising lies so blatantly that it has to make fun of itself and turn corruption into a joke, to question the hustling of customers is like questioning the need to breathe. The Budweiser corporation seems to have done the most with this, especially with their 'Lite' beer, which turns the moral universe of alcoholism into a selling point, as in commercials where the lush professes 'I love you, man' to his father, brothers, girlfriend of the moment – anything to get the drink, an exceptionally weak and tasteless concoction, it may be added.

The class system of capital conduces to endless permutations of deceit in order to conceal its elementary injustice. As persons become personnel, synthetic bonds replace the organic ones of traditional society. The ethos here is 'managerial' and the techniques manipulative, a sign of our times backed by a vast apparatus for the engineering of human relations. As a recent article by one such technician put it in the headline, 'Show Humanity When You Show Employees the Door'. The point is that companies should 'reinforce their cultures and maintain trust even during cutbacks'. This self-evident piece of hypocrisy is no problem for the managerial mind.[16] It goes without saying that people can be made to accept this morality – were this not the case, rebellion would have broken out long ago. Managerial science not only builds on the artifice of humanity even as it reduces workers to disposable things – it drills the workers to treat customers in the same way, training them to put on happy faces, to make prolonged eye contact, and to speak to each and every customer. This lesson, also, most workers internalize only too well. As one Safeway employee said: 'It is just a pride that they have instilled in us that we should treat everybody like we would like to be treated. We talk about being positive all the time. We have classes on wiping out negativity and [having] enthusiasm.'[17] Classes in enthusiasm! Not just classes at the job, it might be added: the classes in school do the same, as do the churches and, of course, the television and movie screens.

In the speeding up of buying and selling, this leading to the reduced utilization time of commodities, or, to put a more ecologically evocative term to it, the systemic production of waste, that is, the throw-away society. Among those wasted, we would have to give first place to human beings. Whereas in traditional society virtue is accorded to all phases of the lifecycle, and includes the wisdom of the old, under capitalism, speed-up affects not only lives, but life itself. In this respect, a recent article in *New York* magazine, titled 'Washed up at 35', was revealing. The article went on to ask: 'Haven't made it yet? Feeling paranoid about the hyperambitious 23-year-old planning his IPO in the next office?' ... 'They're all worried about growing old,' says an 'anti-aging specialist' physician about his corporate clientele. 'They say that companies now demand a very youthful image, and if they can't fit in, they're not going to get the promotion. They might not even keep their job. We're talking about people in their late twenties.' In sum, 'youth has become an increasingly valuable commodity'. Now of course, this has long been the case for capitalism, with its cult of the new and its denial of aging and death. But it is important to note that the trend accelerates, along with capital itself. As a 31-year-old tycoon puts it: 'I only have three years left ... three years before I burn out ... It's a race; things are moving five, ten times faster than they used to ... you have this very short window, if you are going to brand yourself' – the assumption being that becoming a 'brand' is what life should be all about.[18]

Associated with the compression of time, we see a homogenization and compression of space; and with time and space so prepared, capital's penetration of all aspects of the life-world of individuals and communities accelerates.[19] This is not merely a function of population pressure, as its most remarkable feature is the growth of surveillance and behaviour control. The totally administered society is the *telos* of capital, and ingrained in its acceleration.

With the relentless speed-up afforded by advances in information technology, the boundary between work and domesticity is fast disappearing, along with that between body and machine. In this Brave New World, microcomputers and cell phones become bodily appendages forging semi-permanent linkages between workers and the productive system. It used to be that home was the 'haven in a heartless world'; now that polarity is, if not reversed, largely erased: the archetypal person of the near future is entirely absorbed, day and night, into a space–time continuum for the reproduction of capital.

The relentlessly increasing rate of capital turnover devolves into an ever more harried, crowded, and frantic pace of existence. Combined with the financial pressures of living the consumerist life, ordinary people have to work more and more to stay afloat. The spectre of personal indebtedness becomes the fifth Horseman of the Apocalypse – it being said that the average worker is only two paychecks away from losing home and car. More and more, people scramble, becoming increasingly obsessed with money, and slaves to the system. Thus the vaunted capitalist economy, with its endless opportunity, becomes a limitless sink for absorbing life-worlds into itself.

Not surprisingly, this condition is celebrated by the propaganda apparatus: how else could people be made to bear it? Here is a somewhat extended and delirious, but nonetheless paradigmatic specimen taken from the advertising pages of the major media, a full page ad in the *New York Times* of 26 June 1996 (A20), taken out by the American Express Company. The ad is entirely given over to the following text, which sprawls over the page:

Whoever you are, whatever you're doing, we're here to help you plan your children's education. And show you how you can still afford to retire when they get into college. We're here to help you negotiate a second mortgage, afford a second car or go on a second honeymoon. We're here to help you choose a mutual fund, a pension plan and a savings scheme. We're here to help you prepare your taxes. We're here to help you turn your idea into a business. We're here to help you turn your business tip into a vacation. We're here to help you with a few suggestions on where to go. We're here to help you with lawyers, accountants, doctors and bankers. We're here to help you with travel agents, theatrical agents and car rental agents. We're here to help you if you smash your rental car or if you smash someone else's. We're here to help you arrange a weekend in Paris for an anniversary. We're here to help you find the most romantic bistro, the most comfortable hotel. We're here to help you change your dollars into francs, your francs into sterling, your sterling into lira and your lira into any currency in the world and back again. We're here to help you climb the Odessa Steppes [*sic*] and look out from the Leaning Tower of Pisa. We're here to help you with visas, passports and other local customs. We're here to help you if your husband, your wife or your partner falls ill while abroad. We're here to help you cut your costs when you need to fill up on gas. We're here to help you splurge when you want to. We're here to help you save when you don't. We're here to help you ease your workload when it all gets too much. We're here to help you see the world. And we're here to help you pay for a change of clothes if an airline loses your baggage. We're here to help you buy a Mexican sombrero, an Indian topi or one of those Australian hats with all the corks on it. We're here to help you if someone steals your Travelers Cheques. We're here to help you see the stars in Hollywood and the moonlight over San Francisco Bay. We're here to help you see Shakespeare in the park, Mozart in the open air and basketball at the Garden. We're here to help you get seats for football, for baseball, or for the charity ball. We're here to help you help the homeless. We're here to help you settle the bill on a credit card, a charge card or a combination of them both. We're here to help you spread your payments over time or clear a bill all at once. We're even here to help you pay from cyberspace. We're here to help you see your favorite rock group. And go again the next night. And the next. And the next. We're here to help you take up a new hobby or take out an old flame. We're here to help you save for a deposit on a new house. We're here to help you renovate an old one. We're here to help you understand your $401k and perhaps show you ways to save $401K. We're here to help you plan your future. We're here to help you arrange a trip down memory lane. We're here to help you say, 'What the heck!' We're here to help you when you want to say, 'Enough's enough.' We're here to help you play more golf, more tennis, more of what you like. We're here to help you do less paperwork, less work and just plain less. We're here to help you spend more time away with your kids. We're here to help you spend more time away from everyone else's. We're here to recognize a foreign street sign, speak a foreign language and understand a foreign currency. We're here to help you out of a little local difficulty. We're here to help you whether you want to study Pavlov's dog or Schrödinger's cat. We're here to help you retire in some comfort. We're here to help you with cash at over 118,000 ATMs worldwide if you're caught short. We're here to help you at over 1700 Travel Service Offices worldwide. We're here to help you settle the bill at millions of restaurants, stores and hotels. We're here to help you 24 hours a day, seven days a week, 365 days a year. We're here to help you in every town, in every city, in every country all over the world. We're here to help you take advantage of the moment and help you plan for the next. We're here to help you do what you like, wherever you like, whenever you like. We're here to help you see more, escape more, learn more, find more and save more. We're here to help you *do more.*

The ad exhales the seemingly effortless, magical accumulation of the recent giddy epoch of speculative intoxication, and it does so by introducing a new demiurge: the omnipotent, omniscient financial corporation. The consumer just sits back and lets American Express (= money = finance capital =

capital itself) magically provide all in interminable profusion. That such a bizarre idea should arise is a manifestation of the real yet spectral power of finance. With literally trillions of dollars flitting electronically each day through capital markets, with great fortunes made through the manipulation of nothing more than numbers, with billions moving each day through gambling operations, including the supreme gamble of the stock markets, the whole world of capital takes on the character of a casino, in which the linkage between effort and outcome is ruptured, to be replaced by what is readily experienced as mere chance. It is a world in which the very materiality of existence can seem an inconvenient afterthought.

The handmaidens of chance are illusion and magic. That is why Las Vegas, rising inorganically from the desert in a jumbled mass of simulacra, becomes the city of our time. Once the province of the Mob, Vegas increasingly becomes Disneyfied into a spectacular site of fun for the whole family. There is the Sphinx and the Temple of Luxor, there is a building shaped like a bottle of Coca-Cola, here is Manhattan Island, with the Stock Exchange, the Empire State Building, the Brooklyn Bridge, even the replication of the great reading room of the Public Library. All is sign, representation, flows of value lighting up one form, now another, a city like a pinball machine.

In casino capitalism the operative word is 'more', and augmentation expresses the accumulation process in its subjective as well as objective aspect. This signifier is nicely accentuated by American Express in its ad. The only thing left off its list of goodies is restraint. To be more exact, restraint is another item for which the omnipresent corporation can be of help: restraint itself is a commodity. Time and space are now corporate servants. Capital covers all; even 'escape' is permitted so long as American Express sets the terms of escape. Thus less and more are integrated under the sign of finance. But in this calculus, less and more are not equivalent. The former, being incorporated under the sign of the dollar (for American Express – surprise! – will not do this for nothing, and if you do not pay your bill on time, they harass and fine you, then drop you like a leper and turn you over to the credit police), is subordinated to the latter, whose value consists of increasing. Less is therefore another kind of more: American Express will bring you more of less, not less of more. But more leads to still more. Thus it defines no end, only a self-reproducing expansion, the eternal growth of the capital system. A pure logic of power, insensate quantity and

expansion is offered to the sufficiently well-off. The affluent get their munifi-
cent rewards, so great that the typical member of the wealthier classes lives
better than any potentate in history. And the others get the debris.

The culture of advanced capital aims to turn society into addicts of
commodity consumption, a state 'good for business', and, *pari passu*, bad for
ecologies. The evil is doubled, with reckless consumption leading to pollution and waste, and the addiction to commodities creating a society unable
to comprehend, much less resist, the ecological crisis. Once time is bound
in capitalist production, the subtle attunement to natural rhythms required
for an ecological sensibility becomes thwarted. This allows accumulation
itself to appear as natural. People with mentalities warped by the casino
complex are simply not going to think in terms of limits and balances, or
of the mutual recognition of all beings. This helps account for the chorus
of hosannas from presumably intelligent authorities at the nightmarish
prospect of a doubling of economic product in the next 20 years.

Thus capital produces wealth without end, but also poverty, insecurity
and waste, as part of its disintegration of ecosystems. As there is no single
commodity (really, a vast system of commodities) more implicated in this
than the automobile, we might round out this section with some thoughts
about 'automobilia' and its related syndromes, including the newly discovered disease of Road Rage. Automobilia[20] is a prime example of how
rationality at the level of the part becomes irrationality at the level of the
whole. Individually, cars are far better than they were a generation ago:
they are safer, more reliable, more fuel-efficient, longer-lasting and more
comfortable to drive. In the interior of a reasonably advanced car one
encounters 'all the comforts of home': luxurious adjustable seats, cell phone,
splendid sound system, carefully controlled air – the whole package, as the
salesman says. The interior of a car projects an image of a technological
Utopia, which is convenient, since so many people spend so much time
inside them. Step outside the car, though, say on a busy road to fill up with
petrol, and the externalization of a disorder that more than compensates
for the internalized order becomes clear. A horrendous cacophony assaults
body and soul. Unlike a waterfall, even a train that organizes the human
landscape, the cars just roar on; there is no pattern, no particularized,
differentiated tale to be told. There is no integral ecology to it; it is just
endless, consuming traffic – aeons of stored sunlight converted into inertial
momentum so that individuals can go their own way in capitalist freedom.

And it is repeated in thousands and thousands of places, every day and night – carbon dioxide going into the air for global warming; other substances entering the chains that lead to photochemical smog or destruction of the ozone layer; fine particulate matter (think of the hundreds of millions of tyres grinding down against concrete) entering lungs to help create a planetary epidemic of asthma; the above-mentioned noise adding another dimension of pollution; landscapes torn up and paved over, historically breaking down the boundary between city and country while blighting both with strip malls, thickets of garish signs (for how else can people in constant motion see where to shop?) and great swooping freeways on which we hurtle like so many corpuscles in the circulation of capital – the ensemble disintegrating, as has nothing else, the fabric of human ecology.

The ruinousness of automobilia is bound up with its absolutely crucial role in the global economy – combined, to be sure, with the ensemble of densely associated industries such as oil, rubber, cement, construction, repairs, etc., etc.; and equally, from its embeddedness in the entire landscape of lived life, indeed, the very construction of the self. Deep changes in needs accompany the growth of automobilia. If one is trapped within a stifling existence, then driving away from it, even if this is just to go round and round in traffic-clogged circles (contributing, of course, to the clogging), is experienced as a release. This is one reason it is easy for the automobilious giants to spin forth their greenwashed ads that show people blithely moving, no other car in sight, across the very landscapes they are actually wrecking, or to depict ecological advances in the production of cars that are, however rational in the particular instance, simply overwhelmed by the sheer quantity of cars produced.

Looming overcapacity hangs over the automobile industries, as it does for capitalist production in general, with the ability to make some 80 million cars a year, and but 55 million or so able to be sold. Those unrealized 25 million vehicles are a giant splinter in the soul of capitalism, and the goad to endless promotion of automobilious values. Since 1970 the population of the USA has grown by some 30 per cent – while the number of licensed drivers has grown more than 60 per cent, the number of registered vehicles has nearly doubled and the total vehicle-miles driven has more than doubled.[21] Notably, the miles of road added during this period has gone up only 6 per cent. This figure is product of a set of hopeless choices: either perish in nightmarish traffic, or further destroy lived space with gargantuan roads (and eventually perish under even more traffic, which fills newly created highways like gas a vacuum). Even the relatively low figure of 6 per cent translates into major changes in certain strategic locations. One is continually astounded, for example, by the numbers of lanes added to Los Angeles freeways (at some points, eight in either direction by my recent estimate, with additional ones now being added above the roadway).[22]

As the logic of automobilia unfolds, new levels of dis-integration appear, and even people deeply acculturated into the ways of motorcars crack under the strain of contemporary vehicular life. Road Rage, a new 'mental illness', is one outcome, resulting directly or indirectly in some 28,000 traffic deaths a year caused by 'aggressive behaviour like tailgating, weaving through busy lanes, honking or screaming at other drivers, exchanges of insults and even gunfire'. This figure, though provided by chief federal highway safety official Ricardo Martinez, may be speculative; another more recent survey, however, describes 1,500 homicides a year whose instigation is directly traffic-related. According to Leon James, a psychologist from Hawaii, 'Driving and habitual road rage have become virtually inseparable. This is the age of rage mentality.' James cites as contributing factors, a 'tightly wound "controlled" personality type' for whom driving provides a release from 'normal, frustration filled existences' and gives rise to 'fantasies of omnipotence'. Observe that the personality type in question is itself an adaptation to the capitalist marketplace, while the second factor, the omnipotent release from frustration provided by driving, is a basic component of the use-value of automobiles, hammered home by car chases in movies, and the romanticization of auto advertisements. In short, a mental illness Road Rage may be, but one completely within the universe of capitalism's automobilia.[23]

Globalization, or the Establishment of a Planetary Regime to Supervise the Expansionary Process

If penetration, broadly speaking, expresses the expansion of capital culturally, and speed-up its colonization of time, space and personal life, the globalization process reflects the political/economic arrangements through which this occurs. It is the material regime whose social and ecological effects we have been documenting – and the removal of which will have to be achieved if the crisis is to be overcome. In recent years, the term has become something of a buzzword, with technical, cultural and even metaphysical connotations. Here the usage is narrower, and remains yoked to capital, in its ever-present imperial ambition. At one level, then, globalization expresses nothing new, since capital has always been a world system. But at another it is necessary to take into account that the process has in fact reached a new level, with new institutional forms, and, of course, new ecological as well as political implications.

Logically, capital can never rest, but must continue taking over humanity and nature endlessly, albeit unevenly and with constant struggle. This implies an eternally restless dynamism, which is bound to reach novel levels as boundaries are surpassed and recombine. The epoch of globalization reflects, then, the reaching of a certain worldwide stage on which the struggle is to be enacted, and the building of new instruments to operate on it. It is worth observing that for all its power, the triumph of capital still has a way to go, with considerable swathes of the world, for example peasantries, still in the grip of traditional, pre-capitalist ways of production, and others engaged in the so-called 'informal' economy, where the accumulation of capital can only partially take hold. The basic mission of the globalized system is to convert that rough half of the world's economy that still remains relatively outside the engine of accumulation into full, subaltern, participation: to achieve new, 'lean' ways of production utilizing dispersed locations, to take over the natural resources, to consume the labour power cheaply, and to keep commodities rolling so that the values embedded in them may be realized.

The phase of globalization raises important questions as to just where the centre of power resides. A common view, for example, holds that corporations now rule the world, having supplanted nation-states. But while this view calls attention to some highly important issues (it helps focus the mind, for example, to realize that General Motors holds assets worth twice those of the Philippines), the conclusion does not stand up very well to examination. For one thing, corporations are as much the object of globalization as its subject. As we have seen in the instance of Bhopal, the corporation is itself moved by the gigantic force field of capital in which it is suspended, and is given life to the extent that it fosters accumulation. And for another, states play a role in the accumulation of capital just as fundamental as that of the corporation – only imagine what would happen if the process were entirely turned over to the latter, with no governmental presence to regulate and enforce.

So the questions really are about the changing forms of capital itself, along with the changing configurations of state power. As to the former, the epoch of globalization is in part a function of the growing importance of finance capital, that is capital in its money-form. Money was always closer to the heart of what capital is than anything else, and under capitalism the role of money always tends to grow more rapidly than that of things or human beings. Broadly speaking, then, globalization manifests the boundary-breaking effects of a surplus of capital-as-money confronting sluggish human and mechanical materials and striving to set them into motion on an ever-widening scale. In consequence, more pressure is felt throughout the economy and society, and is translated into eco-destabilization along the axes outlined above.

Finance capital is both more liquid and more hungry for immediate reward than any other kind, such as capital embodied in land, machines or people. This is a property of exchangeability and reflects the fact that in its financial form, capital is much purer and closer to its essential being than in any other shape. To repeat, capital is no thing, but a relation that embeds ('invests') itself in things of one kind or another. As it achieves its money-form, then, capital comes closest to being pure relationship: it is coming into itself … but not yet there: never there, yet always moving and dragging the world along with it. For even money has inertia, more in the early years when it was tied to material things such as shells or gold, less and less as it becomes dematerialized and moved about by electronic means. Capital is eternally seeking to shed this burden; yet as it does so, becoming, in effect, less material, its effect on the material earth becomes greater. It spreads faster, farther, draws more of the world into itself, restructuring production, circulation, exchange and consumption to accommodate its ever-growing pressure, in a logic that drives toward bringing the entire earth within the orbit of the dominant economic order.

This induces new modes of organization among existing states. It generates great regional blocks across Europe, Asia and the Western Hemisphere, and creates, so to speak, an office of Hegemon, presently occupied by the USA as that state strong enough to claim the role of global gendarme. But it also brings into existence new *trans-statal* formations to regulate the now expanded ecumene, in particular, through the supervision of trade.

A threefold trans-statal structure ensues. First, trade itself achieves a scale requiring direct supervision. Second, lending institutions are needed to inject requisite funds into the dependent 'periphery' so that trade and other instruments of capital can become stimulated and circulate properly. Finally, an agency is needed to police the debts and other financial irregularities that inevitably arise under this arrangement, and to keep all the parts of the gigantic machine in good working order – a financial cop to go out in advance of the flesh-and-blood, bullet-dealing police and armies. In sum: a trade organization, a global bank and a financial enforcer – a World Trade Organization, a World Bank and an International Monetary Fund – fused into an iron triangle of transnational accumulation, and serving the transnational bourgeoisie.[24]

There are, of course, important distinctions within this apparatus, and between different elements of the state system, just as there always are with any ruling class. The USA has largely called the shots (in the Clinton administration, from the Department of the Treasury, along with the Federal Reserve Bank), and has been in essential charge since the 'American Century' began with the close of the Second World War. It was Richard Nixon who unilaterally took the world off the gold standard in 1971 and allowed exchange rates to float, which is to say, kept them pegged to the value of the dollar, the strongest currency. In this way the USA, which had become a debtor society thanks to imperial exertions in Vietnam, was allowed to remain so without penalty, indeed, became enabled to finance its expansion as the debtor in charge of the show. Not for it the 'structural adjustment programmes' applied to lesser debtor nations by the IMF, that hammer that breaks down civil society and the local economy by selling off public assets, cutting back governmental expenditures and, by orienting the economy towards export, submitting peripheral societies to the WTO-sponsored regime of trade. One law for the lion and another for the ox remains in effect. So much for the simple-minded notion that globalization signifies the decline of the nation-state. *Which* nation-state, it has to be asked: the boss and enforcer, or the subaltern and provider?

In any case, trade, being a direct expression of capital's logic, conquers all. Before the abandonment of the Bretton Woods regime of fixed exchange rates in 1971, cross-border financial flows were some $70 billion a day. Thirty years later, the figure has grown more than twentyfold, to some $1.5 trillion; while in the USA, trade has doubled its share of GDP, spurred by absolute bipartisanship of Democratic and Republican leadership. Quarrel the parties might about abortion and school vouchers, but where the free flow of capital is concerned, there is never any doubt as to what comes first.

As globalization propagates the mechanisms of accumulation around the globe, society after society is swept into the vortex of eco-destruction. Dependent and unequal development accompanied by massive debt becomes the midwife of this process. Wherever a debt is incurred, there will be pressure to discharge it by sacrificing ecological integrity. Indonesian President Suharto, a great friend of globalization, put this clearly after the imposition of a structural adjustment programme. No need to worry, said the amiable leader of the world's fourth largest nation, Indonesia could always exchange its forests for the money owed to the banks. The devastating effects of global debt on nations of the South[25] are discomfiting to global capital – indeed, Jesse Helms, like the Walrus and the Carpenter, was reduced to tears by testimony to this effect. The scandal has led to a flurry of efforts to bring the load down, with some $50 billion in debts being retired in 2000. Alas, the South owed at the time about $2.3 trillion – twenty-six times as much – nor do the terms of forgiveness free it from the wheel of accumulation. As a recent account reported, 'The IMF, the World Bank, the United States and others say that African countries must open up to the global economy – and control wasteful internal spending and inflation if debt relief is to be put to lasting use.'[26] In other words: give us your forests and cheap labour by other means, and we will forgive the debt that you can't pay under any circumstances.

Because of debt's injustice, the IMF is usually considered the heavy villain in the regime of globalization. 'Doctor Death', *Time* magazine called it recently, in an impressive sign that elite opinion is fracturing.[27] This is a reasonable assessment of the organization that has brought at least 90 poor nations under its spell. But the IMF, or 'bad cop' of globalization, should not be singled out as the source of the problem, an impression fostered in a recent essay by Joseph Stiglitz, chief economist of the World Bank from 1996 to November 1999. We met Stiglitz, you may recall, in the last chapter, joining the chorus of world economic leaders extolling the wonders of unlimited growth. Now, however, he has become something of a whistle-blower, and caused something of a sensation by an article in the *New Republic* that confirmed all the worst suspicions as to how utterly secretive, anti-democratic and ruthlessly attentive to short-term profitability is the IMF. Using as examples the handling of the Asian and Russian fiscal crises of

1997–99, Stiglitz leaves no doubt that the placing of 'profits over people', as the saying has it, has caused calamities of Holocaust proportions throughout much of the world. However, he has no intention of calling into question the capitalist system as a whole, but would have us believe that this disaster was the fault of *bad* capitalists at the IMF and the Treasury Department, and that their sin lay in not taking the advice of the World Bank, with its superior economists and good capitalists.[28]

The fantasy is widespread that somewhere a virtuous and all-knowing capitalist can be found, a fairy prince who will rescue the mismanaged global economy. As the World Bank plays 'good cop' in this scheme of things, and no doubt has some well-intentioned individuals working for it (just like any bank, or indeed, Monsanto, Chevron, etc., etc., even the IMF), many are disposed to believe that the Stiglitzs of the world can rescue us with their superior technical wisdom. When plain people go to Lourdes in search of miracle cures, the intelligentsia proclaim them superstitious. Yet many are willing to trust a profit-making Bank that puts technical intelligence in the service of accumulation, a bank that helped finance enterprises such as Union Carbide's plant in Bhopal, and put into place the ecodestructive Green Revolution for which Bhopal was built, and was a great supporter of Suharto, and has built huge fossil-fuel-consuming projects throughout the South while prating of the need to control global warming.

Those persuaded by recent propaganda to think that this leopard has changed its spots might ponder the case of Bolivia, the poorest country in South America. Having been pressured by the Bank to sell off its airline, electric utilities and national train service to private interests, the desperate nation was at length coerced into selling chunks of its water system to a consortium headed by the US construction giant, the Bechtel corporation, along with partners from Italy, Spain and four Bolivian companies – an authentic spectacle of globalization at work, commodifying an essential substratum of life. Thanks to the Bank, the investors only had to put up less than $20,000 initial capital for a water system worth millions. With Bank loans, the consortium set about diverting various rivers – no doubt with the ecological care that usually attends enterprises of this sort – and then, to cover the costs, attempted, again with the Bank's blessing, to force through price increases of as much as $20 a month – this in a country where the median working family income is $100 a month.

Major protests were the result, catapulting new layers of indigenous resistance into prominence, and forcing the Bank and Bechtel to back off. They also led to military responses that killed eight people, prompting World Bank Director James Wolfensohn to say that giving away public services inevitably leads to waste and that countries such as Bolivia need to have 'a proper system of charging'. The highly cultured former Wall Street financier claimed that the privatization of the water supply was by no means directed against the poor, even though the Bank had stated in July 1999 that 'no subsidies should be given to ameliorate the increase in water tariffs' and that all users, including the very poor, should have bills that reflect the full cost of the expansion of the local water system.

No further comment should be required, but this addendum is necessary: that Bechtel was once the province of George Shultz, secretary of state under Ronald Reagan, and that one of the soldiers firing into the protestors was identified as a man trained at the US Army's School of the Americas, an institution located in Georgia and designed to keep the Western Hemisphere in good working order. This put him into the company of the President of Bolivia, the governor of the province, and the mayor of the city – Cochabamba – where the action was centred, all of whom shared the same *alma mater*. Where, then, is the limit of the apparatus of globalization?[29]

Global capitalism exists along a continuum extending from the good grey Alan Greenspan and his Federal Reserve Bank to the most vicious Russian mobster and Colombian drug lord. All are mandated by the great force field and under its spell. In a recent stunning article, the French commentator Christian de Brie describes 'a coherent system closely linked to the expansion of modern capitalism and based on an association of three partners: governments, transnational corporations and mafias ... .[in which] financial crime is first and foremost a market, thriving and structured, ruled by supply and demand'. Each partner needs the other, even if the need must be vigorously denied. In short, an honest look at the system takes us light years from the glowing promises of neoliberalism. Contrary to the official imagery, the actual corporate culture breeds a swarm of pathogens:

> restrictive practices, cartels, abuse of dominant position, dumping, forced sales, insider dealing and speculation, takeovers and dismembering of competitors, fraudulent balance sheets, rigging of accounts and transfer prices,

the use of offshore subsidiaries and shell companies to avoid and evade tax, embezzlement of public funds, bogus contracts, corruption and back-handers, unjust enrichment and abuse of corporate assets, surveillance and spying, blackmail and betrayal, disregard for regulations on employment rights and trade union freedoms, health and safety, social security, pollution and the environment. Not to mention what goes on in the world's growing number of free zones, including those in Europe and in France, where the ordinary rule of law does not apply, especially in social, tax and financial matters.

'An incredible plunder, the full extent of which will never be known' arises, conditioned on one side by state connivance, and on the other by seepage into the underworld. Throughout the planet, but especially in the South, 'workers have to contend with thugs hired by the bosses, blackleg trade unions, strike-breakers, private police and death squads'. There is a hidden synergy, in sum, between the shady practices of corporate capital and the organized criminality of gangsterdom:

> banks and big business are keen to get their hands on the proceeds – laundered – of organised crime. Apart from the traditional activities of drugs, racketeering, kidnappings, gambling, procuring (women and children), smuggling (alcohol, tobacco, medicines), armed robbery, counterfeiting and bogus invoicing, tax evasion and misappropriation of public funds, new markets are also flourishing. These include smuggling illegal labour and refugees, computer piracy, trafficking in works of art and antiquities, in stolen cars and parts, in protected species and human organs, forgery, trafficking in arms, toxic waste and nuclear products, etc.

Occasionally a sign of this appears in some scandal over campaign contributions, in the washing ashore of illegal immigrants from China, or of a submarine purchased by the Russian mafia from disaffected naval officers. There will never be a complete reckoning of the iceberg beneath this tip, although its magnitude can be estimated as an annual 'gross criminal product' of one trillion dollars.[30]

Setting aside the moral implications, the presence of this vast shadowland signifies capitalism's fundamental uncontrollability, and therefore its inability to overcome its crises of ecology and democracy. From this standpoint, the ecological crisis is the effect of globalization viewed from the standpoint of ecosystems, as great waves of capital batter against and erode ecological defences. Similarly, democracy, and not government, is the great victim of globalization. As global capital works its way, the popular will is increasingly disregarded in the effort to squeeze ever more capital out of the system. In the process, the instruments of global capital begin to take on political functions, breaking down local jurisdictions and constituting themselves as a kind of world governing body. But the regime lacks what normal states, even despotic ones, require, namely, some means of legitimation. In the post-aristocratic, post-theocratic world of modernity, democratic advances, even the pseudo-democracy that passes for normal these days, are the necessary glue that holds societies together. Capital's inability to furnish this as it moves toward its realization in the global society has made its operation increasingly look like a global *coup d'état*. This is the great political contradiction of our time, and drives the present surge of resistance.

The Men in Charge

Just between you and me, shouldn't the World Bank be encouraging more migration of the dirty industries to the LDCs [less developed countries]? I think the economic logic behind dumping a load of toxic waste in the lowest wage country is impeccable and we should face up to that ... . I've always thought that underpopulated countries in Africa are vastly under-polluted: their air quality is vastly inefficiently low [*sic*] compared to Los Angeles or Mexico City. (Lawrence Summers, while at the World Bank)

You know, there are some people who are just losers. There are some countries that are just losers. And if you forgive them the debt, it doesn't make a lot of difference. (James Wolfensohn, President, World Bank)

You must cut costs ruthlessly by 50 to 60 percent. Depopulate. Get rid of people. They gum up the works. (Jeffrey Skilling, President, Enron Corporation[31])

To draw out the broad ecological outlines of capitalist society is one thing; to prove that this will inexorably lead to ecocatastrophe unless capital is overthrown is another. Here the question becomes not what capital is doing to ecosystems, human and natural, but whether it can adapt and change its ways, given the gathering breakdown of its natural ground – or to be more exact, whether it can do so in time to permit a mending of its relations with nature. Everyone appreciates how fabulously adaptable capital has been. It has eluded destruction time and again, so much so that its capacity to adapt to ecological breakdown is pretty well taken for granted.

Market society has been fabulously successful in producing wealth. Why not, so the standard argument runs, will it not be just as successful in producing ecological integrity? But where this line of reasoning goes astray is in not realizing that this time, the lesion arises from capitalist production as such. The problem afflicting previous crises was how to resume a pattern of growth interrupted by one stress or another. Now, however, it is precisely the pattern of growth that causes the problem. Yes, capital can produce 'green commodities' or anti-pollution devices; it can even recycle and conserve resources as well as energy. But because it does so as capital, it does so by producing itself before anything else, and this gathering sea of capital will have the effects documented above, essentially washing out the marginal gains achieved by efforts at recuperation. This proposition is no more provable than its converse, the popularly assumed idea that capital will work its way out of the ecological crisis. The question is, rather, whether it is more plausible, and for this purpose we may introduce yet another line of reasoning.

Capitalist production includes all those forces that enter into the generalized production of commodities. But these include the prevalent human dispositions that enter into production. If it is true that capitalism induces a kind of mentality turned away from recognizing nature, we mean for this to be understood as one of the elements (in Marxist terms, a 'force of production') making the ecological crisis more intractable. In plain language, one of the biggest ecological problems with capitalism is the capitalist.

If the ruling class – those persons who through ownership and/or control hold the reins of the system in their hands – were to prove capable of appreciating just how much trouble we are all in, then just maybe they could install necessary changes in time. If, however, they are *structurally incapable* of dealing with the crisis, then this greatly reinforces the indictment made here. I say structural, because the behaviour of elites cannot be reduced to ordinary motivations like greed or domination, as greedy or domineering as they may in fact be. When we are talking of class interest and of how individuals become personifications of great institutional forces, all the innumerable variations that make the human psyche interesting are subjected to a few basic rules, and a remarkable uniformity of behaviour prevails. Of course, an individual member of the elite can rebel and step aside. But what does it matter that a few capitalists think differently from their fellows if their ideas are drowned out by the preponderant force of class opinion? In actuality, a member of the elite who starts seeing things radically differently either gets back into line or is excluded from power; he simply ceases being a member of the elite, and gets replaced by someone more in accord with the needs of capital. For the remainder, the system imposes a powerful and uniform set of constraints, as the dominant social forces induce some psychological elements and inhibit others, while providing ideals, rationalizations and norms of conduct – in short, a kind of moral universe within which behaviour is shaped and given structure.

Each society selects for the psychological types that serve its needs. It is quite possible in this way to mold a great range of characters toward a unified, class purpose. To succeed in the capitalist marketplace and rise to the top, one needs a hard, cold, calculating mentality, the ability to sell oneself, and a hefty dose of the will to power. None of these traits is at all correlated with ecological sensibility or caring, and they are all induced by the same force field that shapes investment decisions.

The three statements by elite figures given above are of course not representative of the public face put to the world by the ruling classes. In fact, Summers has claimed that his remarks were meant to be 'ironic'. If so, however, it is the irony that states a factual truth with a face-saving twist, for the substance of the remark, along with those by Wolfensohn and Skilling, hold a mirror to the actual trajectory of capital. Capital speaks through these powerful figures, in all its ruthless calculatedness, its willingness to jettison the unprofitable, and its reduction of nature to resources and sinks. What they are saying, then, is authentic even if it may be denied. Putting the matter this way removes us from thinking of the capitalist elites as being motivated by 'greed' or some internally driven psychological state. Of course greed plays a role. How could it not when stupendous fortunes can be had for compliance with the rules of the game? But the question is how greed, or the drive for power, or cold and calculating ways of thought, lead to blindness and rigidity. These are the salient traits, and they arise from the intersection of psychological tendencies with the concrete life-world of the capitalist. Consider some of the ways in which this works itself out anti-ecologically.

First, the bigger the system gets – which is to say, the more it fulfills its destiny of expansion – the more grandiose becomes the capitalist way of thought. And the more grandiose, the more removed. If you sit at the heart of the world's financial centres, fly in private jets, manipulate billions of dollars with the tap of a keypad and control a productive apparatus capable of diverting rivers and sending missions to Mars, you are not likely to experience the humility of a St Francis or the patient tenacity of a Rachel Carson. And lacking this, you are no more likely to experience fellow-feeling for the web of life than for the poor people of Africa. In short, ecological consciousness is blocked by the ruling class position.

This grandiosity is greatly reinforced by a sense of personal invulnerability, which insulates capitalists from the consequences of their actions except as these affect the bottom line of profit. Ordinary people are not so protected. The reason that so many people of colour, for example, have toxic waste dumps in their neighborhoods (estimates have run as high as 60 per cent) is transparently that such people do not sit at the command structures of the corporations that pollute. Those who do, by contrast, see to it that the poisons they make stay out of their own neighbourhoods. This keeps the elites away from direct evidence of the destabilizing effects of capitalist production. And it feeds the fantasy that they can always surround themselves with protection against a nature out of balance.

Even if the elites screw up, their reward is ensured. Indeed, consolation prizes are given to executives who fail, a story which caught the attention of the press in 1997. As the *New York Times* put it: 'For top executives, failure – once a wretched embarrassment disguised in corporate spin language or hushed up completely – now pays. Especially if they fail quickly.' Failed top executives at AT&T, Disney, Apple Computer and Smith Barney were sent packing with, respectively, $26 million, $90 million, $7 million and $22 million dollar payoffs – scarcely an incentive to worry greatly about what they are doing. The structural reason for this lies in the increasing turnover at the top – itself a function of the acceleration of capital – that leads executives to demand safety nets and, intercurrently, undercuts loyalty, coherence and larger vision at the upper level of corporations.[32]

Along with this, the ever-growing size of capitalist corporations removes them from contact with nature as an object of care. Insulated by dense and seemingly endless webs of bureaucracy, and presiding over enterprises that typically make anything and everything and throw off subsidiaries like Imelda Marcos changed her shoes, the capitalist bosses have every reason to neglect the immediacy and mutual recognition essential for ecological ways of being. Their order of interrelation is dominated by the entirely anti-ecological principle: the law of exchange. The more money-capital rules, the more is nature reduced to mere abstraction, and the more rationalized are the ruminations of a Lawrence Summers. According to the regime of finance, the economic logic is in fact 'impeccable' to dump more toxic waste in poorer countries. That's simply how one makes more money, which is all that 'counts'.

Another core trait of the capitalist is the fetish of technology. Since technology raises the rate of surplus value extraction, it is a key to profitability, and so becomes invested with the godlike power of capital. The capitalist therefore not only overestimates the technological, he himself becomes like a machine. In his hard, cold calculatedness, he thinks 'instrumentally', that is, reductively and in terms of parts rather than wholes. This is doubly useful in that it permits ready-made rationalizations of one's behaviour, and the isolation and separation of such traits as could stir forth some ecological awareness.

Of course the capitalist does not only think; he is also a passionate, desiring creature. The problem is that capital selects for such passions as are recklessly ecodestructive, particularly the desire to win at all cost. The main mechanism of this is the relentless competition built into the heart of the system, which assures that only the rabidly self-seeking and ruthless are elected to patrol the higher reaches of capital. There is nothing mysterious about this, but its significance is easily overlooked in the macho world of capitalist culture. This is a much more cogent factor in capital's anti-ecological regime than simple greed. The attitude was summed up by recently deposed Coca-Cola president and CEO Douglas Ivester. Friendship, admiration and respect, said Ivester, are not 'really my priority. This is what I really want. I want your customers, I want your space on the shelves, I want your space of the consumer's stomach. And I want every single bit of beverage growth potential that is out there.'[33] Just as capital can never stop expanding, therefore, so can its personifications never have enough. How can people of this sort ever be expected to wake up to the ecological crisis?

The effect is accentuated inasmuch as the regime of finance capital places an emphasis on short-term profitability. The very fluidity sought by capital imposes ever greater demands that profits be realized right away or sooner. This is a main reason why nothing substantial will be done about global warming under the present regime. Sure, all sorts of constructive measures are on the drawing board. But to take them seriously involves the unthinkable measure of cutting into immediate profits. If capitalists could all plan together, this might be possible. But that in turn runs against the law of competition.

One last tendency that keeps capitalists from dealing adequately with the ecological crisis deserves mention. Aside from logical styles or personal passions, we may assess the capacities for judgement of this ruling class. Needless to say, this has to be fairly sound in certain respects if an individual is to ascend the capitalist hierarchy. That is, the tycoon needs to be able to distinguish between his grandiose and aggressive desires and what the real situation will bear. However, this principle applies only to those areas in which profitability is the criterion. Here the capitalist's powers are brought to bear and the results are usually impressive. But where, as with the ecological crisis, the capitalist is simply in over his head and his instrumental kind of thinking and mechanical materialism necessarily misconstrue the real situation, then he is prone to especially great distortions. This is because of his grandiosity, his immersion in the discourse of 'spin control', public relations and other kinds of manipulation, and also from an induced character trait quite common among those who live by the market, namely, a kind of 'optimistic denial'. The capitalist has to be thoroughly realistic on one level, but insofar as he is immersed in commodity exchange, he is also subject to a high degree of wishful thinking. Success in the imponderable market depends a great deal upon instilling confidence and assurance that such and such will really sell, for whether such and such actually sells depends in part upon whether people believe in it. This attitude, so essential to huckstering and 'hustling customers', is normally balanced by shrewdness of one kind or another. However, where, as with the ecological crisis, the shrewdness is misplaced because the situation is incomprehensible, then the all-too-human traits of denying reality and resorting to wishful thinking come to the fore. Since no one in fact can predict the outcome of the ecological crisis, or any of its constituent ecosystemic threads, the way is left open for optimistic denial, in short, minimization of the dangers, and inadequate responses taken for opportunistic motives rather than from a real appreciation of the problem.

The Indictment

Capitalism bestrides the world because of its fantastic ability to produce wealth – and to induce the wealth-producing side of human nature. The result is the most powerful form of human organization ever devised, and also the most destructive. Capital's advocates claim that its destructivity can be contained and that capital, as it matures, will peacefully overcome the rapacity shown in its phases of primitive accumulation, the way Sweden advanced from its Viking past. Give us a little more time, they argue, and globalization will truly become the tide that raises all boats and not just the yachts of the wealthy, while the general increase in wealth will enable the earth that is harbour for these boats to be made snug and bright.

An opposite conclusion is argued here. I hold instead that with the production of capitalist wealth, and as an integral part of it, poverty, eternal strife, insecurity, eco-destruction and, finally, nihilism are also produced. These concomitants may be externalized and exported, so long as production is local and restricted. But as capital matures and becomes global, the escape routes are sealed and its cancerous character is revealed – penetrating all spheres of human existence, destabilizing the ecologies of space and time and subjecting the earth to an increasingly authoritarian and corrupt regime. Now everything is sacrificed to accumulation, and with the closure of the circle of globalization, there is no further room to externalize.

The ecological crisis is the name for the global ecodestabilization accompanying global accumulation. Capital has shown a phenomenal resilience and ability to absorb all contradiction in its logic of exchange – this is a main reason why various modes of revolt have come and gone, leaving only bitter memorials behind, as Che Guevara has become the name for a brand of beer. In the ecological crisis, however, the logic of exchange itself becomes the source of destabilization, and the more it is drawn into the picture, the more corrupt and unstable becomes the relation to nature. Capital cannot recuperate the ecological crisis because its essential being, manifest in the 'grow or die' syndrome, is to produce such a crisis, and the only thing it really knows how to do, which is to produce according to exchange-value, is exactly the source of the crisis.

The logic of this argument is not yoked to the appearance of some sudden overwhelming calamity, or to the more likely concurrence of a great number of smaller weakening blows leading to collapse, or even to the possibility that the system will muddle through. It is predicated rather on demonstrating the utter unworthiness of capitalism to shepherd civilization through the crisis it has engendered through cancerous expansion. The above-mentioned contingent disasters may happen one way or another, or some or all of them may not happen at all – but we must be perfectly clear that they are primed to happen, and that capitalism, far from providing remedies, makes them more likely the more it fulfils itself.

That is why, in this excursion through the peculiarities of capital and capitalism, I have emphasized the anti-ecological features of capitalist production rather than the particulars of its relation to the crisis. Only the barest suggestion has been given of the innumerable instances of environmental assault: of the great propaganda system and its greenwashing campaign; of the betrayal of ecological responsibility by the established media; of the perfidy of individual politicians and parties; of the co-option of environmental groups; of the complicity of the scientific establishment; of the tangled legal system; and of the efforts to suppress and intimidate environmentalists. Good books have been written about all of these things – and in Chapter 7 I return to some of them in assaying the adequacy of current ecological politics.[34]

But we should not lose sight of the whole picture in attending to particulars: there is a single world-dominating order, and even though it still has not reached everywhere, it cannot be reformed, cannot be satisfied with less than everything, and has the institutions in place for its purpose. No set of individual reforms can encompass what capital means, or drive it out by the root. Therefore, no matter how meritorious or necessary any particular reform may be, the fact remains that it is capital as a whole that has to be confronted and brought down, as daunting as the prospect may be.

Notes

1. Slatella 2000: D4.

2. The term derives from the phenomenological philosopher Edmund Husserl.

3. The elective was under the auspices of the Tropical Medicine Faculty at Columbia University's medical school, which had formed a liaison with the Aluminum Company of America, proprietors of a large bauxite mine in the small town of Moengo. Suriname lies roughly 5° north of the Equator, and presents an essentially Amazonian ecology, with rivers discharging into the Caribbean sea. In the remoter jungles lived a dwindling group of Caribe Indians, while closer to the sea, though still in dense

rainforest, dwelt the 'Bush-Negroes,' descendants of escaped African slaves. It is to these latter that the observations apply.

4. See Kovel 1997a. McDonald's has formed marketing linkages with Coca-Cola, as well as other icons of globalized capitalist culture, such as the Olympic games.

5. Watson 1997; Jenkins 1997; Fiddes 1991.

6. Crossette 2000a; Gardner and Halweil 2000. According to Worldwatch, 1.2 billion are now overweight, matching the number of starving people. Another 2 billion comprise the 'hidden hungry', with bad diets. In 1999, 400,000 liposuctions were performed in the USA, and 80 per cent of malnourished children lived in countries that reported food surpluses.

7. Crossette 2000b. The UNICEF report is the first comprehensive survey of the phenomenon, and details violence, worst for the poorest, at every aspect of the life cycle, from aborted female foetuses, the killing of female babies, underfeeding of girl children, lack of medical care, sexual abuse, and fatal beatings of grown women. This pervasive violence, which beyond doubt represents a major increase from the level of traditional society, comes from those closest to women and reflects the general break-up of intimate life in a world whose communal structure is destabilized by capital's penetration, along with closely related manifestations like massive migration. By contrast, in traditional societies, for example those of the North American Indians, rape and the abuse of women were among the most severely punished and rarest of crimes. This was one reason why many settler women in the American colonies 'defected' to the Indians.

8. Public Citizen 1996.

9. Engels 1987; Bowden 1996. This extraordinary account focuses on the subculture of photographers and TV journalists who document the madness.

10. Nathan 1997.

11. Ordonez 2000.

12. 'Nano' refers to the contraction of machines to the level of individual molecules, the word referring to one-thousandth of a 'micron', i.e., a millionth of a millimetre, the scale of molecular processes. See Drexler 1986. Although the later phase of a technology may replace an earlier one, as the electronic calculator makes the mechanical slide-rule obsolete, the overall effect is additive and combinative. Thus gigantic jet planes incorporate electronic technology without ceasing to be huge; or computers guide the development of molecular-scale technologies, then become incorporated into such technologies.

13. DeBord 1992.

14. Thompson 1967; White 1967.

15. Marx 1963: 41.

16. Kanter 1997: A22. The author, a professor of managment at Harvard Business School, accurately observes that despite the then success of the economy, an 'undercurrent of cynicism (along with fatigue from increased workloads)' was rife – in fact, 46 per cent of employees of 1,000 large corporations feared layoffs in 1997 as compared with 31 per cent in 1992. Meanwhile the remaining workers suffer from yet another mental illness, 'layoff survivor sickness', characterized by anger, depression, fear, guilt, risk aversion, distrust, vulnerability, powerlessness and loss of motivation – accompanied by an increase in stress-related claims. This occurred in an economy that was widely deemed to be 'as good as it gets'.

17. Bass 2000. The only level of conflict reported in the article, based upon research done at Penn State University, was that the behaviour stimulated sexual harassment by male customers, who mistook the robotic friendliness for a come-on. Otherwise internalization was quite successful. Note the mutilation of the Golden Rule: the worker wants to treat everybody as she herself is treated. So she treats them as means to the end of accumulation, just as she is treated. But the only coherent interpretation of the moral law, as Kant realized, is to treat persons as ends in themselves, not as means, or things.

18. Williams 2000.

19. Harvey 1993.

20. The term is from Freund and Martin 1993, a valuable study.

21. Purdom 2000.

22. As bad as the situation in the USA may be, it is dwarfed by the traffic-generated nightmares of cities in the 'newly industrializing countries'. In NICs, an even more unregulated capital induces scenarios such as that in Sao Paulo, Brazil, where the rich have taken to using helicopters to avoid roads 'hopelessly clogged with traffic' and subject to the 'carjackings, kidnappings of executives and roadside robberies [that] have become part of the risks of everyday life for anyone perceived to have money'. However hard it may be to enter the Kingdom of Heaven, it is easier for a rich man to buy a helicopter than for a poor man to buy a car in São Paulo – nor is parking much of a problem, as the gated communities where many rich people reside offer ideal setting for landing-pads. The noisy monsters have predictably become status symbols ('Why settle for an armored BMW when you can afford a helicopter?' goes one slogan), as some 400 flit through the air and create an even more nightmarish environment for the average citizen (Romero 2000). Gated communities, with private police forces and the like, are a major accompaniment of the ecological crisis as it affects urban space in the age of automobilia. I recall reading that in the USA, nearly 30 per cent live in such fragmenting enclaves.

23. Wald 1997; Turner 2000.

24. The World Bank, set up along with the IMF at the 1944 Bretton Woods conference, was originally designed to help with post-war European reconstruction. It then shifted to the Third World, made major infrastructural loans (which included financing the plant at Bhopal) and became increasingly involved with 'adjustment' of peripheral economies in order to integrate them better with the needs of global capital. The IMF, by contrast, was originally set up to maintain the standard of fixed interest rates established after the war. After 1971, when these rates began to float, it turned to making loans to troubled economies and clearing them for further capital investment by the Bank, hence its involvement with the notorious structural adjustment programmes. As for the WTO, it emerged finally from its chrysalis in 1995 after its predecessor, the General Agreement on Tariffs and Trade, finished its preliminary organizing.

25. George 1992.

26. Murphy 2000.

27. Pooley 2000, an article focusing on the case of Tanzania.

28. Stiglitz 2000, in which we find: 'The IMF staff … frequently consists of third-rank students from first-rate universities. (Trust me: I've taught at Oxford University, MIT, Stanford University, Yale University, and Princeton University, and the IMF almost never succeeded in recruiting any of the best students.)' So that's what we need – as they put it in the Vietnam era, the 'best and the brightest.'

29. Barlow 2000; also http://www.brain.net.pk/diama; and egroups.com/groups/ waterline.

30. De Brie estimates about one-third to one-half of this in drugs, the rest divided between computer piracy, counterfeiting, budgetary fraud, animal smuggling, white slaving, and so on. In other words, a good estimate of simply the transborder crime amounts to some 20 per cent of world trade. Allowing that only one-half of that ends up as profit, and that one-third of this is lost in money-laundering operations, the net realized annual profit from international crime stands at some $350 billion. De Brie 2000; see also Bergman 2000.

31. *Multinational Monitor*, June 1997, p. 6. Summers' now infamous remarks were made in an internal World Bank memo in 1991, when he was an underling economist for that institution. The outrage was such that he went on to become secretary of the treasury and president of Harvard. Wolfensohn was responding to suggestions that the World Bank write off the debts owed to it by developing countries.

32. Dobrzynski 1997.

33. Deogun 1997. Alas, poor Ivester, his dreams came to nought, and he was eventually sacked for not delivering on them.

34. Some works I have found valuable in tracking the various concrete forms taken by the crisis are: Athanasiou 1996; Karliner 1997; Beder 1997; Tokar 1997; Steingraber 1997; Fagin and Lavelle 1996; Colburn et al. 1996; Pring and Canan 1996; Rampton and Stauber 1997; Lappé et al. 1998; Shiva 1991; Gelbspan 1998; Gibbs, 1995; Ho 1998; Thornton 2000.

Part II
The Domination of Nature

5 On Ecologies

To say that capital is ecodestructive is to claim that under its regime, large swathes of the natural world are becoming undone. However troubling, this is straightforward enough. But we have also said in a number of places that it is 'anti-ecological', which is not quite the same thing. The latter term introduces a new notion, that the word 'ecology' signifies something to be valued in our relationship within nature, and that capital does not simply degrade one portion of nature or another, but violates the whole sense of the universe. Obviously, this obliges us to say a thing or two about what that sense might be, and, in a more general way, what it means to talk about nature.

The notion of nature is as elusive as any in the repertoire of thought. Nature palpably exists irrespective of what we say about it. And yet nature only exists *for us* insofar as we say anything about it. All propositions about nature, from the most esoteric investigations into cosmology, to the regulations for dumping wastes, to the writings of ideologues left, right and centre – including, to be sure, the thoughts written down here – are mediated by language, which, besides being an imperfect mirror of reality, is densely social and historical. Practically speaking, then, there are two layers of our imprint upon nature: first, the natural world has been substantively re-arranged by human influence, to the extent that one would be hard-pressed to find any configuration of matter on the surface of the earth and a good ways above and below it that has not been altered by our species-activity;[1] and second, that all propositions about the natural world are, first of all, social utterances. When we speak, or become aware, of something called 'nature', we are apprehending something that also has a history, at the least, because the ways of speaking about it are social practices, and also, in the great majority of instances of interest to us, because the 'natural' entity has itself received a human, historical imprint.

The term 'ecology' and its various meanings also has a history, in this case conditioned by the gathering crisis that bears its name.[2] It stands to reason that when the integrity of the natural world is under ever-growing threat, the notions used to account for that integrity and its disintegration will come into prominence. In the century-and-a-quarter since it appeared on the intellectual landscape, ecology has managed to acquire a great deal of significance. As used here, the term has a fourfold meaning:

- A technical discipline within the natural science of biology devoted to the study of the interrelationships between living creatures and their environment. Here the crucial variables are usually the populations of diverse life-forms as they interact with the rest of nature.

- An object singled out for ecological study, that is, not populations as such but locations within the totality of the earth. We can talk of this as a more or less definite place, as, for example, the ecology of a local pond or of the Amazon basin – which at a certain scale may take the name of a 'bioregion'. Or we may think of it as a sub-set of the natural world with certain internal relations, such as the atmosphere, or the endocrine system of higher animals. Here the object in question has systemic properties, that is, it is a structure of interrelating elements defined both spatially and temporally; hence the name *ecosystem* to define a principle object of our study. Ecosystems are bounded but also inter-related (for example, the endocrine system is related to the circulatory system, or the oceans to the atmosphere). In fact, there is no such thing as an ecosystem-in-itself; all are interconnected, in ways that concern us greatly. We use the term *ecosphere* to refer to the world regarded according to the principles of ecology, in other words, it is the earth as seen 'eco-systemically'. And from a still higher level of abstraction, we can think of nature itself as the *integral of all ecosystems*. This notion, of an integral, means also that we think of 'wholes' composed of parts but distinct from the sum of those parts. In philosophical language, we are develop-ing not a hierarchical systems-theory, but a dialectic of emergence.

- A dimension of the human world. This is essential, unless we take the nonsensical position that humanity is outside nature. Needless to say, developing a social view of ecology may not be to every natural scientist's taste. And in any case it requires us to extend our method by introducing dimensions peculiar to the human world, such as language, meaning and history. These attributes give us our identity as a natural species. Once we begin looking at things this way, moreover, there is no reason not to talk of the ecology of cities, of neighbourhoods, of families, or, indeed, of minds.[3]

- Since values are uniquely human phenomena, we logically extend the scope by taking into account ethical positions with ecological content; and since an ethical position is a guiding aspect for action in the world, we talk of ecological politics as well. It is in this latter sense that we indict capital as 'anti-ecological', just as the indictment of its 'ecodestructiveness' refers to the second, ecosystemic, sense of the term. What it may mean to act ecologically, or to hold 'ecocentric' values, is a problem integrating all dimensions of ecology, and the solution of which, to be termed 'ecosocialism', is the aim of this study.

Ecological thinking concerns relationships, and the structures and flows between them. At one level, this is mere common sense; at another, it turns the world upside down and commits us to a world-view and philosophy of nature very much at odds with the dominant system. Nature as such vastly exceeds the phenomena of life, yet life may be justly regarded as being at the same time both a special case of nature, and, in a way we only dimly perceive, as a potential of nature – something that nature generates under specific circumstances.[4] Life is unitary, in the sense that the basic molecular architectures of humans, redwoods and slime moulds all indicate a common ancestor. Yet life is also inconceivably – to our dim awareness – multiform, in a profusion that has arisen over 3.5 billion years through ceaseless interactions between living creatures, and with their non-living surround. It follows that all ecosystems that contain living beings also relate to the rest of nature, whether this be other creatures, the immediate surround of the earth's macro-physical environment: i.e., the 'environment', or the molecular, atomic or sub-atomic realms, or the extension of nature into the cosmos. A slender, filamentous connection throughout the great reaches of nature, to be sure, and scarcely likely ever to be fully plumbed by our science, but existent so long as we take the relatedness of elements within nature with full seriousness. From this standpoint we think of nature as the integral of all ecosystems, extending in every direction and beyond the limits of the planet. Talking of integrals means talking in terms of organisms, and of wholes – in other words, the systematic introduction of an ecological vision commits us to positing reality as an interconnected web whose numberless nodes are integrated into holistic beings of ever exfoliating wonder – or would be so, until capital got hold of them.

What is Life?

The boundary between the living and the non-living is not sharp, which is to be expected if life is a potential form of being hatched by nature. Nature is *formative*, that is, it has the dynamic potential to generate particular nodes of existence; and life represents a way-station of its formativeness. Were nature a diffuse continuum with no differentiation among its parameters, such as pertained at the moment of the 'Big Bang', and will return at the extended moment of its 'heat death', then there would be no-thing at all, no particularized aggregation, no allocating of time and space, of dust, of energic differentials, of galaxies, stars, planets around stars, seas and land on the planet, rocks on the land, pools of water, concatenations of chemicals in the air and in the waters, cycles of temperature and light – in short, none of the differentiation that is the lot of the cosmos in the aeons between its alpha and omega points. So the category of existence is occupied by the 'some-things' that exist. These comprise *beings* insofar as they internalize their existence, that is, make their 'is-ness' part of themselves. In this way, every-thing has being insofar as it is not other-things. This 'being of beings' relates to and to a degree incorporates the other-things, making them internal to itself even as they become objects. Beings are temporal: they evolve as they come in and out of existence, and with their evolution comes a fuller internalization. In other words, a motion of inwardness toward subjectivity accompanies a more highly differentiated objective existence. In one line of development, this eventually results in the emergence of consciousness and mind. What we call 'development' takes place on a terrain of being, and through greater subject–object differentiation – whether expressed in terms of the maturation of a child or as the evolution of life.

Life manifests a kind of being that self-sustains and replicates – that propagates its own form, through the presencing of definite individuals along with the capacity of said individuals to reproduce. But nature is not only formative: it is also dissipative of form – indeed, were it not, form itself could not exist. Thus it is that for our universe, there is a trajectory between alpha and omega points, between an undifferentiated moment of origin and an end – unimaginably distant[5] – at which all beings cease to exist because differentiation itself has ended. The passage of this great loop is registered in the famous laws of thermodynamics, though not accounted for by them. The First Law expresses the insight of ancient natural philosophy, as in the Epicurean doctrine that 'nothing comes of nothing'; it holds that matter and energy are conserved in physical systems. The Second Law surpasses this by introducing the notion of form and the dissipation of form. If 'entropy' is a logarithmic measure of the probabilistic disorder of a given physical system, the Second Law states that for such a system, whether it be the air in a room, a living body, or the earth as a whole, so long as neither energy nor matter is added to said system – that is, so long as the system is 'closed' – then its entropy will rise with time. An increase in the randomness of its elements, or, from the other side, a loss of form, will therefore emerge absent the input of energy. More, the direction of this change defines 'time's arrow'. Thus an ice cube melts, 'with time', in a glass of water, replacing a relatively improbable state with a more probable one – that is, one corresponding to a greater number of system possibilities in what physicists call phase-space.[6] Similarly, when we die, the exquisite combination of molecules that has existed in this living form is returned to the great flux of the universe. It is living form that maintains that exquisiteness – to which we, as self-reflective living creatures, respond aesthetically.

There are a number of themes here that need a bit of unpacking. First, we understand life to stand in a degree of tension with the universe that gave it existence. The universe, or nature, has within itself to give birth to life, as a 'natural' potential of the cosmos. But at the same time, and through the workings of the same nature in its Second Law, life stands against certain laws of the universe. Life must be ... and life cannot remain. Poised between these poles, life must continually *struggle* for its existence; if it does not, it passes into death.

In the current orthodoxy the term 'struggle' is endowed with Hobbesian and Social-Darwinian meanings: struggle is the war of all against all, and the survival of the fittest in a regime of continual mutual aggression. This notion was not Darwin's, and it is not only ideologically distorted, but factually wrong. By no means do all creatures behave in this way. In fact, no creature, not even the 'king of the jungle', endures wholly through predation; while for the simplest creatures, those microscopic cellular beings on which the entire biosphere rests, the Social-Darwinian notion is without meaning. As the British palaeontologist Richard Fortey points out, the first 'sustainable' systems, the mat creatures or 'stromatolites' whose lineage goes 3 billion years back to the Precambrian (roughly 2.4 billion years before the emergence of more complex multicellular organisms), and that still endure in certain protected locales, are composed of layers of prokaryotic bacteria, the topmost, 'thin as a sheet of paper', doing photosynthesis, the lower layers breaking down the waste products of the upper by fermentation, the whole given structure and nutrient by trapped grains of minerals.

> It was a sustainable system, an ecosystem in miniature. If this truly reflected the state of the nascent biological world it is clear that cooperation and coexistence were a part of life close to its inception. Existence at base can be thought of as reciprocal rather than competitive ... These humble structures are the birth of ecology.[7]

Given that for the considerable majority of the time life has been on earth it has existed as static mats of micro-organisms undergoing biochemical exchange with the rest of nature, the meaning of 'struggle' includes forms of cooperation as well as competition and predation; indeed, the former would be more fundamental than the latter. The stromatolites had no organs, they gathered not, nor did they hunt, nor were they hunted, and for a period longer than so-called higher life has existed. Yet they lived and had 'ecologies'. For the stromatolites – and, at bottom, ourselves – to struggle means therefore to engage in transfers of matter and energy required to sustain a certain formal organization in relation to the Second Law. Dead, the numberless atoms of our substance are essentially unchanged; their mutual positioning (including the positioning into more complex molecules), however, is drastically rearranged. The absence of life signals a reorganization in the direction of randomness and disorganization, mainly carried out in this epoch through the agency of other living beings who rebuild their substance from the elements of the old.

Life, then, is what sustains organization – to be exact, organization at low entropy. The ensemble of energic and formal processes required for this constitutes the specific life activity of a given creature or species. The hunting, gathering, and so on of 'higher' organisms is a more elaborate way of proceeding down the path, grounded in the necessities of a more elaborate formal structure. Each creature must extract energy in order to struggle, so as to maintain its form, which is to say, to endure. And this means that each creature is insufficient in-itself, for insofar as it individuates, it also separates, and that from which it is separated is therefore related to it, connected yet different. Those who do not come together in this way are the non-existent.

All living beings have internal and external relations of parts to wholes. This quality, that life must exist in relation to other life and to nature as a whole if it is to contend with the Second Law, defines the notion of eco-system, and on a far deeper level than that of a mere collection of bodies. Ecosystems constitute places of 'putting together'. They are the sites where creatures interact in ways potentially conducive to their emergence and sustenance. Ecosystems are the loci of nature's formativity, active ensembles where being comes into existence. Ecology in the larger sense is the dis-course of such ensembles, and is built into the fabric of terrestrial life, from the infinitesimal micro-organism to the ecosystems now being destabilized.[8]

Life emerges on this planet – we may set aside the question of life on other planets – owing to a fortuitous set of circumstances within the range of cosmic possibility. Here nature originates life, which then, through struggle and in its ecosystemic places, proceeds to evolve. But evolution is conditioned at every step by the flux of ecosystems. Life's own activity, played out in ecosystems (along with other natural influences, such as meteorites or solar flares) is what prods living beings along, changing the terms of the struggle for existence and leading to evolutionary development. Ecology is therefore integrally tied to evolution – one may say that any given ecosystem is a synchronic slice through evolutionary time. Life is defined anti-entropically, insofar as its chief feature is the sustenance and creation of form. Living systems display degrees of order incomprehensible to the crude mind. Whether we look at the obvious proportions and sym-metries of organisms or, more impressively still, the fine molecular structure wherein each atom seems to be positioned as in a tiny workshop, it would seem that life not only disobeys but positively flouts the Second Law. This is exactly what the struggle for existence is about. Dead, the corpse of a once-alive creature very quickly falls into line with the principle of rising entropy. The work of life, and the intricate dance of energy and form that goes into it, are essentially enterprises to stave off and reverse the Second Law. Far from refuting the Second Law, then, life affirms its power by struggling against it.[9]

The struggle of life against entropy does not abolish the Second Law, because living creatures are anything but closed systems. Whether they convert ambient sunlight into usable form through photosynthesis in the plant kingdom, or eat the products of this activity in the substance of animals, life is constantly taking in low-entropy energy to sustain its form. A considerable degree of evolved biochemical activity consists of the capacity of living beings to capture energy in small packets, principally of high-energy phosphate bonds, so that the fine structure of life's workshop can proceed. Here, in the astounding nano-factories of the cell, the principle permitting the emergence of life in the first place is institutionalized: reactants are held together, energy is transformed into small and usable amounts, and the whole tiny architecture is repeated trillions of times over, as life builds and propagates itself.

Through it all, the net entropic pattern remains very much in line with the Second Law: insofar as life can be put in the position of a (relatively) closed system, it will increase the entropy of the totality comprising itself and its surround. For the earth as a whole, it is not so clear. It is very likely to be the case that life's capacity to draw down the energy of the sun (and to a lesser extent, that of more immediately gravitational sources like tides and geothermal hot spots) has so overridden the constraints of closed systems as to have produced, at least until quite recently, when the ecological crisis has reversed the pattern, an actual decrease of entropy on the planet. At least, that is the way I would regard the 'Gaia' principle, according to which the earth itself is a super-organism, with the capacity to self-regulate and even to exhibit signs of a kind of consciousness.[10]

It would seem the case that whatever Gaian tendencies are evinced by the global ecosystem are manifestations of the cumulative effects of evolution upon the planet, made possible by the genius of life to subject the globe to its ordering effects. In this scheme, the 'closed' system is the earth + space, with respect to which the overall increase in entropy is accounted for by harmless re-radiation of degraded solar energy into the latter. Meanwhile, organic evolution achieved for the earth as a whole what the life process does for individual beings, namely, an increase in order and dynamic form.

If ecology is the readout of life's formal organization at any point in time, then evolution is its forward temporal motion. Therefore the ecological state of things at any moment is like a snapshot of evolution about to happen. This should not be interpreted, however, as a teleologically ordered process, pulled from beyond by God – or in the more ideologically understood sense, that evolution awaits its fulfilment in an equilibrium under the guidance of the current ruling class or master race. The notion of formativeness in nature requires, rather, a more dynamic reading. For if ecology were ever in a steady state, then there would be no pressure to evolve, and nothing of the beauty and intricacy of living form. It is lack, and conflict, and the ceaseless interaction between living beings and their surround, that condition the evolution of life. Equilibrium as such is not a property of life, while, generally speaking, those functions within which a kind of balance obtains are better thought of as a metastable equipoising: the 'holding together' of elements in creative formation. Heraclitus seized the root of things when he posited ceaseless motion, with its absencing and presencing, as the way of the universe.[11]

Therefore when we talk of the 'stability' of ecosystems, we do not imply a static condition, or even one of simple equilibrium. We mean, rather, a state of being with an irreducible indeterminacy, within which one might say, 'life goes forward': evolving new (though not 'higher') species, and introducing those formal shapes and dynamic processes into the ecosphere that comprise its work on earth. Since it is in the nature of ecosystems to move and evolve, we do better to evoke their *integrity* than their stability. The notion of integrity includes stability as a rate of change and emergence compatible with the working of any ecosystem. Even at its 'climax' the forest continues to evolve. At the physiological level, the immune system is stable if it is capable of changing by introducing new antibodies to meet new contingencies. Ditto for the circulatory system, which has to keep maintaining its existent vessels, and extending new ones into traumatized areas.

To speak of the integrity of something means recognizing that it exists as the integral of its parts. In a word, it is a Whole. Preserving ecological integrity is a matter, therefore, of preserving Wholes, and fostering their emergence and development. I say 'fostering' meaning that we have a choice as to whether to do this or not – a choice that depends in part on whether we value the integrity of ecosystems. As to why we should do so, one might say that our own survival depends on it, but also and necessarily because to value this way means to fulfil our own nature, to find its integrity as well. The ordering effects of life on earth are not merely a matter of overcoming entropy. They also result in those entities and patterns that we find beautiful – and this sense of beauty is no indulgence, but the participation in that nature from which being arises. If we wonder at the beauty and elegance of nature, then, we are nature appreciating itself, and our wonderment is part of the form of nature itself. We have the choice as to whether to try to foster the continuance of life. By choosing 'no', that is, choosing to continue on with the way of life that leads to ecological disintegration, we are also choosing against ourselves. And this leads us to ask just who we are.

On Human Being

A natural creature, beyond doubt, the same basic set of molecules, including DNA, the same submission to the entropy principle, the same fundamental ground plan, caught up in evolutionary time and dependence upon ecosystems. Like all natural creatures, the human one has an imprint. The bat has sonar, the whale special capacities for diving (and its own kind of sonar), the bee its quantum dance, the venus flytrap its signature form of carnivorousness. Each creature in nature has its 'nature', its way of being, its point of insertion into the ecosystemic manifold, its peculiar mode of struggling. We regard 'human nature', or 'hummingbird nature', or 'bee nature', or 'maple tree nature' in this light – both holistically, as the species-specific way of struggle in an ecosystemic world conditioned by the entropy principle, and also at a more concrete level, as the ensemble of powers, potentials and capacities that enable this way to be expressed. There is nothing mystical about the fact of particular species-nature: it is simple logic. To be is to struggle, and each point of difference in being is a different mode of struggling. In this way, living forms arise and take their place in eocsystemic manifolds, each, in their way, better, each *as* their way.

The notion of human nature is often unpopular with people of progressive persuasion, who see in it a system of essentialist chains: men *are* in essence like this (from Mars); women *are* like that (from Venus); blacks are this way; Chicanos that way, and so on – always with the more or less unstated proviso that in a stable social order they will remain that way, generally at a subaltern rank. Nature – and human nature – in this view are essences, false reductions of what humanity is, and therefore a fetter on what it can be. But this point of view, however well-intentioned, is mistaken. Essentialism is undoubtedly wrong, both morally and philosophically, because it imputes to the object a thing-like inertia that violates its range of potential being; it is, we might say, a kind of reification. But there is no *a priori* reason to place the blame for essentialism on the idea of nature. The categories of nature need not inherently limit human freedom and potential, although they can be used in this way – and always will be drawn upon as such by ideologues of authority and repression. They need not, in other words, conflate humans with other creatures, any more than they reduce elephants to hummingbirds.

The idea of social or cultural determination is often opposed to determination by nature, as though the former had a built-in reassurance of freedom. But there is no reason why this need be so. Essentialist views, say of blacks and Latinos, can just as well be expressed in culturalist as in racist terms. Classically, racism is a biological essentialism, the object being considered an (inferior) sub-species of the human type. But this essence can just as well be transferred to ethnicities or other cultural structures, where it becomes the 'culture of poverty', or the 'black family', or, as the latest wrinkle has it, the culture of believing one's group to be racially oppressed, all of which allegedly traps the groups in question into a universe of self-defeating social assumptions.[12]

In any case, the notion of human nature is necessary for any in-depth appreciation of the ecological crisis, and its lack is a sign of the crisis itself. Without such a view, humanity is severed from the remainder of nature, and a genuinely ecological view is replaced by mere environmentalism. If we have no nature, then nature is always outside us, a mere grab-bag of resources and instrumental possibilities. Nor can the ties linking humanity and nature be given as a set of physical transfers between people and their 'environment'. Creatures struggle as organismic totalities, that is, full beings who act in the ecosystemic world and are acted upon by the world, not as leaky bags of dull matter.

All creatures co-evolve with their surround, in the course of which they actively transform their surround. Nature gives rise to form, and living creatures are trans-forming forms. That is why to talk of environment instead of ecologies violates the nature of things. Life actively changes the world, from other creatures to the very configuration of the rocks and the composition of the air. The atmosphere we breathe was made by living creatures, and so was the soil. The form of every creature is determined by other creatures.

Humans are also trans-forming, but with a core difference that defines human nature: we have evolved the inwardness, potentially inherent for all beings, into a subjectivity, or self, which has the capacity for an *imagination*

– an internally represented world – and we act upon and transform reality through this imagination. I do not mean that we live only in the imagination, as that would mean not living at all, nor do I mean that the imaginary world is more important than the world it represents: I argue only that the capacity to represent the world internally, to work it over in thought, and to remember and anticipate it as well as to actually inhabit it, is what makes us human. The specifically human is a whole motion, encompassing inner and outer worlds and mutually transforming both. The signature of human nature lies in this motion as a whole, while the various powers that compose our nature are the components necessary for this motion to occur. These powers and their various substrata all evolve ecosystemically, just like the rest of nature, with the highly important distinction that a co-evolving human sphere, mediated by the imaginary world, arises alongside the sphere of non-human existents – alongside, then interpenetrated with, colonizing, and, in the time of ecological crisis, destructive of the non-human order. This does not mean that we go against nature and do or become just as we please – an illusion expressing a pathological imagination. Our lives remain conditioned by the realities of nature, from quantum flows, to coarse Newtonian mechanics, to the hegemony of the entropy principle. No matter how ingeniously we may fashion nature – including the manipulation of the genome and the creating of new kinds of life – we are still doing no more than learning its laws so that we may use them for human purpose. Nor, it must be emphasized, does this remarkable capacity make us the high point or end point of evolution, for every creature standing at the end of its line of evolution is, with respect to the genealogy of nature, as high as any other. However, it does give us a kind of power such as no other creature has remotely possessed, and, with this power, various delusions and opportunities.

Teasing apart some of the threads of human nature, we find the following:

- An ensemble of somatic elements, rapidly evolving owing to the marked selection advantage conferred by human nature: a relatively huge brain, elaborate voice box, opposable thumb, upright posture, and the like, providing the material substratum of specifically human ways of being.
- Of special importance was the emergence of language as the specific human mode of communicating and representing the world. This involved 'hard wiring' of the evolving brain, coordination with the evolving

speech apparatus, and, decisively, integration with evolving forms of sociality, the result being that the powers of individuals could be combined.

- Human sociality implies *society*, as a kind of super-body, with a *culture*, transmissible through generations as a shared system of meanings. Society and its culture become the locus of that parallel, imagined universe that comprises the human order in its varying relationships to nature.

- The boundary of the super-body with pre-existing nature is made by means of *technology*. Tools are extensions of the body as well as transfer points of the body into material nature, and of nature into the body. Technology is always socially determined and the bearer of meanings constructed through language. It is not a collection of tools but a fabric of social relations, certain threads of which are nature transformed into tools.

- Human being entails a new order of subjectivity. All beings, we have observed, possess a potential interiority implied by their difference from other beings – the fact that they are some-thing and not others. Human nature appears as that development within which this interiority acquires internal structure through the particular forms taken by our consciousness under the influence of language. All creatures are present to each other. Language involves *re-presentation*: a sphere of interiority arises where what is presented is presented back – re-presented – owing to its signification with language. Hence the real is, so to speak, doubled. This re-presenting is formative of the imaginative space of subjectivity. The imagined world is just as much a part of human ecology as are chemical messengers for dog ecology or moth ecology.

- As this space of interior representation attains identity, it becomes a *self*. Its form is given by a degree of consciousness of itself, clothed by language with the words 'I' (as the subject phase) and 'me' (as the object phase). The radically augmented power of the human species is generated here, in the space where the world is created within the self, which then defines a social collectivity that acts upon the world.

- An ensemble of relations is involved here – not just intelligence, and the practical skills, but desire as well, which conditions and drives the practical intelligence. This arises from the radical formlessness of human instinctual structures, which are reshaped according to culture. Correlated with this are the processes of separation and individuation that occur out of the matrix of childhood. Culture implies intergenerational transmission, which rests upon the facts of childhood, something no other species remotely undergoes.[13]

• The sociality of humans is unique – though neither more nor less so than that of bees, coyotes, baboons, dolphins, and so on. It cannot be reduced to that of any other social animal, no matter how many amusing parallels may be found. This is because of the centrality of the self in human existence, and also because this self is always and necessarily a social product, formed through language and mutual *recognition* between the developing person and others. This foundation gives the human self a permanently dialectical quality – that is, it is formed in and lives through a set of contradictions that arise as the self is formed in mutual recognition of others, and later, in contradiction between individual interest and social bond. The mark of the other is always upon the self, and so are its vulnerability to loss and fear of solitude, facts that are to loom large in our relation to nature.[14]

• The uniqueness of human being and its relation to desire, and the dialectics of the self and recognition, means also that sexuality and gender play a uniquely powerful role in human existence compared with all other creatures. The significance of this for the ecological crisis will be examined in the next chapter.

A common feature of this ensemble is a unique tension developing between humanity and nature. From one side, a fully embodied creature, obeying all the laws of the universe; from the other, a stubborn, proud and wilful creature who distinguishes the self from nature and even chooses to protest the natural. We can say it is a potential, then, of human nature to *quarrel with nature and even to reject the purely natural given*. This notion, dialectical to the core, may serve to encapsulate and signify human nature as a whole. It appears in phenomena as ubiquitous as the need to cook food, and to adorn the body, and as fundamental as technology – for each tool, as an extension of the body, is also a kind of protest against the limits of the natural body. And it marks the deepest strata of our psyche as we relate to the ends of life. Every creature fights for life, but only a creature defined by selfhood will ponder death, fear death, deny death, or develop religion as a reaction to the perceived limits of existence. Thus one of the most distinctive features of humanity in the archaeological record is funerary evidence. Even the simplest trace of a burial condenses all that is specifically human: an awareness of death, that is, of the finitude of our self; a protest against death; care for the person who died, along with presumed grief and sense of loss; signification, or representation, along with technology; and as a condition for the whole ensemble, society and culture. Nothing of the sort obtains for other creatures.[15]

Defining human nature as a tension with nature enables us to avoid essentialist positions, or confining the human being in any kind of prescriptive strait-jacket. It allows for the quirkiness of human beings, and our playfulness and aesthetic side. It also says something about human creativity, as the restless need to remake the world and to make other worlds, and about the sense of beauty that uniquely marks the species. And it does this while yet rooting us in nature and allowing for the immense range of ecological modes of being that characterize us, including those leading to and potentially leading out of the ecological crisis.

The general function we have been describing may be identified as *production*, as the term for what human beings do, as part of nature, to express the formativity of nature by mediating it through the human world. When we produce, we *trans-form* nature. We use the term 'labour' to express in a general way the human propensity to produce, being careful to distinguish this meaning from the degraded (or 'alienated') sense of toil that characterizes the products of domination, as we discuss below. Similarly, an economy enters the picture when production is socially organized, and there is a division of labour, so that human powers are more elaborately expressed.

Both social production and consumption are direct extensions of human nature, in that each transforms nature through an engagement with the imagination and the ensemble of human powers. Production – and the human capacity of labour – are, as Marx insisted, a matter of looking ahead: every object which gets made exists in the imagination before it does so in reality. Just so is every commodity defined, as we have observed, by its *use-value*, and this, too, is necessarily a function of need, which in turn is a function of want, which in turn can be a function of desire. No purely mechanical or utilitarian accounting can give a sense of the use-values of commodities, and therefore, of the economy itself: the imagination needs to be invoked.[16]

But we are not done with human nature. There are yet other, more complex qualities to be noted:

- The emptiness that always shadows the self and the peculiar set of powers conferred by human nature creates for humanity a capacity not seen elsewhere in nature, namely, a reaching beyond itself, along with the potential – by no means expressed in all instances – of achieving a universal perspective, and of reaching toward the Whole. Broadly speaking, this refers to our spiritual life, the forms taken by which, or lack thereof, are very much part of the ecological crisis.[17]
- In addition, we recognize that the peculiar position of the self, poised as it is between the entropy principle and the looking-forward of production, with desire for lost objects, projection into the future, and ambitions for universality – that all this leads to a special, socially conditioned temporality specific for each society, and produced in its myth and narrative. Human nature, by rejecting the given and making its world, configures an account of itself according to time: it produces *history*.[18] We have said something already about the special temporal conditions of capitalism, with its speed-up and binding of time; however, every society has a special temporality, wrought from the arrow conferred by the entropy principle, and manifesting the tension with nature that will always be an aspect of human being.
- All of the powers of humanity, spiritual and practical, are available for addressing the social order and have the potential for transforming it, through a revolution if necessary. If nothing in nature stands still, how much more so is this the case for human beings and society! All things pass, and for us, the relevant question is whether the capitalist order will pass away before it causes humanity to pass away. But capital cannot pass away of itself; it has to be ushered out, through the transformation into an ecologically sane society.

Ecosystemic Integrity and Disintegration

Ecosystemic boundaries provide structural scaffolding for what is within an organism (the 'organs' and other internal ecosystems – nervous, endocrine, immune, and so on), as well as the point of differentiation between ecosystems. The nature of the ties between organisms in a particular ecosystem is given by the specific activity of each being, and is never singular. Trees in a forest are linked through the myriad creatures who relate to them as food, shelter or nesting place, as well as through their access to water, air and sunlight; and also directly between each other, through a subterreanean network of fungi, root hairs and the like that effectively links all the trees into a superorganism.

Existing systems theories, including informational theories, tend to posit a mechanical and crudely hierarchical set of relations between ecosystemic elements. This leads to hopeless contradictions in the relations between humanity and nature, which have prevented the emergence of an integral view, and divide those who sever humanity from nature from those who would submerge it in nature. So long as mechanistic reduction holds sway, the set of ecosystems will be put together essentially like a motor car, with each system being a part such as the starter or the tyres. What is needed is recognition of the fact that the formativeness of life introduces a radically different element, which we here simply call the Whole, and is manifest in the dynamic fluidity that obtains within and between ecosystems. Elements of living ecosystems do not exist as separable parts; they also exist in relation to the Whole, which is non-reducible to any of its parts, which plays a role in determining them, and cannot exist without them. What is individual exists in relation to the Whole, therefore, and this relationship must be included in any concrete account of things. Our very being is given this way, and, for humans, endowed as we are with intense interiority, it appears as spirit. The Whole is the formative notion of the ecosystem: it is a kind of *logos* that constitutes the intelligence of the ecosystem, which intelligence is drawn upon by individual beings within the ecosystem and, in our case, eventuates in consciousness. When we, or any other creature, are truly thinking, we are thinking in respect to the Whole; there is a sense in which it can also be said that the Whole is thinking through us.

The boundary-processes between elements in an ecosystem determine its integrity. These processes are as varied as life-forms themselves, and cannot be reduced to any common property beyond the interplay between formativeness and the constraints of entropy and other fundamental physical laws. Yet we can say that the integrity or 'health' of an ecosystem is a function of how these boundary processes, of whatever kind, relate organisms to each other internally, to other ecosystems externally, and to the Whole. The integrity of an ecosystem can be expressed in relational terms;

we might say that it depends upon the degree of *differentiation* between its elements, where this term describes *a state of being that preserves both individuality and connectedness*. From another angle, to the extent that organismic beings *recognize* one another, they are both distinct and connected: they become themselves through active relation to the other. In this usage, recognition need not imply any defined subjective element. It is rather any mutual signalling that preserves both connection and individuality. Nor does differentiation always imply harmony or equilibrium. It can allow for interactions between organisms that result in the death of one or more of them; but a death, nevertheless, that provides for the preservation of the Whole.[19] The ecosystem consists of the comings and goings of all its constituents; this ceaseless motion builds up the Whole, within which, therefore, the death of individuals is just as important as their particular lives.

If differentiation is the key to understanding ecosystemic integrity, what makes for ecosystemic disintegration? Here we introduce a formal process that interrupts the dialectic of individuality and connectedness, and leads to the *separation* of elements, or, from another angle, of their *splitting*. What splits apart the elements of an ecosystem, either from each other, or, what amounts to the same thing, from the Whole, will impede the development of that Whole, block the evolution of new forms, and eventually destroy the individuals within it. Splitting entails a breakdown of recognition. Whatever will fragment an ecosystem, separating its constituents and depriving them of the range of their mutual interactions, will block the formation of the Whole, and to that degree impoverish the development of the organisms within that whole, cause a deterioration of their internal state and even, perhaps, lead to their extinction.

This can be viewed as a process of physical separation – the so-called 'island effect' by which ecosystems sink below the size that permits the optimal interaction of their organismic elements[20] – but also as the introduction of disruptive elements into the ecosystem, either new organisms ('pests' and pathogens), or new substances that block the life-processes and so annihilate ecosystemic existence. The introduction of methyl isocyanate into Bhopal was an example of splitting as annihilation. A similar discussion could be resumed at a more subtle level for pollutants that have been inserted into the biosphere – as, for example, by organochlorines that mimic hormones and fragment the integrity of the endocrine ecosystem[21] – and also by capital, which separates the producer from the means of production, as well as through the effects of money, to be discussed below. All of these modalities introduce self-perpetuating splits into ecosystems, which disintegrate them. What is split away leads not to a renewal of being but to emptiness and withering, physically but also subjectively, as when traumatic memories are split off, or parts of the self become alien.[22]

The ecological crisis is a great and proliferating set of ecosystemic splits, both natural and human, subjective as well as objective – a fraying of the fabric of the ecosphere. But what was frayed can also be mended, the way a broken arm can be mended. Here the break in the bone splits apart the functional unity of the limb, which the healer mends by figuring out how to hold together the broken parts so that nature's reintegrative process can resume. So it is with damaged ecosystems: ways must be found to restore and hold together elements to create a flourishing ecosystemic boundedness. There are important homologies to this in the ordinary functioning of nature, for example, the structural dynamics of the cell, where small packets of energy are deployed through the exquisite arrangement of ribosomes in mitochondria, 'holding together' the intricate array of molecules so that the synthesis of low-entropy compounds – and structures composed of these – can go forward. It is not too far-fetched to claim that these conditions formally reproduce those attending the origins of life itself. Another example, in which I should hope every human participates, is the holding of children, the animate communication with them, and, then, necessarily, the letting go when the child is capable of moving on her own. This is the way individuality and connectedness become integrated in a human life. The great intricacies of raising children are variations on this simple theme; they amount to the provision of safe spaces in which an entropically unlikely interaction of elements can take place. Nothing fancy, yet more than three billion years of evolution enter into it.

It is important to recall in this time of despair that humanity, the greatest pest in nature, is not necessarily pestilential. All production – our giving form to nature – is an ensemble of order and disorder, and an entropic gamble. By 'producing production' ecologically, we bring the odds of that production in the direction of ecosystemic integrity. The artist's fury to rearrange the given is akin to the gardener's tearing of the soil. 'The cut worm forgives the plough,' wrote Blake, knowing that destruction and production are conjoined sides of a dialectic.

Gardening, taken at large, can vary from a crude appropriation of capitalist consumerism (pesticides, heavy equipment, and so on), to inspired modes of 'organic' intervention, including the practice of 'permaculture', which engages a conscious effort to design gardens as full ecosystems.[23] All good gardening consists of differentiating a pre-existent given by the holding together of disparate elements (seeds, water, good soil, compost, mulch, light) so that ecosystem development can occur. Conscious preparation is necessary, and culturally transmitted knowledge. Thus gardening is a social process, enhanced to the degree that a fully realized association enters the picture. In fact, a community garden is an excellent model of a pathway toward an ecological society, as we will discuss later on.

The whole of history enters into each garden plot, and is perennially reopened there. These filaments extend back to the origins of humankind, and reveal the authentic core of our nature – which is to intervene creatively in nature. Long before the Neolithic revolution had opened a path toward hierarchical society, humanity had learned to read the book of nature and to follow its generative way. It was a hard learning, whose lesson is lost in a facile romanticization of 'first peoples'. For the very first humans were by no means always kind to nature, nor should we expect this of them. Marauding bands of archaic peoples, for example, were quite likely the species exterminators of mastodons, along with many other species. And why not? Why should the powers of collective action and technology afforded by human being not have gone haywire again and again under the circumstances of Palaeolithic existence, just as they have since? There is no surprise in that. The wonder is, rather, that at least some of the same creatures learned from their mistakes, learned to care for nature, and to divine the essentials of an ecocentric way of being.

If we look back to those forms of production that are not only pre-capitalist but essentially pre-market (in that the elements of private property, money and exchange are peripheral to life), we find humanity capable of the whole range of ecological relations, creative as well as wanton. The latter is written in many extinctions and false starts, while the former may be summarized as follows: *that under original conditions, the human being is not merely capable of living in 'harmony with nature'; more fundamentally, an unalienated human intelligence is itself capable of fostering the evolution of nature even as it itself evolves.* In this sense, what we call 'nature' is to some degree a human product itself, so that ecology and history have a common root. If evolution is mediated by the activity of creatures through ecosystems, should not the consciously transformative activity that is the human trademark also be an evolutionary force?

Consider the Amazon Basin, a hotly contested zone of the ecological crisis. It is recognized that an immense proportion of living species – including innumerable species as yet undiscovered by us, along with many that are extremely useful – are found in this great womb. What accounts for this prodigious diversity? There is no single 'efficient cause', in the sense derived for the ecological crisis as a whole, but there are distinct efficient causal patterns, a major one of which involves human intervention. The principal mode of species diversification is known as 'allopatric speciation' – briefly, the divergent paths taken by common gene pools as the creatures bearing those genes are separated and undergo different development under varying ecosystemic conditions. The famous example is the varied evolution of finches in the Galapagos Islands, discovered by Darwin. As different populations from the stem species moved to different islands, they ceased interbreeding and divergences began to appear under the different island conditions – which had been further changed by species activity – until eventually new species appeared.

In the hot and moist Amazon Basin, the immense, varied yet relatively unbroken terrain, some six million square kilometres in area, creates an exponentially greater gene pool for the purposes of recombination. However, the very unbrokenness of the terrain can be seen to work against the project of speciation. For despite the great range of soils and habitats, there are few islands, or mountain ranges, or impassable bodies of water to provide the ecosystemic differentiation to allow allopatric speciation to take its course 'naturally'. One would think, rather, that the oceanic scale of the rainforest would cause related gene pools to intermix constantly, thereby inhibiting the profusion of new species.

Such reckoning omits, however, to take into account a creature able to create new ecosystems and demarcate them from others in a fluid and shifting way. More, this creature, left to its own devices, will for quite a few millennia live in small communities and as a result build a great number of micro-ecosystems.[24] The indigenous peoples of the Amazon not only created new ecosystems, they deliberately made these in a way that encouraged diversity of species – for instance, by planting different configurations of trees that would attract varying patterns of game species. Moreover, they engaged, like many Indians of the Americas, in the controlled burning of the landscape. Utterly unlike the mass burnings by alienated and desperate workers and peasants that have been destroying the rainforest for the past two generations, this kind of burning is conducted in small batches, at carefully controlled times and rates, and by the individuals who directly inhabit the land. As Susanna Hecht and Alex Cockburn comment for the Kayapó (who at the height of their society tended an area roughly the size of France), the burning 'is coupled with activities that compensate for its potentially destructive effects'.[25] The result is actual enhancement of fertility (necessary given the peculiar conditions of the rainforest) and the provision of micro-ecosystems for rapid speciation.

Here humanity writes with its labour on the surface of the Amazon basin to bring forth new and richly varying life forms. Far from being a congenital enemy of nature, then, humans can be a part of nature that catalyses nature's own exuberance. This ecologically creative activity is reserved, however, for those whose human ecology is closely configured to the varying natural ecologies with which it interacts, so that the combined human–natural ecosystem is integral and differentiated rather than dis-integrated and split. It needs be realized that this kind of behaviour requires that the earth not be treated as private property, or, what comes to the same thing, that the labour that undertakes it is freely differentiated. It is under such 'original' conditions that human intelligence and consciousness learned to take an ecocentric form. This way of being creates people who differentiate nature and know the individual plant species one by one,[26] who live in the small, collectively managed communities that provide an immense range of opportunities for allopatric speciation, and who develop the existentially alive culture whose lessons are ours to learn.[27]

Notes

1. See, for example, Goudie 1991. Alongside the manifest and immediate effects are others more pervasive and subtle, such as the spread of substances on currents of air and water to every spot on the earth. Thus polar bears turn out to have huge con-centrations – in fact, the highest anywhere – of pesticide residues sprayed thousands of miles away. Of course, we should keep a sense of proportion: only an infinitesimal portion of the substance of the universe has been altered by human activity. It's just that this speck of dust happens to define our existence.

2. The best single account of the history of ecological thought is Worster 1994.

3. As in Bateson 1972.

4. See, for example, de Duve 1995. Working within an entirely materialist frame of

reference, de Duve, a Nobel Laureate, insists that because of the large number of linked successive steps necessary for the emergence of life, this could not have been a freak or random event, rather, 'the universe was – and presumably still is – pregnant with life' (1995: 9). See also Fortey 1997. Where de Duve builds from the atomic level to the ever-growing complexification of living form, Fortey presents a panoramic view of the whole march of evolution.

5. According to Paul Davies (1983), we have some 10^{100} years to wait for this, a comfortable interval. The relatively imminent cosmological catastrophe, which will surely wipe out the earth itself whether or not humans are still on it, is the scheduled turning of the sun into a red-giant star, whose dimensions will reach the orbit of this planet in a mere 5 billion (5×10^9) years – roughly the time the earth has been in existence. So we are halfway there.

6. As for the Second Law, the mathematical physicist Roger Penrose raises the question of its cosmological relationships in an extremely interesting contribution. The entropy principle defines time's arrow – i.e., it determines whether t or t' is the later for any closed system according to which one corresponds to greater entropy for that system. Penrose asks how this can be more than a circular definition, in which entropy increases with time, while time's arrow is defined as that direction in which entropy increases. 'Something', he wonders, '*forced* the entropy to be low in the past ... [W]e should not be surprised if, *given* a low-entropy state, the entropy turns out to be higher at a later time. What *should* surprise us is that entropy gets more and more ridiculously tiny the farther and farther we examine it in the past!' Penrose observes that we take in low-entropy food in order to sustain the low entropy necessary for life. But '[w]here does this supply of low entropy come from?' Ultimately, as we know, from photosynthesis, the foundational way that life on earth struggles for existence. But this is to say that we draw low entropy from the sun (whether we eat plants that bind solar energy into living form or other creatures who eat the plants). 'Contrary to a common impression,' continues Penrose, 'the earth (together with inhabitants) does *not* gain energy from the sun! What the earth does is to take energy in a low entropy form and then spew it *all* back into space, but in a high-entropy form [radiant heat, i.e., infra-red photons, replacing higher frequency visible photons].' Thus there are few photons of high energy coming in and relatively more of lower energy going out – an increase in entropy. Now, this is because 'the sun is a *hot-spot* in the sky', in which energy is concentrated, and this in turn is because of the 'gravitational contraction from what had been a previously uniform distribution of gas (mainly hydrogen)'. The sun, like any star, heats from this contraction until thermonuclear reactions set in and keep it from contracting further and hence burning itself out. It follows that gravity is the ultimate source of the sun's energy – and through it, life on earth (and, to be sure, fossil fuels). Indeed, gravity is the ultimate cause of nuclear energy as well, the heavier isotopes of uranium, and so on, arising in the gravitationally compressed interior of neutron stars – and of course it is the direct source of geothermal energy along with the energy of tides, the two other energy variants of relevance to life on earth. Deep sea hot vents are loci of forms of life not dependent upon photosynthesis, and, in certain views, may have been the cradle of life on earth. Tides, of course, are an active component of many important ecosystems, especially coral reefs. In sum, gravitational clumping determines the Second Law, through the initial spreading out of matter and energy through all space in the 'Big Bang', and its secondary coming together through gravity. (In contrast to a thermally driven system, where uniformity is equivalent to higher entropy, a gravitationally driven system is at its most ordered, least probable, state when uniform; hence the appearance

of form as such may be more properly assigned to that phase of the development of nature in which non-gravitational modes of energy engage and interact with gravitational modes.) At this point the argument passes into the uncertainties of quantum gravity and ceases to be relevant to the present work. The point to be emphasized is the ultimate linkage between cosmological forces and the great regulatory principles of life and terrestrial ecosystems: the fundamental unity of nature. Penrose 1990, 410–17, Ch. 7 *passim*. Italics in original.

7.　Fortey 1997: 65. Fortey points out the great variety of stromatolite forms that evolved over the next billion years, including reefs – essentially one creature extending hundreds of miles. The arrival of animals destabilized the stromatolitic mats, which had prepared the way for more complex forms by creating atmospheric oxygen. Now they endure only in special environments where nobody is there to eat them. The evolutionary biologist Lynn Margulis follows a similar, though much more daring, line of thought in her 'endosymbiosis' theory. See Margulis 1998.

8.　We set aside the question of the formal organization of cosmological nature. Here the levels of energy and the form taken by matter is so remote from that occurring on earth that the notion of ecology makes little sense. The term, after all, derives from the Greek *oikos*, or home. Strictly speaking, we would have to substitute another term for the 'ecosystemic' extension into the cosmos.

9.　The classic text is Schrödinger 1967. First written in 1944, before the discoveries of molecular biology, this is one of those inspired leaps that shows the power of a good theory to look ahead.

10.　Lovelock 1979.

11.　'Opposition unites. From what draws apart results the most beautiful harmony. All things take place by strife' (Fragment 46 in Nahm 1947: 91). Edward Hussey writes of Heraclitus: 'the perpetual struggle of opposites and the justice that balances them are indistinguishable and both equally present in every event' (Hussey 1972: 49). Within contemporary biology, there is heated debate about the question of equilibrium and struggle. Chaos theory captures something of this flux, with its doctrine of 'strange attractors', non-linear processes, and the capabilities of butterfly wings to set off typhoons. As the *Oxford Dictionary* puts it: 'scientifically, chaos denotes the behaviour of a system which is governed by deterministic laws but is so unpredictable as to appear random, owing to its extreme sensitivity to initial conditions.' Glieck 1987 provides a popular introduction. Botkin 1990 presents the impact of this on ecology as such. Missing from these theories are notions of dialectics, as developed below, in the next chapter, and in particular, a coherent relation to human ecologies. I am generally in support of the position argued by Richard Levins and Richard Lewontin (Levins 1985), especially the essay 'Evolution as theory and ideology', pp. 9–64. Both the notion of progress and that of equilibrium are taken to task by these distinguished biologists.

12.　See my *White Racism* (Kovel 1984) for a discussion of how the biologization of race-as-pseudospecies has come about, particularly with regard to white-over-black racism. These days, racial essentialism is still prevalent as a discourse, only now, well-rewarded savants write long, thickly researched tomes in which the 'Black Problem' is located in a cultural, rather than a biological, framework. But an essence by any name remains a reification frozen out of historical time. See, for example, Herrnstein and Murray 1996; Thernstrom and Thernstrom 1997.

13.　To add a bit to this highly compressed account: the enlarged brain and upright posture necessary for freeing the hands comprise a kind of evolutionary contradiction, for the latter results in a rigid pelvis, which has difficulty in allowing the former to be born. This was 'solved' by allowing the brain to be born immature and having it undergo a considerable amount of development *ex utero*. This plays a central role in the replacement of instinct with cultural learning, and also in the peculiar importance of childhood to human beings. The need for protracted child care in a slowly maturing creature who has to be carried about for a long time owing to the loss of clinging instincts (which persist only in vestigial form, as in the Babinski sign known to neonatologists) has had incalculable influence on our cultural inheritance.

14. Hegel, Nietzsche, Freud, Lacan and others – all beyond present scope – stand in the line of those who uncovered this relationship in Western thought; though it may also be said that the entirety of our spiritual traditions are built upon figuring it out.

15. A caveat: almost all of these points will be contested by those who point to the care given by elephants to their dead, or to the use of language by whales, and so forth. Lest there be misunderstanding, let me emphasize that species chauvinism is not my intent. To establish an ensemble of human-natural traits is not to locate these in any particular species, but to say, rather, that any species with the power to adopt them can arrive at the ambivalent position of humans. If my Max dog recognizes me, that gives him a degree of human being, just as severely demented people have lost that attribute. But there is a specific putting together of these things that is distinctively human, which other, perhaps more sensible, creatures do not share.

16. The architect, in contrast to the bee, 'raises his structure in imagination before he erects it in reality. At the end of every labour-process, we get a result that already existed in the imagination of the labourer at its commencement' (Marx 1967a: 178).

17. For a discussion, see my *History and Spirit* (Kovel 1998b).

18. 'Neither nature objectively nor nature subjectively is directly given in a form adequate to the *human* being. And as everything natural has to have its *beginning, man* too has his act of coming-to-be – *history* … History is the true natural history of man' (Marx 1978b: 116, italics in original).

19. For human society, this has been expressed in terms of sacrifice, with its many ramifications.

20. Quammen 1996.

21. See Colburn et al. 1996.

22. From the other side, the appropriation of split-off parts of the self, accompanied by the letting go (as against the splitting off) of desires, is a sign of the development of the human being, and the core gesture of healing.

23. The brainchild of a Tasmanian, Bill Mollison, permaculture designs living environments using architectural principles and taking into account the whole range of global to local interrelations. In certain settings, such as South India, microclimatic changes have been induced that reverse generations of ecological degeneration. In others, substantial food production has been achieved in urban settings. See Mollison 1988. The website http://www.kenyon.edu/projects/permaculture/ gives an index of the impressive scope of this movement.

24. This discussion is principally drawn from Hecht and Cockburn 1990. Another important factor is the frequency of flooding that divides and in effect shuffles the landscapes. Thus there is no singular efficient cause here. As Hecht and Cockburn point out, people tended to follow the flooding and therefore to work synergistically with nature in the production of new areas for allopatric speciation.

25.   Hecht and Cockburn 1990: 44. Timing is essential, as is planting before the blaze so that agricultural succession begins immediately after the fire, followed by crops of other cyclical variety, so that a rich and complex ecosystem is rapidly restored. Proper attention is also paid to recycling ashes and so on, as well as the technique of 'cool burning', which controls pests but allows desired plants to flourish.

26.   The ethnobotanist William Balée has shown that the Ka'apor Indians of north-east Brazil were able to name and use 94 per cent of the plant species in a sample area of two and a half acres. This is extreme. But most forest populations (not just aboriginal Indians) know and use about 50 per cent of the plant species. Cited in Hecht and Cockburn 1990: 59.

27.   Two authors who both explored and celebrated these ways are Stanley Diamond (Diamond 1974) and Pierre Clastres (Clastres 1977).

6 Capital and the Domination of Nature

The Pathology of a Cancer upon Nature

What is the root of capital's wanton ecodestructivity? One way of seeing this is in terms of an economy geared to run on the basis of unceasing accumulation. Thus each unit of capital must, as the saying goes, 'grow or die', and each capitalist must constantly search to expand markets and profits or lose his position in the hierarchy. Under such a regime the economic dimension consumes all else, nature is continually devalued in the search for profit along an expanding frontier, and the ecological crisis follows inevitably.

This reasoning is, I believe, valid, and necessary for grasping how capital becomes the efficient cause of the crisis. But it is incomplete, and fails to clear up the mystery of what capital *is*, and consequently what is to be done about it. For example, it is a commonly held opinion that capitalism is an innate and therefore inevitable outcome for the human species. If this is the case, then the necessary path of human evolution travels from the Olduvai Gorge to the New York Stock Exchange, and to think of a world beyond capital is mere baying at the moon.

It only takes a brief reflection to demolish the received understanding. Capital is certainly a potentiality for human nature, but, despite all the efforts of ideologues to argue for its natural inevitability, no more than this. For if capital were natural, why has it only occupied the last 500 years of a record that goes back for hundreds of thousands? More to the point, why did it have to be imposed through violence wherever it set down its rule? And most importantly, why does it have to be continually maintained through violence, and continuously re-imposed on each generation through an enormous apparatus of indoctrination? Why not just let children be the way they want to be and trust that they will turn into capitalists and workers for capitalists – the way we let baby chicks be, knowing that they will reliably grow into chickens if provided with food, water and shelter? Those who believe that capital is innate should also be willing to do without police, or the industries of culture, and if they are not, then their arguments are hypocritical.

But this only sharpens the questions of what capital is, why the path to it was chosen, and why people would submit to an economy and think so much of wealth in the first place? These are highly practical concerns. It is widely recognized, for example, that habits of consumption in the industrial societies will have to be drastically altered if a sustainable world is to be achieved. This means, however, that the very pattern of human needs will have to be changed, which means in turn that the basic way in which we inhabit nature will have to be changed. We know that capital forcibly indoctrinates people to resist these changes, but only a poor and superficial analysis would stop here and say nothing further about how this works and how it came about. Capital's efficient causation of the ecological crisis establishes it as the enemy of nature. But the roots of the enmity still await exploration.

A great deal of ink has been expended in trying to decide just what is the core of our estrangement from nature, but little of it has any real explanatory value. It is perfectly possible and quite desirable, for example, to identify, as do the Deep Ecologists, certain central and controlling ideas that define a pathological relation to nature, notably the 'anthropocentric' delusion that sees nature, in all its intricate glory, existing like so many planets around the human sun. No understanding of the ecological crisis would be complete without such a dimension. But it is a dimension only, that outlines the subjective shape of an ecodestructive complex without connection to the objective side of things, and with no clue as to how it arose – or, therefore, as to how it can be overcome. A mental attitude explains no more than some of the internal circuitry of a phenomenon, and until its origins and relationships with the world are spelled out, is just an empty and vague abstraction.

Similarly, many authors are ready to talk of 'technology' or 'industrialization' as the active elements in the crisis, since it is obvious that it is through such means that nature is being laid waste. But to stop at this point is not only incomplete, but evasive and politically opportunistic, since it is patently the case that the industry in question, and the tools it uses, are instruments of capital accumulation, and have been so since the beginnings of the modern world.[1] No tool, no large-scale organization of technology, can exist in itself: industry, and all the qualities internal to it, are products and expressions of a given mode of social organization, and cannot be conceived apart from it. The world teems with brilliant innovations that deserve application as ways of checking the ecological crisis, but will not be used because they run against the exigencies of accumulation. The same can be said for 'science', also routinely hauled out as the culprit responsible for our estrangement from nature, which is said to be reduced 'scientifically' to a mere object for dissection. Well, yes, this does happen, but the questions must again be posed: which science, in the service of which interests, and shaped by which social forces? No doubt an estranged science plays a tremendous role in the domination of nature. But estrangement of this kind must itself be explained, and in the explaining, we push back the origins of domination.

Science, technology and industry are today all subsumed into the capitalist system. Yet capitalism as we know it did not spring full-grown into the world. It combined many precursors, which took root in peculiar cultural soils. The economies that resulted were not the bearers of any particular essence, but reflected, like the personalities of individuals, specific integrations, some of which have been more deadly to ecologies than others. For example, our variety of eco-destructive capitalism was a peculiarly European concoction, and, as such, deeply influenced by the dominant Christian religion, spiritual edge of an extremely powerful and by no means ecologically friendly world-view.[2] The attitude of Christianity toward nature long pre-dates capitalism, and extends from its Judaic roots, as in the passage in *Genesis* (1: 26) where Yahweh gives Adam 'dominion over the fish of the sea, and over the fowl of the air, and over the cattle, and over all the earth, and over every creeping thing that creepeth upon the earth' – all of which is not only compatible with but mandated by the belief that 'God created man in his own image, in the image of God created he him (27).

No other world religion, and certainly no tribal religion, incorporates the domination of nature so directly into its *Logos*. It bears emphasis that this attitude was strongly contested within Christianity – indeed, some of the greatest saints, Francis and Teresa of Avila being the most famous, are defined by rebellion against it, just as the Church itself would strive to contain the capitalist monster once it arose from European soil. Religions are dialectical: they express domination as well as the protest against domination, and at times the release from domination. Nevertheless, there is a definite balance of forces at play, and for Christianity, the preponderance of these forces was expressed in what would have to be called an anti-ecological direction. This is best shown by the striking hatred of the body that marks the history of Christendom, along with its obsessive preoccupation with feelings of guilt.[3]

Many societies could have led the way into the capitalist era, including China and India, which were more highly developed by far than Europe in the fifteenth century, while being more at home with nature. It is impossible to say whether their accession to capitalism would have resulted in an ecologically friendlier outcome. But the luck was with Europe, which had its shipping lanes along the trade winds that led to the 'undiscovered' Americas. And so the civilization whose previous development had primed it for the domination of nature became capitalist in the sense that we recognize the beast, especially after emergence into harsh and life-denying Calvinism.[4]

Yet this relationship does not entitle us to declare Christianity the villain of the piece, either, since the crisis is quite capable of being reproduced without it; indeed, in its current phase, virtually all traces of the religious origins of capital have been effaced. In the final analysis, a religion is itself the ambivalent product of a certain kind of society. Thus the evocation of Christendom again raises the question of origins and pushes back the quest until it disappears into the mists of human beginnings. Here, however, we reach a ground that can enable a reasonably coherent – if highly attenuated and schematic – image of how the domination of nature arose, and what led it to mutate into capitalism. It goes without saying that what follows is adapted to the purposes of this work and does not represent a full rendition of the story and the many questions attached to it. The reader must decide for him- or herself whether the light it casts will compensate for the brevity of treatment.

The Gendered Bifurcation of Nature

The first map of the human species was drawn according to 'him' and 'her', in that produced configuration of sexuality known as *gender*. Gender is the original dividing line within humanity: all constructions of humankind, whether within humanity or between humanity and nature, are inscribed by it. There is nothing more 'material' (to the common origin of the words, *material* and *mother*). Sex is of the earth, and the primary dividing lines between genders were between earth-transforming labour. From this matrix (there is the root again) arose the beginnings of domination, and all future dominations, including that effected by capital, are shadowed by that of male over female.

This is not an exercise in politically correct male-bashing, but the recognition that the history of domination would be radically incomplete unless the role played in it by the construction of the masculine gender were acknowledged. The actual origins must remain shrouded in an impenetrably distant past. Nevertheless, everything that is known (though all-too-often ideologically denied) about the human species compels the reconstruction of the following, which we state succinctly and according to the ideas already developed about human nature, so as to bring out the essential points: [5]

- In the original, hunter-gatherer, phase of society, the first differentiation of labour occurs according to sex, generally speaking, with males hunting and females gathering – along, needless to say, with their work of reproduction. Note that this labour produces the gender itself, and that its origins were a genuine differentiation, with mutual recognition, fluid social relations and self-determination. Such can still be seen in the cultural remnants we have of these peoples, and by the reconstruction of the quality of self-experience derived from it: the 'dream-time' of Australian first peoples, the wandering of souls, the manifestations of Trickster, and so forth.[6]
- The phase encompasses the great span of human prehistory, and entails a great range of human–natural transformations, including the domestication of animals and the origins of agriculture. Though without domination, the original division of labour set forth males as the takers of life and females as life's givers. Moreover, the death-dealing tools of the hunt, and the fact of its often being carried out by roving bands, prepared a way for something worse.
- Here a sporadically occurring event may be postulated of whose existence we may be certain even though no concrete first instance can be brought forward. Its agent was masculine, not as individual hunter, but as a subset of the collective: a group, or band of hunters. Its stimulus

would vary, being composed however of internal as well as external forces, the latter being, say, a threat to survival, such as disease or drought, which compelled a search for new resources; while the former was a function of the psychodynamics of the male group. In any case, the event in question was a transformation of the hunt into a raid, with the object being now not the obtaining of food and skins from animals, but the expropriation of productive labour from other humans, taking not the life of another creature, but the life-giving and building power of one's own kind.[7]

- This necessarily involved the seizure of women and children from a neighbouring collective. We would suppose a threefold violence: killing or driving off the males from the attacked collective, denying the self-determination of the seized women and children, and the forcible sexual violation of the captives.

- This act was a profound mutation in human being. It created a whole new conjuncture, which in time became a structure. First, the possibilities of exploiting another's labour are introduced, always in the direction of male over female. Second, the potentials for enduring social divisions are grounded in this, again male over female; these are to extend from the hunting band, to the warrior band, and to the ruling class, with any number of intermediate and modern variations, such as the Vatican Curia, the NFL Superbowl champions, corporate Boards of Directors, the Joint Chiefs of Staff, the Politburo, secret societies such as Yale's Skull and Bones. There is a sense in which the whole world has been run by male groups since the beginnings of history. Third, the genders are further produced by this, with sharply opposed identities constituted by master and slave. And fourth, violence – physical force along with the culture glorifying this – had to become institutionalized in order to hold on to what had been stolen.

- The structures imposed by the original seizure of female labour had dramatic expansive possibilities. Social violence entered the lists of the dangers to which societies are exposed. The violence invited retaliation and/or defence, and it came to define ever larger social aggregates with expansive dynamics, as each particular group underwent a compulsion to achieve power relative to others. Internally, the drive toward power caused struggles for leadership and social control. The result, after innumerable twists and turns we are unable to detail here, was the emergence of the

Big Man, the Chieftain, the King, the Emperor, the Pope, the Führer, the Generalissimo and the CEO.

We would emphasize again that these principles would be variously applied across a vast range of situation. There is no need, either, to imagine a single such event radiating outward to encompass the rest of humanity. But what has to be underscored is the absolute dynamism of this event, and the fact that it amounted to a real mutation of human society as potent as anything from the realm of genetics. Out of the nexus of original male violence arose codified property relations, as a way of holding on to what had been taken: hence the notion of legitimacy follows that of violent seizure. Similarly, the institution of patriarchy emerged, as a system of apportioning women and assuring ownership and control over children – a never ending dilemma for the man who sows his seed and moves on, as the Big Man must. Property in this sense is not primarily that which attaches to the self, like clothing or jewellery (although in stratified and wealthy societies, the control over personal consumption is quite significant), but rather the power of producing – and re-producing – life and the means for life. The control over labour generates civilization, and this originates in the forcible control over women.

It follows that domination and property are gendered from the beginning.[8] This means that a basic alienation is introduced at the foundations of society – alienation being the reflex, at the level of human being, of ecosystemic splitting. The dominant male identity is formed in this cauldron. From the beginning, its reference point is the other males in the hunting/ warrior group, with whom it associates and identifies; coordinatively, it comes to shun and deny recognition to the subjected female. A purified male-Ego comes to define the dominant form taken by the self, which enters into the exfoliating system of splits constituting the emergent civilization. Subjectively, this alienation becomes inscribed as a progressive separation from the body, and from what the body signifies, namely, nature.[9]

A polarization between the human and the natural worlds ensues, with masculinity occupying the human (= intellectual, far-seeing, spiritual, power- ful and active) pole, and femininity the pole of nature (= instinctual, limited and body-based, inconstant, weak and passive). The *gendered bifurcation of nature* has been set going, to configure the relations between genders, and between humanity and nature, all the way to the ecological crisis.

The path leading from the first violent expropriation of labour to the heights of capital passes through the solidification of property and the appearance of class as a defining element of society. Class institutionalizes property and emerges *pari passu* with the introduction of splitting into human ecosystems. Although violent expropriation is a necessary step in domination, it is insufficient in itself as a way of producing and reproducing life. Secondary forms of recognition become essential to hold the social ecosystem together and harness its forces. Class is one such, operating in the sphere of production as patriarchy does in that of reproduction. Class codifies the formal arrangements for the ownership of productive property and the control over labour. The rule of law is layered over that of violence, and internalizes violence. Labour has become unfree.

Unlike gender, class is grounded not in physical difference or biological plan, but in the formalization of the productive core of human being. Since the free exercise of transformative power expresses human nature, class is a violation of human nature, and with it, of nature itself, even if it is not grounded in the physical body. But class relationships never appear in pure, unadulterated form, however, as the splits they impose would tear society apart. They occur, rather, embedded in a further institutional turn, which emerges and takes the form of the *state*. It is the class/state nexus that comprises the decisive leap between archaic society and what we call civilization. With this, history as such begins, and the cyclical, differentiated time of original society is transformed according to the hierarchical ground plan of class. Now society has a controlling agency to tell its story to itself – a story, however, given over to conflict because of the institutionalization of class. States impose writing, through their cadres of technicians; they impose universalizing religions such as Christianity through their cadres of priests; and they impose laws through their judges and courts; they impose violence and conquest with their armies, and also the legitimation of violence and conquest. Everything thereafter is marked with contradiction, stemming from the state's original dilemma, that it stands over the whole of society, but is for society's ruling classes.

States carry forth all those notions we call 'progress'. They also, however, implement the domination of nature, in all the forms taken by nature – women certainly, but also the other peoples conquered by those states which achieve imperial status. As enslaved and dominated peoples become incorporated into the domain, they acquire the status of Other – barbarians, savages, human animals, and eventually (with the growth of science), ethnicities and races – all of which categories cluster with the female at the 'nature' end of the bifurcation within humanity.

This discussion may help clarify a vexing issue on the left as to the priority of different categories of what might be called 'dominative splitting' – chiefly, those of gender, class, race, ethnic and national exclusion, and, with the ecological crisis, species. Here we must ask, priority in relation to what? If we intend prior in *time*, then gender holds the laurel – and, considering how history always adds to the past rather than replacing it, would appear as at least a trace in all further dominations. If we intend prior in *existential* significance, then that would apply to whichever of the categories was put forward by immediate historical forces as these are lived by masses of people: thus to a Jew living in Germany in the 1930s, anti-Semitism would have been searingly prior, just as anti-Arab racism would be to a Palestinian living under Israeli domination today, or a ruthless, aggravated sexism would be to women living in, say, Afghanistan. As to which is *politically* prior, in the sense of being that which whose transformation is practically more urgent, that depends upon the preceding, but also upon the deployment of all the forces active in a concrete situation; we shall address this in the last section of this work, when we deal with the politics of overcoming the crisis.

If, however, we ask the question of *efficacy*, that is, which split sets the others into motion, then priority would have to be given to class, for the plain reason that class relations entail the state as an instrument of enforcement and control, and it is the state that shapes and organizes the splits that appear in human ecosystems. Thus class is both logically and historically distinct from other forms of exclusion (hence we should not talk of 'classism' to go along with 'sexism' and 'racism,' and 'species-ism'). This is, first of all, because class is an essentially man-made category, without root in even a mystified biology. We cannot imagine a human world without gender distinctions – although we can imagine a world without domination by gender. But a world without class is eminently imaginable – indeed, such was the human world for the great majority of our species' time on earth, during all of which considerable fuss was made over gender. Historically, the difference arises because 'class' signifies one side of a larger figure that includes a state apparatus whose conquests and regulations create races and shape gender relations. Thus there will be no true resolution of racism so long as class society stands, inasmuch as a racially oppressed society implies the activities of a class-defending state.[10] Nor can gender inequality be enacted away so long as class society, with its state, demands the super-exploitation of woman's labour.

Class society continually generates gender, racial, ethnic oppressions and the like, which take on a life of their own, as well as profoundly affecting the concrete relations of class itself. It follows that class politics must be fought out in terms of all the active forms of social splitting. It is the management of these divisions that keeps state society functional. Thus though each person in a class society is reduced from what s/he can become, the varied reductions can be combined into the great stratified regimes of history – this one becoming a fierce warrior, that one a routine-loving clerk, another a submissive seamstress, and so on, until we reach today's personi-fications of capital and captains of industry. Yet no matter how functional a class society, the profundity of its ecological violence ensures a basic antagonism which drives history onward. History *is* the history of class society – because no matter how modified, so powerful a schism is bound to work itself through to the surface, provoke resistance ('class struggle'), and lead to the succession of powers. The relation of class can be mystified without end – only consider the extent to which religion exists for just this purpose, or watch a show glorifying the police on television – yet so long as we have any respect for human nature, we must recognize that so funda-mental an antagonism as would steal the vital force of one person for the enrichment of another cannot be conjured away.

The state is what steps forward to manage this conflict so that the ruling class gets its way without causing society to fly apart. It is the state's province to deal with class contradiction as it works itself out in numberless ways – to build its armies and use them in conquest (thereby reinforcing patriarchal and violent values), to codify property, to set forth laws to punish those who would trangress property relations and to regulate contracts between in-dividuals who play by the rules, to institutionalize police, courts and prisons to back up those laws, or to certify what is proper and right in the education of the young, or the marriage of the sexes, or establish the religions that justify God's ways to mere man, or to institutionalize science and education – in sum, to regulate and enforce the class structure, and to channel the flux of history in the direction of the elites. The state institutionalizes patriarchy as well as class, and hence maintains the societal ground for the gendered bifurcation of nature. Furthermore, inasmuch as the modern state is also a *nation*-state, it employs the attachment of a people to its land as a source of legitimation, and thus incorporates the history of nature into myths of wholeness and integrity. All aspects of the domination of nature are in fact woven into the fabric by means of which the state holds society together, from which it follows that to give coherence to this narrative and make a difference in it, we have to attend to the state and its ultimate dependance upon maintaining the class structure. All of this is to play a basic role in the unfolding of contemporary ecological struggles, as we discuss in the next section.

The Rise of Capital

> Capitalism only triumphed when it becomes identified with the state, when it is the state. (Braudel 1977: 64)

Class relationships separate people from their vital power. Capital goes further: it separates our vital power from itself, and imposes a double estrangement. The arena within which this occurs is the labour market, and the instrument of its occurrence is that most strange and interesting concoction of the human mind, money.

As the saying goes, money makes the world go round. But there are three different aspects to money, which ascend in mystery, though all are bound together in reality.[11] The first, simplest, and most rational as well as the most ancient, would be money *as an instrument of exchange and trade*. We say 'rational' because without some independent element that enables goods to be compared to each other, economic activity, indeed, society itself, would remain palaeolithic. At this level, the money-function allows raw materials, instruments of production and finished goods to be brought together from varied sources, making a wider human intercourse possible.

The second way we know money is *as a commodity*, something that can be acquired, traded, and, crucially, accumulated. There is, from this angle, a history of money that passes from common concretions like shells or exchangeable possessions such as cattle,[12] to metallic coin, to the abstraction into paper notes of one kind and another, onwards into the ever-increasing dematerialization taken by the money-form until today, in the digital age, it covers the globalized world with a shower of bytes. To explore these aspects would distract us from the task at hand. However, one of them, the propensity for dematerialization, is of absolute importance, as it leads to the third and most puzzling, as well as most relevant, aspect of money.

What installs our system as the enemy of nature is the property of money as *the repository of value*. The notion of value, so difficult to grasp, yet so compelling for civilization, provides a window on to the pathology of power. Where money is concerned, value is an abstraction of the exchange function: thus from the particulars of exchanging one item for another, we arrive at 'exchangeability-in-general'. But it is also the convergence of exchangeability with desire. Value is the projection of human want into nature – including human nature and the qualities of the self. It is the setting up of an alternative, monetized world, with no fixed connection to the original world.[13] Thus value does not exist in nature, though the creature who devises it does. As Georg Simmel put in in his magisterial work on money:

> The series of natural phenomena could be described in their entirety without mentioning the value of things; and our scale of valuation remains meaningful, whether or not any of its objects appear frequently or at all in reality ... Valuation as a real psychological occurrence is part of the natural world; but what we mean by valuation, its conceptual meaning, is something independent of this world; is not part of it, but is rather the whole world viewed from a particular vantage point.[14]

There are distinct universes of value, by no means all economic. The infant values the breast, the child her dolls, the Buddha contemplation, the ecocentrically minded the biosphere, the fetishist a high heel, and so forth. Nor are all abstractions evil, to say the least, else we would regard mathematics as a crime, or the abstracting of Marx when he developed his notions of value in order to emancipate labour. Abstractions – including quantification – need not be pathological so long as there remains a differentiated path back to the sensuous-concrete, such as we see in the most fruitful science; or when, as in the case of 'pure' mathematics, abstractions are bracketed away from the external world. That is, the mathematician does not confuse his abstractions with reality – unless he is psychotic, and even if he is psychotic, he lacks the means to bring reality under the sway of his abstraction. Not so for capital, which converts the sensuous world into abstraction for the purpose of value. Since the sensuous world remains sensuous, that is, ecosystemic, this conversion becomes a splitting of devastating proportion and leads to a new order of domination.

Whatever is produced tends to serve some purpose, and meets a need, even if this be frivolous, destructive or fantastic. Thus a kind of value adheres to all made objects according to the needs these meet, or, to choose another word, their utility. For made things, *use-value* represents the conjugation of labour and nature, and occupies the boundary between human nature and nature at large. And because human nature entails participation of the imagination, there is no use-value that does not include some subjective and imagined dimension – whether this be the cosiness of a good blanket, the taste of wine, the anticipation of the potential life lying embedded in a seed, and so forth.

Use-value is essentially concrete; it is a *qualitative* function, composed of sensuous and intellectual distinctions with other aspects of the world, including other use-values. Being qualitative, it retains the essential feature of differentiation, that distinct elements can recognize one another and form links and associations. Use-values can be deformed when they come to express alienated ways of being – what else can be said, after all, about use-values such as are expressed by a TV game show, or any of the commodities that reflect false needs – sports utility vehicles, lite beer, fashion magazines, hand guns, and so on. But because they are also concrete, they can be restored, as a 'used' article can be mended or made to shine. Indeed, the mending of the ecological crisis requires precisely such a restoration.

Not all use-values are attached to commodities. However, all commodities have a use-value, since no one would purchase anything or exchange it for something else unless it has some utility.[15] But they also have another kind of value, arising from the fact of exchangeability that attaches to all commodities: *exchange-value*. Here, in sharp contrast to use-values, the sensuous and concrete are eliminated by definition. All that is retained as the mark of exchangeability is quantity: this item, x, is exchangeable for so many of y, which in turn is exchangeable for so many of z, and so forth, with no intrinsic end. Any concrete quality will break the chain; only number suffices, and money becomes the embodiment of that number. Hence money is fundamentally quantity, which becomes its use-value. Simmel again: 'The quantity of money is its quality. Since money is nothing but the indifferent means for concrete and infinitely varied purposes, its quantity is the only important determination so far as we are concerned. With reference to money, we do not ask what and how, but how much.'[16]

There is nothing else in the universe like it. Use-values require the participation of nature, but exchange-values are made by quantifying nature. The ascension of quantity over quality gives these relations the capacity for evil once the value function is advanced to the centre of the social stage, as in capitalism. In this loss of the sensuous and concrete, the abstracting function is abandoned to the delusions of power. Precisely because nature has been detached, with its limits and interrelations, in short, its ecosystems, there is no longer any internal limit to the value function. It can expand effortlessly. Pure quantity can swell infinitely without any reference to the external world, even though the quantity-using creature remains very much in that world. And if there is some will-to-power in the creature who makes for himself this value function, carried forward from traditional modes of domination, then that, too, can go to infinity.

Along the way, possibilities for recognition are sundered. Simmel points out two aspects: that valuation takes place in the human being, i.e., 'part of the natural world', and that it is not the world in itself, but 'rather the whole world viewed from a particular vantage point'. The abstraction into money sets loose these two formally distinct parts of value to wander their separate ways – and the creature who subsumes both those ways, *Homo œconomicus*, or the capitalist personification – is split internally and from the world. Hence the value that stalks forth in the economy is also the route that turns our differentiation from nature into a regime of splitting, which is to say, into one of self-perpetuating eco-disintegration.

The transformation of capital from an ancient part of the economic system into the world-devouring monster reproduced by capitalism occurred when the value function became attached to labour itself. For this to have taken place, an extensive series of prior developments, affecting the history of money as well as labour, was necessary.

Long before capitalism arose as such, rulers appreciated the power of money and foisted it upon the masses – who proved significantly reluctant to take the bait. In a far cry from Adam Smith's ideological notion, that the species has an innate propensity to barter, truck and exchange (in other words, that capitalism is part of human nature), the use of money was distinctly an acquired habit, often enough requiring coercion. With regard to Europe, which as the cradle of the capitalism we know deserves special attention, Alexander Murray has pointed out a kind of turning point occurring around the first millennium, in which a society not simply unacquainted with money but actually resistant to it was converted into one whose wheels were to become increasingly lubricated with lucre.[17] In Carolingean times, coins were introduced from above into a matrix that had no 'use' for their exchange-value, and where they were treated primarily in their second function, as a commodity to be exchanged along with others. Many coins were melted down for bullion, others were given directly to the poor, others were converted into ornaments and silver chalices, while others still have been found unused in various storage sites. Fines and penalties such as flogging had to be imposed to rouse the people of the 'Dark Ages' into the glories of exchange. Murray concludes that money was considered 'strange and suspect', and holds 'psychic inertia' responsible. But I would think that the said inertia was grounded in an intuition of the wreckage inherent in the strange function of value, a prescience, shared for a time by the Catholic Church, that the same money could become a wedge breaking down the integrity of communal life-worlds. In any case, there can be no doubt that medieval monetarism eventually speeded up economic activity and prepared the way for capitalism. By facilitating exchange, money increased its own value, fostered avarice, led to usury, and created demand for its own accumulation. The production of money surged – thus England had ten mints in 900, and 70 a century later, and banking, which first occurred to people in the ancient era, came into Europe with the founding of the Bank of Venice in 1171.

The expansion and centralization of trade, banking functions and urbanism fostered rationalization and technological progress. As the location of Europe's first bank in Venice suggests, this side of the process was advanced in the Mediterranean and mostly in the Italian city-states. Venice, along with Genoa and Florence, became the leading centres of the early manifestation of finance. Later the Luso-Hispanic plunder of the Western Hemisphere (opened by the Genovese Columbus) provided bullion for the finance capital that allowed Europe, whose economy had remained backward with respect to Asian centres until the mid-eighteenth century, to buy its way into hegemony.[18]

As for the labour relation, this was furthest developed in Northern Europe and especially through agricultural transformations in England. Here the critical factor became what Marx referred to as the separation of the worker from the means of production – which in pre-capitalist society meant the land, and, more generally, nature. In one of Marx's many summaries of this he puts it as follows:

> One of the prerequisites of wage labour and one of the historic conditions
> for capital is free labour and the exchange of free labour against money, in
> order to reproduce money and to convert it into values, in order to be
> consumed by money, not as use value for enjoyment but as use value for
> money. Another prerequisite is the separation of free labour from the objec-
> tive means of its realisation – from the means and materials of labour. This
> means above all that the worker must be separated from the land, which
> functions as his natural laboratory ... the relationship of the worker to the
> objective conditions of his labour is one of ownership: this is the natural
> unity of labour with its material prerequisites. [Under these circumstances]
> the individual is related to himself as proprietor, as master of the conditions
> of his reality. The same relation holds between one individual and the rest.[19]

The separation required violent expropriation.[20] The rate of dispossession
began accelerating after the mid-sixteenth century, as bullion from the
Americas began entering the European economies. It took place most
systematically in England in the form of the 'enclosure' of the commons,
i.e., of commonly owned land; it took place elsewhere in Europe as the
precondition for the coming of capitalism to that subcontinent; it took
place throughout the 'New World' and Africa as millions upon millions
became dispossessed so that the great capitalist enterprises and slave trades
could fatten; and it continues to take place today, with the expropriation of
community gardens in New York City, or wherever peasants stand back-
wardly in the way of accumulation, as, for example, in Mexico, where
NAFTA fosters their being driven by cheap imports of corn off the *ejidos*[21]
and into the *maquiladoras* or across the border – and also across that half of
the world which lies vulnerable to globalization. The separation of peoples
from the means of production and their communal heritage transfigures
the notion of property and creates the social foundation of the capitalist
mode of production; it is a gesture continuously reproduced as capital
penetrates life-worlds. Separation in this regard has two aspects: the physical
and juridical removal of producers from the appropriation of their own
lives; and alongside this, the alienation or estrangement, between the worker
and the product made, the method of work employed, relations with other
workers (and by extension, all social relations), and finally, from their own
human nature. The fourfold sense of alienated labour was drawn by Marx
in his early philosophical writing; later, in the mature synthesis of *Capital*,
it became amplified as the famous concept of commodity fetishism, an

insight into the way value-driven production mystifies the nature of things made, so that commodities relate as persons, and persons as things, in a veritable frenzy of estrangement.[22]

Separation/alienation/splitting is the fundamental gesture of capital. It applies to the expropriation of peasants, but also forcefully to the industrial system, where technological prowess in the service of value-expansion puts the finishing touches to the domination of nature. The Industrial Revolution brought in its wake work-discipline, as individual human labour had to become integrated with machinery and coordinated on an ever-expanding scale. Just as early medieval people were coerced into accepting the logic of money, so were early modern people coerced into accepting the logic of the bound time of accumulation. Wages are convertible to capital only if placed in a rigid schema of linear temporality, inasmuch as an abstract interval is the only way of computing the exchange-value of labour-power, or of measuring the surplus value wrung from it. For this computation, technology in the form of clocks was required, along with new modes of socialization and a religious and moral culture to put it all together and justify the whole arrangement in the eyes of God.[23]

Science, technology and industry, therefore, are all bundled together and, under the aegis of capital, come to express its powers of splitting. In capital's early phase, the inner connection to the gendered bifurcation of nature were strikingly revealed, in the blood shed in the great witch crazes of early modern Europe, and through ideologues of science such as Francis Bacon. As the system matured, its latent powers of ecodestruction would come to the fore under the aegis of industrialization.[24]

Industrialization is not an independent force, then, but the hammer with which nature is smashed for the sake of capital. Industrial logging destroys forests; industrial fishing destroys fisheries; industrial chemistry makes Frankenfood; industrial use of fossil fuels creates the greenhouse effect, and so forth – all for the sake of value-expansion. Most important, the technically driven production of the industrial order demands an expanded energy supply, for the purpose of which fuels such as coal, natural gas and petroleum are by far the most likely candidates. Such fuel represents past ecological activity: numberless residues of chemical bonds developed by living creatures in interaction with sunlight over hundreds of millions of years, now turned to heat energy to propel the instruments of industrial society. Each drive to the mall to buy wasteful plastic junk made from fossil fuel degrades aeons of ecological order into heat and noxious fumes. I have read somewhere that in a single day the industrial world consumes the equivalent of ten thousand years of bio-ecological activity, a ratio, roughly, of 3–4,000,000 to one. With this squandering, and the associated tossing about of materials of every sort, the entropic potentials inherent in social production reach levels of eco-destabilization on an expanding scale. The staggering pace of entropic decay has become noticeable only recently because the earth is sizeable enough to have buffered its effects until the past thirty years or so, since when we have had a clogging of the 'sinks' along with an ever rising level of production.

The phenomenon of separation expresses the core gesture of eco-disintegration, for separation in the physical and social sense corresponds to splitting in the ontological sense. Splitting extends the separation of elements of ecosystems past the point where they interact to create new Wholes – or, from another angle, to the point where the dialectic that constitutes eco-systems breaks down. It follows that the ecological crisis is not simply a manifestation of the macro-economic effects of capital, but also reveals the extension of capitalist alienation into the ecosphere. And as this alienation, and the whole structure of the system, is grounded in the relation between capital and labour, it also follows that the ecological crisis and capital's exploitation of labour are two aspects of the same phenomenon.

The historical matrix for this occurred when persons of the nascent ruling class subjugated labour into the system of exchange-value, turning their power to transform nature into a commodity on sale for a wage. The wage relation, in which one's capacity to work is given a money equivalent and sold on the market, is much older than capitalism itself, nor was it the only form of labour within emerging capitalist markets,[25] nor, needless to say, is it a necessary evil in each and every instance where it appears. But its generalization into the means by which capital itself is produced permanently alters the landscape of human being in an anti-ecological direction.

Capitalism became a full-blown system when the political, economic, legal and cultural conditions were finally put together into a self-expanding machine for turning human beings into salaried workers on the fertile plains of labour markets. There were many turns in this road, but the definitive one came when the class of capitalists took full control of the state during the various bourgeois revolutions. Then all the state functions mentioned above were subsumed into the purposes of capital. The goal of production became accumulation of value, use-values became subordinated to exchange-values, surplus-value production became the alpha and omega of the economy, and ecological relations were abstracted away from their mutual differentiation and fragmented. In its latest, neoliberal-globalized stage, increased gender exploitation becomes the rule for the great masses of humanity, even as upper-class women within the metropolis achieve substantive gains within the bourgeois order. Racial and ethnic schisms persist alongside, and as a defense against, the ultimate atomization that is capital's *telos*. Everywhere differences – of wealth, of status, of values – increase, layered over strata of homogenization. Non-recognition of fellow creatures is built into society, which thereby undergoes a motion toward nihilism. Human nature became separated from itself, and what had been only a logical potentiality became a historical actuality whose logical outcome is the complete submission of the globe to the regime of value.

Philosophical Interlude

No more than an extended set of notes, really, since to do justice to the topic requires another volume, while to ignore it completely leaves too many threads of the argument dangling. In fact, we have been intervening throughout in philosophical debates, without explicitly saying as much; here we need only say a little further, so as to round matters out before launching into the question of how to transform capitalism.

The Australian eco-philosopher Arran Gare develops the notion of a kind of 'wrong turn' taken by civilization, one manifestation of which was the postulation of a higher realm of being over the world of mere matter. We might call this the philosophical reflex of the domination of nature; that it took at first the shape of NeoPlatonism, that is, at the cradle of Christianity, is less important for us than the fact that an idea of this sort keeps reproducing itself according to historical specifics. This was the mutation that engendered Christianity's flight from the body, leaving in its wake a space of abstraction from which the line to capital can be drawn. As Gare's account makes clear, proponents of this attitude infest thought in many non-religious guises, for example, *mechanical materialism*, which installs the deadening of matter by neglecting nature's formativity, or *social Darwinism*, which naturalizes capitalist competition, seeing it as a fundamental principle of life. [26]

While it is nonsense to reduce ideas to material interests (since material interests include ideas and are shaped by ideas), it is necessary to regard all thinking as conjunctural, as no philosopher can do else but try to make sense of the world as he or she has been thrown into it. All thinkers have positions, and take positions, of which their philosophies are necessarily expressions. Before there was NeoPlatonism there was Platonism, which first elaborated the idea of essences; and we know enough about Plato to recognize the impulse behind his thought to establish philosophers as rulers, in the meantime subduing the common people with a strong state that condensed class relations into abstract principles while mystifying them with propaganda. Wherever, then, there is postulated a 'higher reality' standing over mere reality, we may expect the thinker in question to have, somewhere in mind, the installation of a class system with, needless to say, himself on the side of the rulers. This went for Plato and, in recent times, for the great Martin Heidegger, whose ontology cannot – and more to the point, should not – ever be separated from his explicit Nazism.[27]

Heidegger is of signal importance, as his thought is regarded very seriously by deep ecologists, particularly in regard to the critique of techno-logy, where he even takes to task the notion of efficient cause.[28] He asks: is not the notion of efficient cause itself a concomitant of technological domination? Does it not therefore perpetuate the estrangement from nature and ultimately the ecological crisis? For Heidegger, the efficient cause does not stand apart from the instrumental cause, as we have claimed, but is essentially instrumentality writ large.

Why, he argues, seek a '*causa efficiens*' that 'brings about the effect that is the finished [product],' and becomes 'the standard for all causality', but at the same time drowns out the other Aristotelian causes: the *causa materialis*, or material out of which a thing is made; the *causa formalis*, the shape or form into which it enters; and the *causa finalis*, the end to which it is put? The authentic technological attitude does not privilege any aspect of causality, but rather sees all four as 'the ways, all belonging at once to each other, of being responsible for something else'. From another angle, Heidegger posits a much more intimate and nonlinear relation between cause and effect than conveyed in the notion of efficient cause, seen as a kind of demiurge standing behind the world and moving it.

The notion is developed in relation to a silver chalice made as a sacrificial vessel. Using terms such as 'indebtedness', 'considering' and 'gathering',

Heidegger conveys how a tool-using human can take responsibility for the 'bringing-forth', or *poiesis*, of new being. In his later period (this essay was first composed as a lecture in the early 1950s), Heidegger saw the truth of being as a 'presencing'; hence, 'Every occasion for whatever passes beyond the nonpresent and goes forth into presencing is *poiesis*, bringing-forth.' Far from being anti-technological, then, Heidegger sees technology as, ideally, an elementary form of the 'coming into being' that is the human contribution to the real; it is to be set alongside nature's bringing-forth, or *physis*, by which is meant 'the arising of something out of itself', like the 'bursting of a blossom into bloom'.

Bringing forth gathers the four modes of causality, hence revealing, or presencing, is the highest mode of technology. Following the Greek sense, Heidegger locates this true meaning as *techne*, and groups the technical approach to reality with 'the arts of the mind and the fine arts'.

> Whoever builds a house or a ship or forges a sacrificial chalice reveals what is to be brought forth, according to the terms of the four modes of occasioning. This revealing gathers together in advance the aspect and the matter of ship or house, with a view to the finished thing envisioned as completed, and from this gathering determines the manner of its construction. Thus what is decisive in *techne* does not lie at all in making and manipulating nor in the using of means, but rather in the revealing mentioned before. It is as revealing, and not as manufacturing, that *techne* is a bringing-forth. (p. 295)

Under conditions of our estrangement, things have not worked out this way: 'the revealing that holds sway throughout modern technology does not unfold into a bringing-forth in the sense of *poeisis*'. Instead, it is a 'challenging ... which puts to nature the unreasonable demand that it supply energy which can be extracted and stored as such'. The earth is now reduced to a repository of resources; and this degrades both mineral and agricultural practice. It is an 'expediting' directed toward 'driving on to the maximum yield at the minimum expense'. There is a 'monstrousness that reigns here', for the description of which Heidegger sets out another set of ontological terms, to go along with challenging: 'setting-upon', 'ordering' and 'standing reserve' (this being a kind of hypostasis, in which 'everything is ordered to stand by, to be immediately on hand, indeed to stand there just so that it may be on call for a further ordering').

Heidegger integrates this critique in the term 'en-framing' (*Ge-stell*). This accounts for the dependance of modern technology on physical science; more deeply, it suggests the way in which being is frozen and constrained under the spiritually desolate condition of modernity. From this point, Heidegger derives many of the phenomena inherent to this way of technical being, from the reduction of God to a mere *causa efficiens*, to the self-estrangement of 'man'. 'Where this ordering holds sway, it drives out every other possibility of revealing.' Thus enframing technology becomes hegemonic, and the very possibility of truth withers.

But Heidegger concludes his essay optimistically: there is a 'saving power' growing in the midst of the danger posed by enframing. For there is a 'granting', too, in the midst of technology, and this can be gathered as a saving power. How? If we 'ponder this arising,' and, in recollection, 'watch over it'. In this way we can get beyond the notion of technology as an instrument, not through 'human activity', but by 'reflection': we can 'ponder the fact that all saving power must be of a higher essence than what is endangered, though at the same time kindred to it'. Specifically, Heidegger calls for the enhancement of an artistic dimension, not for aesthetic purposes alone, but as his Greeks did, for the purpose of revealing: 'The closer we come to the danger, the more brightly do the ways into the saving power begin to shine and the more questioning we become. For questioning is the piety of thought' (p. 317).

Taking his cue, let us question Heidegger, though perhaps not with piety. Begin with the question of universality. A thinker of Heidegger's magnitude, one of the philosophical luminaries of the twentieth century, must, one should think, stand for the *whole* of humankind if he is to command respect. And indeed he claims to do just this, if only through his continual reference to 'man' as the subject and object of his discourse, viz: 'Who accomplishes the challenging setting-upon through which what we call the real is revealed as standing-reserve? Obviously, man. To what extent is man capable of such a revealing?' (p. 299). We may translate this: who is the agent of the pathological relation to technology that is causing the ecological crisis? The answer to this is, self-evidently … man. At this point, however, the questioning of Heidegger may commence. For the usage of an undifferentiated 'man' as the agent of technological degradation is a highly dubious way to confront the ecological crisis.

Who is this 'man?' Logically, it is either somebody or everybody, and if the latter, it is either all of us as an undifferentiated mass, or all of us in some kind of internal relation – a hierarchy such as patriarchy or class, as we have discussed: in other words, some articulation of the social world.

The articulated view opens onto an effective understanding of the crisis. But it is not the one chosen by Heidegger, who, instead of articulating the real character of humanity, splits it into two equally unsatisfactory moieties. Manifestly, he speaks for an undifferentiated notion of 'man'; concretely and practically, however, he speaks only for the Northern European elites. Heidegger really speaks just for some people, but as this would absolutely violate the spirit of his discourse and the supreme abstraction of his language he ascends into the fuzzy realm of a falsely universalized subject.

How do we know that Heidegger speaks just for the dominant classes of Northern Europeans? There is the matter of his personal history, which was only evaded and never repudiated during the years when this essay was gestated. The younger Heidegger was acutely aware that philosophical syntheses are reflective of real struggles and cannot be fulfilled unless the philosopher intervenes in these struggles. In this spirit he connected his philosophical project of curing the malaise of modern society to National Socialism, as the party capable of healing this lesion by taking state power in Germany.[29] The Nazi career of Heidegger was one of the great intellectual scandals of the twentieth century, and the shame of it undoubtedly contributed to a certain gnomic tendency in his later thought, such as we see in essays of this kind, where elliptical phrases, neologisms and scurrying through the language of antiquity for authenticity maintain the illusion that no specific programme for transformation need be enunciated. But Nazism was nothing if not a specific project. Whatever else can be said about the Third Reich, there can be no doubt that whoever signed up to its principles (and Heidegger was a party member) affirmed a radically racist view of the world, within which, of course, the Northern European elites occupied the master role.

We can see directly within the present text how Heidegger refuses to define a specific agent for the crisis, however much its logic may demand this – and also why the question of efficient cause is distasteful to him, as this methodology, used faithfully, would disclose his dreadful partiality. And so Heidegger talks movingly of the revealing expressed in the making of a silver chalice, but glosses over the history that has degraded craftmanship – or its spiritual associations as described. For who makes chalices any more? Why not address the people who make Barbie dolls, or methyl isocyanate, or overpriced sneakers, or cluster bombs – and who can stop doing so if they are willing to starve, or lose their health insurance, or not make the mortgage payments on the house? Are not the real conditions of their labour the causal elements in the deterioration of their *techne*?

Heidegger talks elsewhere of the 'forester' who no longer 'walks the forest path in the same way his grandfather did' because he is 'today ordered by the industry that produces commercial woods' thus making him 'subordinate to the orderability of cellulose'. Yes, yes, excellent to talk of this, but why not go on to the 'industry' as a causal mover – not because of the essence of 'industrialization' that it bears, but because it is set going to serve the lord of capital that reduces trees to cellulose? Nor should this be talked of only in metaphorical terms: who is this industry? There are real people involved, who personify the great forces of the capital system yet must also be held morally, politically and legally responsible, as the management of Union Carbide should have been held responsible for Bhopal.

Similar reflections are in order for the peasants whose downfall Heidegger laments – and who fell, and continue to fall all over the world, because of the encroachment of the same profit motive. And of course, the same goes for one of his most important insights, that there is something active at work in the world that 'puts to nature the unreasonable demand that it supply energy which can be extracted and stored as such'. Does this something simply arrive, like Athene, from the head of its father? Or is it the product of a vast transformation only understandable in terms of the inexorable force of capital? Is it the self-caused exfoliation of an original estrangement, carried out without any mediations in the real world? Well, then, one still has to explain the many simulacra of said mediations, such as stock exchanges, oil pipelines, credit cards, police and armies.

If one draws all the appropriate inferences that point to such a conclusion, but refuses to name it as such, then one is mystifying, and as with all mystifications, supporting the status quo. It is striking how closely Heidegger's critique of technology can be applied to the capital system, yet never bridges across to this most obvious point. This is not to deny that his critique runs far beyond the ordinary insights derived from political economy. Heidegger's insights are, as he intended, profound: they advance our view of what is wrong and what has to be done to right it in a way that no political-economic analysis of the ecological crisis possibly can. But what is merely profound swims at an inaccessible and meaningless depth. More, it can be used for malignant purposes. We dwell on Heidegger not just because of his philosophical eminence, but essentially because reasoning of this sort has been repeatedly used for malignant purposes. Behind the discourse of 'ecology' can lurk, therefore, a spectre of fascism. We return to the theme in Part III.

Philosophy can and should be an active force extending the reach of political economy. In this regard, it seems to me necessary to postulate a methodological principle that embodies the paramount goal of reintegrating ecosystems. We have seen how the world of capital is riddled with the sequelae of splitting, and how ecosystemic integrity is critically dependent upon differentiation. It follows that we need to overcome splitting with differentiation, in thought as well as practice. We need, therefore, a method incorporating the notion of differentiation.

Let us recall some conditions for this. A differentiated relationship is one in which elements of an ecosystem are brought together in a process of mutual recognition that respects their wholeness and integrity. There are three terms here, each needing explication. The elements are presumed different, yet capable of entering into a relationship; the entering upon this relationship requires the specific activity of an agent; and, finally, the mutual recognition implies identity-in-difference: entities are what their being is, yet this being is defined in the relationship to the other. In this case, we are speaking of bringing different ideas together, and, as we have seen for other aspects of differentiated production such as gardening, holding them so that the life within them can be expressed as the formation of an integral whole.

A moment's reflection will tell us that we have been speaking here of a process broadly defined as *dialectical*. And since we may claim some lineage from the ancient Greeks too, we may recall that for these progenitors of philosophy, dialectic meant the bringing together of different points of view for the purposes of argument, and in the interests of arriving at truth.[30] Dialectic was not a mere pluralism but a consciousness of the radical unfulfilment of the merely individual mind or ego, and of the hidden relationships of differing points of view. Dialectics recognizes both the limits and powers of the mind: that we are limited in our knowing, owing to the unfathomable reaches of nature which can be grasped intuitively at best, and owing, also, to the peculiarities of human selfhood, with its 'dialectic' of separation and attachment ... but that we are also powerful because of the capacity of the imagination to become visionary, seeing beyond the given and transforming the real. Hence dialectics as practice is the bringing together of minds in a dialogical spirit of open discourse – a process the fulfilment of which requires a free society of associated producers, that is, a society beyond all forms of splitting, in particular those imposed by class and gender or racial domination. Without this, the genius of those forced into the subaltern position will wither, while the logic of the masters will be fatally corrupted by power.

There is, in addition to dialectics as practice, the question of dialectics as logic, or theory, which we can only barely pursue here, to say that it must be an abstraction from practice that remains in contact with practice – that is, differentiated and not split off from it. Here the prime dialectical category is *negation*, as that which both is and is not itself. In line with this, dialectic must be capable of guiding practice as well, so that for dialectical realization, theory is practical, and practice is theoretical – a condition known generally as *praxis*.[31]

Finally, in this highly compressed account, we need to enquire as to the 'dialectics of nature'.[32] It is plain, first, that any such notion cannot privilege the 'higher reality' over mere being, as this aggrandizes ecosystemic splitting into a metaphysic. The notion of dialectic is grounded in the formativeness of nature – it is, one might say, nature's formativity refracted through the human mind, the flux of nature, its absencing and presencing, made word. As differentiated ecosystems will tend to bring forth life, so is dialectic the location of human creativity. But we do not project the laws of dialectical logic into nature, for the twofold reason that these laws are abstracted from human practice, and that human practical activity, including the workings of thought, is conducted at a great remove from the ultimate workings of the universe. No matter how science may approximate the knowing of these, there is no way that human practice can be usefully affected by the great reaches of the cosmos or the unfathomable fine grain of matter and energy – except to be in awe of their splendour.

The precondition of an ecologically rational attitude toward nature is the recognition that nature far surpasses us and has its own intrinsic value, irreducible to our practice. Thus we achieve differentiation from nature. It is in this light that we would approach the question of transforming practice ecologically – or, as we now recognize to be the same thing, dialectically.

On the Reformability of Capitalism

The monster that now bestrides the world was born of the conjugation of value and dominated labour. From the former arose the quantification of reality, and, with this, the loss of the differentiated recognition essential for ecosystemic integrity; from the latter emerged a kind of selfhood that could swim in these icy waters. From this standpoint one might call capitalism a 'regime of the ego', meaning that under its auspices a kind of estranged self emerges as the mode of capital's reproduction. This self is not merely prideful – the ordinary connotation of 'egotistical' – more fully, it is the ensemble of those relations that embody the domination of nature from one side, and, from the other, ensure the reproduction of capital. This ego is the latest version of the purified male principle, emerging aeons after the initial gendered domination became absorbed and rationalized as profit-ability and self-maximization (allowing suitable 'power-women' to join the dance). It is a pure culture of splitting and non-recognition: of itself, of the otherness of nature and of the nature of others. In terms of the preceding discussion, it is the elevation of the merely individual and isolated mind-as-ego into a reigning principle. [33]

Capital produces egoic relations, which reproduce capital. The isolated selves of the capitalist order can choose to become personifications of capital, or may have the role thrust upon them. In either case, they embark upon a pattern of non-recognition mandated by the fact that the almighty dollar interposes itself between all elements of experience: all things in the world, all other persons, and between the self and its world: nothing really exists except in and through monetization. This set-up provides an ideal culture medium for the bacillus of competition and ruthless self-maximization. Because money is all that 'counts', a peculiar heartlessness characterizes capitalists, a tough-minded and cold abstraction that will sacrifice species, whole continents (viz. Africa) or inconvenient sub-sets of the population (viz. black urban males) who add too little to the great march of surplus value or may be seen as standing in its way. The presence of value screens out genuine fellow-feeling or compassion, replacing it with the calculus of profit-expansion. Never has a holocaust been carried out so impersonally. When the Nazis killed their victims, the crimes were accompanied by a racist drumbeat; for global capital, the losses are regrettable necessities.

The value-term that subsumes everything into the spell of capital sets going a kind of wheel of accumulation, from production to consumption and back, spinning ever more rapidly as the inertial mass of capital grows, and generating its force field as a spinning magnet generates an electrical field. This phenomenon has important implications for the reformability of the system. Because capital is so spectral, and succeeds so well in ideologically mystifying its real nature, attention is constantly deflected from the actual source of eco-destabilization to the instruments by which that source acts. The real problem, however, is the *whole mass* of globally accumulated capital, along with the speed of its circulation and the class structures sustaining this. That is what generates the force field, in proportion to its own scale; and it is this force field, acting across the numberless points of insertion that constitute the ecosphere, that creates ever larger agglomerations of capital, sets the ecological crisis going, and keeps it from being resolved. For one fact may be taken as certain – that to resolve the ecological crisis as a whole, as against tidying up one corner or another, is radically incompatible with the existence of gigantic pools of capital, the force field these induce, the criminal underworld with which they connect, and, by extension, the elites who comprise the transnational bourgeoisie. And by not resolving the crisis as a whole, we open ourselves to the spectre of another mythical creature, the many-headed hydra, that regenerated itself the more its individual tentacles were chopped away.

To realize this is to recognize that there is no compromising with capital, no schema of reformism that will clean up its act by making it act more greenly or efficiently. We shall explore the practical implications of this thesis in Part III, and here need simply to restate the conclusion in blunt terms: green capital, or non-polluting capital, is preferable to the immediately ecodestructive breed on its immediate terms. But this is the lesser point, and diminishes with its very success. For green capital (or 'socially/ecologically responsible investing') exists, by its very capital-nature, essentially to create more value, and this leaches away from the concretely green location to join the great pool, and follows its force field into zones of greater concentration, expanded profitability – and greater ecodestruction.

There are crises within capitalism, which both generates them and is dependent upon them. Crises are ruptures in the accumulation process, causing the wheel to slow, but also stimulating new turns; they take many shapes and have long or short cycles, and many intricate effects upon ecologies. A recession may reduce demand and so take some of the load off resources; recovery may increase this demand, but also occur with greater efficiency, hence also reduce the load. Thus economic crises condition the ecological crisis, but have no necessary effect on it. There is no singular generalization that covers all cases. James O'Connor summarizes the complexity:

> Capitalist accumulation normally causes ecological crisis of certain types; economic crisis is associated with partly different and partly similar ecological problems of different severity; external barriers to capital in the form of scarce resources, urban space, healthy and disciplined wage labour, and other conditions of production may have the effect of raising costs and threatening profits; and finally, environmental and other social movements defending conditions of life, forests, soil quality, amenities, health conditions, urban space, and so on, may also raise costs and make capital less flexible.[34]

But capital gets nature whether on its way up or its way down. In the USA, the boom-boom Clinton years witnessed grotesque increases in matters such as the sowing of the ecosphere with toxic chemicals,[35] while the sharp downturn that accompanied the George W. Bush presidency was immediately met by rejection of the Kyoto protocols. From the standpoint of ecosystems, the *phase* of the business cycle is considerably less relevant, then, than the *fact* of the business cycle, and the wanton economic system it expresses.

Economic problems interact with ecological problems, while ecological problems (including the effects of ecological movements) interact with economic problems. This is all at the level of the trees. For the forest, meanwhile, we see the effects on the planetary ecology caused by the growth of the system as a whole. Here the dark angel is the thermodynamic law, where mounting entropy appears as ecosystemic decay.[36] The immediate impacts of this on life are what energize the resistance embodied in the environmental and ecological movements. Meanwhile, the economy goes on along its growth-intoxicated way, immune to the effects of ecosystem breakdown on accumulation, and blindly careening toward the abyss.

The conclusion must be that irrespective of the particulars of one economic interaction or another, the system as a whole is causing irreparable damage to its ecological foundations, and that it does so precisely as it grows. And since the one underlying feature of all aspects of capital is the relentless pressure to grow, we are obliged to bring down the capitalist system as a whole, and replace it with an ecologically viable alternative, if we want to save our species along with numberless others.

Notes

1. In *Capital* Marx (1967a) makes clear how technology and the industrial mode of organization are necessities for maximizing surplus-value extraction, the *sine qua non* of the production of capital. At this point we need also to anticipate the commonly made point in support of the thesis that industrialization is to blame, namely, that it was during the regime of the USSR, hell-bent on industrialization presumably in opposition to capitalism, that an immense amount of ecological havoc was wrought. I deal with this question in Chapter 8.

2. This is not to assert the doctrine of European exceptionalism, which has been thoroughly debunked by scholars such as James Blaut and Andre Gunder Frank (Blaut 1993; Frank 1998), who have decisively shown that there was no innate European genius that gave command over the capitalist world. However, there were cultural differences between Europe and other, more advanced nations, such as China and India, at the dawn of the modern era, and it is a fair question to ask whether those differences, which prominently included Christianity, played a role, not in the superior virtue of the West, but in the development of its pathology, and with it, the pathology of capital.

3. DeLumeau 1990 documents bodily estrangement in compelling detail. For a view of Christianity that parallels many of the arguments taken here, see Ruether 1992.

4. In Needham 1954, Joseph Needham summarizes his magisterial study of Chinese science. As for Calvinism and capitalism, we cannot take up this famous debate here. See, of course, Weber 1976 and Tawney 1998, as well as Leiss 1972; Glacken 1973.

5. The most compelling exposition of this theme so far as I know, and the one to which this account is the most indebted, is Mies 1998. See also Salleh 1997; O'Brien 1981.

6. My best guide to this mode of being was Stanley Diamond (Diamond 1974).

7. At present, roughly two-thirds of actual social production is carried out by females. This figure is probably the best estimate for the actual productive efforts of women in archaic hunter-gatherer societies (Mies 1998).

8. As Mies (1998) emphasizes, this account is within the frame of classical Marxism, with its central role given to the exploitation of productive labour. At the same time it challenges Engels' understanding of the primacy of cause. In Engels' canonical view, social production develops, so to speak, in a gender-neutral way until a surplus is gathered, which then becomes expropriated through violence, leading to class and gender domination. However, it is more cogent to invoke the violent control of female productive labour as the original lesion. For Engels (1972), the seizure of property appears the result of innate aggression instead of an event that became historically generalized into domination through the development of systems of force. The implication is important, for if innate aggression is the motor behind the seizure of surplus, then the entire Marxist project is brought down, and one might as well adhere to Freud's account in *Civilization and its Discontents* (Freud 1931).

9. The account given here condenses a wealth of psychoanalytic knowledge deriving

from a core contradiction in male-dominated societies, viz. that the female dominated by the grown male was once represented by his mother at an infantile moment in the lifecycle when he was utterly dependent and lacked all of those powers that came to be his stock in trade. It may be presumed in what follows that this nexus reverberates throughout the history of humankind, inscribed in the dialectics of desire. See Chodorow 1978; Kovel 1981; Benjamin 1988.

10. For a discussion, see Kovel 1984.

11. For a good discussion of Marx's development of these ideas, see Rosdolsky 1977: 109–66.

12. From *pecus*, the Latin word for cattle, comes 'pecuniary'.

13. That is, I may value air because I need it to live, or I may not. Where air is concerned the brain stem disregards what the 'I', or self, demands, and goes on breathing. However, there are innumerable instances wherein we live in refusal. Kierkegaard, Nietzsche and Dostoevsky were much preoccupied with this conjuncture, which represents a breakdown of Hegelian rationalism as the nineteenth century increasingly exposed a civilization in crisis.

14. Simmel 1978: 60.

15. Daydreams have utility, which can be private or shared, as between friends. But they cannot join the economy until embedded in a material object. Even as such, they need not have exchange-value – as, for instance, in a gift economy, or where they are bartered for another concrete item, or where they are dreamt for personal satisfaction.

16. Simmel 1978: 259.

17. Murray 1978. Islamic society, by contrast (along with China, India and others) was well acquainted with the use of money, and was not overtaken by Europe in this respect until the Crusades. This striking backwardness of that area of the world that would come to dominate capitalism centuries later is a remarkable fact. One would speculate that money represented a kind of taboo, or forbidden desire.

18. Arrighi 1994; Frank 1998.

19. Marx 1964: 67.

20. See especially Polanyi 1957.

21. A restoration of the commons gained as a result of the Revolution from 1911 to 1920, and under savage attack under NAFTA.

22. Marx 1978b; Sheasby 1997.

23. Thompson 1967.

24. The witch craze was an assault on the female gender unmatched in the history of any other civilization. It was part of the suppression of 'pagan', that is, earth- and female-centred religions that stood in the way of Christian patriarchy; and specifically the driving out of female and naturopathic healers on behalf of an embryonic male-dominated medical establishment. See Ehrenreich and English 1974. As for Bacon, his rendering of science as an exercise of the phallus – indeed, as a kind of rape of Mother Nature – is explored in Carolyn Merchant's pathbreaking *The Death of Nature* (Merchant 1980). It is equally necessary to point out Bacon's paramount role in defining scientific progress as integral to capitalism – and also, because the two developments are but sides of the same coin, that he was, in Merchant's words, the 'inspiration behind the Royal Society' of 1660, the first state-sponsored research institute (p. 160). It was the state, then, that organized the scientific revolutions that gave birth to industrial capitalism, and did so profoundly within the terms of the gendered bifurcation of nature.

25. Slavery being an infamous feature of early capitalist development, continuing today, and in fact on the rise. But slavery fails to provide flexible labour markets and restricts the moment of consumption. Thus it cannot be generalized within capitalism, as is the case for wage labour.

26. Gare 1996a.

27. For a discussion of the relations between spiritual/philosophical systems and historical structures, see Kovel 1998b.

28. Heidegger 1977. All quotes in this section are from this text. See also Zimmerman 1994.

29. Farias 1989.

30. Kovel 1998a.

31. Of modern Marxists, Raya Dunayevskaya was most faithful to the need for a philosophical moment in order to unify theory and praxis. Her great achievement was to reconnect Marx to Hegel's *Science of Logic* (Hegel 1969). See Dunayevskaya 1973, 2000.

32. Derived from the famous work of Engels; see Engels 1940.

33. The term, of course, has many psychological implications, most famously Freud's tripartite version of the psyche, in which the ego's non-recognition of the 'id', or the 'it-ness' of the world, that is, nature, was given the status of normality instead of being seen as a psychological reflex of capital. Here we see the ego ontologically, from the standpoint of being and not the psyche. For discussion see Kovel 1981; 1998b; also Lichtman 1982; Wolfenstein 1993.

34. O'Connor 1998a: 183.

35. For example, in 1999, a fine year for capital, the amount of the 644 toxic chemicals tracked by the EPA rose 5 per cent over 1998, to 7.8 billion pounds.

36. This line of thought was developed by the Romanian-American economist Nicholas Georgescu-Roegen, who had the insight that '*our whole economic life feeds on low entropy*' (Georgescu-Roegen 1971: 277; italics in original). It follows, although Georgescu-Roegen does not emphasize the point, that an out-of-control, expanding economy will hasten entropic decay.

Part III

Towards Ecosocialism

Introduction

Let me summarize where the argument stands:

- The ecological crisis puts the future at grave risk.
- Capital is the reigning mode of production, and capitalist society exists to reproduce, secure and expand capital.
- Capital is the efficient cause of the ecological crisis.
- Capital, under the charge of the present transnational bourgeoisie and headquartered chiefly but not exclusively in the USA, cannot be reformed. It can only grow or die, and hence reacts to any contraction or slowing as to a mortal threat.
- As capital keeps growing, the crisis grows, too: civilization and much of nature is doomed. Indeed, it is not unwarranted to ask whether this will prove to be the way of our extinction as a species.
- Therefore, it is either capital or our future. If we value the latter, capitalism must be brought down and replaced with an ecologically worthy society.

Let me add two conditions to this assessment, the first very well-known but numbing to contemplate; the second scarcely appreciated but profoundly important:

- Capital rules the world as never before; no alternative to it now commands the interest, much less the loyalty, of any substantial body of people.
- Capital is not what most people take it to be. It is not a rational system of markets in which freely constituted individuals create wealth in healthy competition. It is, rather, a spectral apparatus that integrates earlier modes of domination, especially that by gender, and generates a gigantic force field of profit-seeking that polarizes all human activity and sucks it into itself. Capital is spectral because its profit is the realization of a

"value" deriving from estranged human power. This has been instituted in private ownership of the means of production, along with a peculiar system of domination – exploited wage labour – in which persons are split internally and between each other and nature. The implication is brutally simple. In order to overcome capital, two minimal conditions need to be met: first, there must be basic changes in ownership of productive resources so that, ultimately, the earth is no longer privately owned; and second, our productive powers, the core of human nature, have to be liberated, so that people self-determine their productive power.

These two conditions go together: capital's power is so uncontested because the conditions for seriously changing it are far too radical for the great majority of people to contemplate, much less support. We should be under no illusion whatsoever: the scale of the envisioned changes, and the gap between even a dawning awareness of what would be entailed and the presently prevailing political consciousness is so enormous as to make a person want to forget the whole thing. Why, it would be reasonable to ask, bother to burden us with ideas so off the scale of what society now proposes that to raise them would seem the work of a lunatic?

I am not insensible to this line of reasoning. The fantastic unlikeliness of an ecological transformation has often occurred to me – say, during a walk through midtown Manhattan, loomed over by the 'cloud capp'd' towers of corporate capital, the mighty banks, the whole gigantic symphony in stone, steel and glass consecrated to the god of profit – or when I find myself surrounded there by the hundreds of thousands of scurrying people set into motion by that great force field like so many wind-up toys in the game of accumulation, and am led to wonder whether any of them is ready to think in the terms drawn here. Faced with the appalling evidence of just how far we have to go – not just the direct strength of the system but its indirect strength deriving from the weakness of its adversaries, and the way the crisis sinks the mind and drains the will – the idea of dropping the whole affair and settling back into creature comforts has often come.

But then one thinks of the stakes, and the compelling argument that leads to capital's indictment as nature's enemy, and there is no question of whether to continue. Nor can we allow the current imbalance of forces to sow doubt, or to confuse or vitiate the issues. When a physician deals with a grave illness, s/he must not waste effort in brooding about how difficult the case is, but work instead to see as clearly as possible what is the problem and what can be done. In a word, one does what one can. —don't give up

It is time to concentrate on making changes, first on the wide range of what already exists, and then on possibilities for radical transformation. There is no point in wringing our hands and backing away from this task, and everything to be gained, literally a world to be won, by pursuing it conscientiously. — the stakes are too great, we can't retreat

Moreover, the time is becoming auspicious. The spirit of struggle arises, chiefly against globalization. Signs of a radically new political direction abound, combining decentralized spontaneity with the growing awareness that capitalism itself is the problem. A new generation is emerging, to engage the crisis of the times creatively.

The name given in what follows to the notion of a necessary and sufficient transformation of capitalist society for the overcoming of the ecological crisis is *ecosocialism*.

7 Critique of Actually Existing Ecopolitics

In this chapter we consider approaches to the ecological crisis that, while working to mend the relationship with nature, for one reason or another do not call for the replacement of capitalism by a system grounded in the restoration of the means of production to freely associated producers. Inasmuch as the permanence of capitalism is widely acknowledged, while its essential ecodestructivity and inability to correct itself are almost as widely not acknowledged, what will be discussed comprises pretty much the whole of present-day ecopolitics, and, therefore, the starting place of any future ecopolitics. This should be borne in mind during what follows, the occasionally sharp tone of which is sounded in order to radicalize the current discourse. It goes without saying that the existing approaches are in many cases admirable, and comprise real points of attack. But if capital is the core problem, we urgently need a new strategy that sees beyond present lines of activity.

There are a number of ways of thinking about the many sides of ecopolitics. Bearing in mind that we are dealing with different levels of abstraction, much overlapping, it is useful to consider the subject from four angles: logics of change, economic models, ecophilosophies and patterns of movement, along with a few generalizations pointing the way toward the conception of ecosocialism as such.

Logics of change

Working within the system The 'system' here means various arms of the state, including regulatory agencies and the judiciary, as well as the extensive and varied set of established non-governmental organizations, and elements of capital itself. Obviously, it is a life's work to keep track of so large and complicated an apparatus, and we can do no more than set forth certain underlying principles in discussing it.

It is unnecessary to detail once more how corporations and politicians are in bed with each other, and just how inadequately the state takes care of ecosystems.[1] But these facts say nothing about whether or not it is desirable to work within them to make a change. After all, everything in capitalist society is conditioned by capital, from the raising of children to the writing of this book. Similarly, degrees of resistance to capital can be found in the strangest places. While it may be a safe bet to conclude that the legal system is stacked to benefit the rich and powerful, it is not true that the law is reducible to economic interest, nor that it is impossible to secure real gains through the courts. By the same reasoning, corporate executives and other personifications of capital are only relatively consumed by it. In each of them, therefore, there may be glimmers of conscience, or if not that, at least common sense. Then there was Al Gore, the first high US government official in whom the germ of an ecocentric philosophy may be said to have lodged. Gore's sensitivity to the matter of global warming led him to an important role in passage of the Kyoto Protocols in December 1997;[2] thus if Kyoto, however limited, is on the whole a good thing, then Gore, and by definition, 'the system', are capable of some degree of ecological sanity, hence cannot be dismissed *tout court*.

It is significant to see an ecocentric awareness appear in someone so highly placed. But mere awareness is ambivalent, and can be used for deception as well as constructive action. This certainly proved the case for Gore, Clinton, and, by extension, the Democratic Party, which had effectively betrayed its working-class constituencies for some time before their adminstration.[3] Clinton's redefinition of himself as a 'New Democrat' in 1984 solidified the development, which had been building for decades, since anti-communism crippled the left and labour entered its long decline. The centrist motion of the Democratic Party went into high gear after the accumulation crisis of the 1970s jolted capital out of its 'Fordist' phase of accommodation with labour, and reset it on the path of accelerated accumulation and globalization known as neoliberalism. Reagan was the bearer of this in the US political landscape, while Clinton carried it through at the social democratic end of the established spectrum, Thatcher and Blair performing the same functions for Britain.

Neoliberalism's passion for unrestricted market forces is expressed in the fancy for pollution credits, applied first to toxic industrial emissions by Bush I in 1989, and now proposed with respect to greenhouse gas emissions.

Clinton/Gore were ardent proponents of this scheme, as are those 'responsible' industrial democracies who continue to uphold the virtues of Kyoto in the wake of Bush II's rejection. Yet the trading of credits is essentially a capitalist shell game. It not only frees corporate hands but, by creating a new commodity tradable in places such as the Chicago Board of Trade, enables yet more value to be accumulated. The idea of tradable credits owes a great deal to Stephen Breyer, rewarded by Clinton with a Supreme Court seat,[4] as well as to major environmental NGOs, most notably the Environmental Defense Fund, which see no contradiction in rationalizing pollution and turning it into a fresh source of profit.[5]

The story offers useful lessons in the co-option of the mainstream environmental movement as this passes from citizen-based activism to ponderous bureaucracies scuffling for 'a seat at the table' Capital is more than happy to enlist the mainstream movement as a partner in the management of nature. Big environmental groups offer capital a threefold convenience: as legitimation, reminding the world that the system works; as control over popular dissent, a kind of sponge that sucks up and contains the ecological anxiety in the general population; and as rationalization, a useful governor to introduce some control and protect the system from its own worst tendencies, while ensuring the orderly flow of profits.

Foundations tend to be created by rich people to soften the contradictions of that which enabled the rich to become so in the first place, and are basically no further from capital than the state. Like the state, the foundation is relatively free to express a more universal interest – and some of them are, like religion in Marx's view, the 'heart of a heartless world', and able to support marginal or even radical projects. However, taken all in all, the foundation's basic function is to rationalize the given society and not to overturn it. The same can be said for the 'think-tanks' lavishly funded by capital to generate ideas for its reproduction; and, unhappily as well, the universities, those putative centres of free inquiry where a growing number of environmental studies programmes train people to manage nature.

The 'system', then, is what is on the ground, of this time and place, which is that of capital's breakthrough into reckless globalization. Yes, 'the system works' – for the ruling interests that bring about the ecological crisis; and its environmentally conscientious wing is structurally bound to reproduce the *status quo*, no matter how many virtuous acts it performs in doing so. No doubt the laws currently on the books provide in principle for a *is it already to late?*

much better world, and even one considerably closer to an ecological society. Just so did the Constitution of the USSR under Stalin guarantee full democratic rights to the Russian people. There is, in sum, no reason to believe that the system can change itself from within.

This is no blanket dismissal, but a reminder that radical change requires a coordination of forces from within and without the system – and that those in the former position will have to adopt a divided consciousness, doing the world's work, but in a spirit of preparing ground for its transformation. The struggle for an ecologically rational world must include a struggle for the state, and since the state is the repository of many democratic hopes, it is a struggle for the *democratization* of the state – just as it would be a struggle for the fulfilment of the rule of law over the principle of egoism, or for universities to express their universality, or, in general, to remind the system of its broken promises, and to insist that they be kept. This potential is perhaps best realized through the work of radical lawyers, who can effectively exploit the contradiction between promise and reality. But it applies as well to electoral politics – of which more below.

Voluntarism   A voluntaristic act is one that arises from good intention, say, the desire to recycle waste, or work in a community garden, and more or less stays there, without special connection to social movements consciously directed towards the ecological crisis. Thus it is an action taken towards an individual manifestation of the crisis, and taken primarily on moral or aesthetic grounds.

Such actions, lists of which can be found in mass-marketed literature of the 'xx things you can do to save the planet' type, stand as much chance of overcoming the ecological crisis as handing out spare change on the subway does of overcoming poverty. I put this bluntly, not to question the virtue of voluntarism, but as a challenge for it to go further and build those linkages necessary for effective action. A voluntaristic act is a point of potential, something available for connection to other acts, and other frames of reference. If it stays in itself, it will tend to be drawn off into individualism, which is to say, to remain split off, isolated and transient. If, on the other hand, it connects itself to a larger project, then it can enter into a process of differentiation, a bringing together that is the heart of ecosystem formation and integrity.

While there is nothing wrong with any ecologically voluntarist act so

things happen in stages. why can't this be stage 1?

nice but prolongs system that attacks the world

long as it is done with a good heart and a mind towards restoring the earth, there is nothing inherent to it, either, that leads anywhere. Moral exhortations may *feel* as though they generate larger purposes, but this is an illusion. There is no *solidarity* inherent in the moral impulse, and unless that which makes for solidarity is added, voluntarism will stop at its own border. Certainly the world is better off because of recycling, but it is not that much better off, nor does the range of improvement much exceed the localities in which these acts are taken. This raises questions concerning localism itself, so widely held as a value by the green movements. Yes, local movements are capable of reproducing themselves and spreading to encompass the whole ecosphere. But that simply leads to the question of what will suffice to make this universalization happen, which in any case is not voluntaristic action.

To the contrary, market forces have been applied to configure voluntarism according to the demands of capital. Thus recycling is reinforced by various sanctions and rewards, for example, laws in places like New York City, or incentives to avoid dumping-costs in smaller localities. In this way, citizens are induced to provide free labour to the huge and growing industries that profit from 'waste management', and voluntarism becomes ancillary to the capitalization of nature.[6]

However admirable individual acts of charity or ecological sanity may be, they tend either to be co-opted, or to remain merely local and lose the thread of effective collective action. A lovely garden is a wondrous thing, and indicates the species potential for fostering ecosystem development and even for bringing new life into the world. But given the current predicament, it is a signpost and not an end. Voltaire's advice, 'Il faut cultiver nos jardins' – in other words, let us tend individually to immediate and concrete satisfactions and ignore large-scale projects of social transformation – made sense in a world whose dominant forces were religious absolutism and fanaticism. In a world organized by global capital's force field, it rings with defeatism.

Ultimately, the touchstone of voluntarism is this: that it is an ecopolitics without *struggle*, struggle against the inertia and fear within, and the great weight of capitalist rationalization and repression without. It is the easy path at a time when sacrifice and heroism are called for.

Technological answers   It is a widely held assumption that technological means of overcoming the ecological crisis are at hand. With the cracking of the genome, with astounding feats of information technology and tele-communications, with the emergence of extremely low-polluting energy devices such as fuel cells (the product of whose combustion is water vapour), with the whole broad advance of science – and with a nice boost from the propaganda machine – the conflict between humanity and nature can be made to seem eminently resolvable. In an important sense, this is, if not absolutely true, at least operationally plausible – for if the technology did not, or could not, exist, then it would make no sense at all to agitate for an ecologically rational world.

But this is only a truism. Those of us old enough to recall the launching of the atomic age will recall how nuclear energy was going to be 'too cheap to meter', just as the discoveries of antibiotics were supposed to herald the eradication of infectious disease. If we know better now, it is a sign of growing ecological consciousness that events in nature are reciprocal and multi-determined, and, across such a broad scale, never neatly predictable. What remains much less appreciated is that technology can never be ap-preciated outside of its social relations. Ross Perot's campaign dictum, 'If it's broke, fix it', was a sign of the crudity that regards social problems as essentially mechanical and susceptible to tinkering, that is, to manipulation from the outside by a disinterested expert, as a mechanic would fix the transmission on a car. This is mechanical materialism of a vulgar sort, which sees technology as something added on to society and not an integral part of society.

In the specific case of capitalism, technological innovation has been the *sine qua non* of growth, and, because it cheapens the cost of labour, indispen-sable to surplus value extraction. The more technology, roughly speaking, the more growth under a capitalist regime – and since growth, capitalist-style, is the efficient cause of the ecological crisis, it shouldn't take a genius to sense the ambivalence of technological solutions to the crisis. If, for instance, energy were suddenly made free and unlimited and inserted into the capitalist system as it now exists, the results could be as catastrophic as giving an alcoholic unlimited drink. Free energy would, for example, so lower the costs of producing and operating motor vehicles that the world would rapidly fill up with as many cars as Los Angeles, collapsing infra-structure, tremendously increasing resource depletion, paving over the remainder of nature, and leaving humanity to kill itself off in a spasm of road rage. Limits of energy and materials are, in this sense, brakes on rampant growth, but capital, nature's cancer, tolerates neither limit nor boundary. It goes where the profit is, and the more cars, the more profit.

The above example is revealing but also conceals the fact that, barring some kind of Buck Rogers breakthrough,[7] the prospective energy reckoning is not a happy one, and moots all fanciful predictions. In short, 'limits to growth' exist, no matter what the director of the IMF thinks, and the current energy brouhaha is a sign of their drawing near. As a result of this, certain good things are being stirred up, such as the search for more fuel-efficient cars, even if this has for its chief motive the putting of more cars on the road. Along the same lines, resource substitution is always on the agenda, but this, too, requires great inputs of energy, and, in the case of plastics and other synthetics, the direct transforming of petroleum and coal. It is a plain illusion that the informational commodities on which modern, 'post-industrial' capitalism has learned to thrive sit more lightly on the earth.[8] The infrastructure for the information age is as impressive in its way as the railroads, and much less likely to be recyclable – for the simple reason that informational commodities require the miniaturization of highly complex assemblies involving many substances, in contrast to the relatively homogeneous bases of older industrial processes. How are we to reclaim economically the many rare metals joined together in even modest personal computers, as these become obsolete the day before they are made? Do we burn them in huge numbers – as I have been told takes place in China – and thereby release yet more dioxin into the ecosphere?[9]

So long, therefore, as growth is the alpha and omega of the economy, we will be eternally chasing our tails in an ever-widening circle of accumulation. Meanwhile, the industrial system remains utterly dependent on fossil fuels inputs that are radically non-renewable. I say 'radically' to underscore the fact that the whole of capitalist society runs on high-energy chemical bonds laid down by living beings and concentrated over hundreds of millions of years. Thus we rob the past. The only substitute for this needed concentration is the utterly unacceptable alternative of nuclear power, with its indisposable wastes. Other modalities, principally the vaunted solar alternative, are simply too diffuse and too expensive to concentrate to serve the needs of contemporary society, much less one that continues to grow according to the plan of the capitalist elites. It is too easily forgotten that in using solar power, one is starting with what nature had long ago concentrated into the low-entropy fuels we get at the petrol station. It is life's gift of low entropy that is essential to the industrial system and that cannot be replaced except at ruinously high expenditures of energy. Electric cars may be non-polluting, but the generation of electricity is not – nor should we forget that even before the vast increase in electrical generation required to propel our motor vehicle fleet, there is tremendous pressure to expand the electrical generation grid, now breaking down in places such as California. Again, hydrogen fuel cells offer a non-polluting energy supply of great promise – but how are we to obtain the hydrogen except by splitting methnae or water molecules, once more requiring prodigious amounts of electricity?[10] In their haste to excoriate the admittedly gruesome energy schemes of the Bush administration, environmental liberals often overlook the fact that the president is simply being candid in stating that what he asks for is what capitalism demands.

It scarcely bears saying that all measures of increasing the renewability and efficiency and decreasing the pollution of energy sources – that is, all 'soft-energy paths'[11] – are to be endorsed, and for the same reason one endorses recycling. What cannot be supported is the illusion that these measures of themselves can do more than retard the slide toward eco-catastrophe – a fall that may become precipitous once the inevitable occurs and fossil fuels become uneconomical to extract, that is effectively run out, as expected within the next half-century.[12]

Only a basic change in patterns of production and use can allow eco-logically appropriate technologies to have their beneficial effect. But this means a basic change in need patterns and in the whole way life is lived, which means an entirely different foundation for society. To the extent to which expectation of technological fixes blinds us to this, technology may be said to stand in the way of resolving the ecological crisis.

But in truth, technology does not stand in the way: it is part of the way. Technology is not a collection of techniques and tools but a pattern of social relationships centring on the extension of the body as an instrument for transforming nature. This can be seen by comparing patterns of pro-ducing foodstuffs – the prevalent capital-intensive industrial farm, and the so-called 'organic' alternative.

An organic farm is no more 'natural' than agribusiness, but it is pre-dicated on certain kinds of relationships that are distinctly foreign to capital as well as resonant with the ways of spontaneously evolving ecosystems. For example, instead of using chemical inputs to control pests or accelerate growth, other organisms are introduced or composting is employed – in each instance, a conscious enhancement of an original process is chosen instead of a substitution for it. From another angle, this introduces a certain indeterminacy and complexity into the practice of agriculture. Smaller and more intricately put-together systems, configured to the concrete contours of the land, replace the monocultures that homogenize landscapes. Thus the specificities of sites are developed rather than written over, as under capital. Finally, there is a great deal of intense personal engagement, with strong aesthetic and even spiritual potentials. This results from organic agriculture's surpassing of the homogenized and quantified monocultures of agribusiness, with its reliance on high inputs from fossil fuel and alienated labour.[13]

Organic agriculture also greatly surpasses voluntarism inasmuch as it reflects a deep and sustained commitment – or, what comes to the same thing, as it manifests highly developed social production. But this same fact also points towards the great vulnerability of organic farming to the vicissitudes of capital. Submission to the terms of markets, where price structures, interest rates, and so on are set by the benchmarks of big business, greatly hems in the organic farmer, and will continue to do so as long as he or she repeats the error of voluntarism by not challenging the market and struggling to transform it. And of course this cannot be done in isolation from other struggles.

All of which leads to a look at non-socialist efforts to reform the economic system.

Green Economics

In the wake of the collapse of twentieth-century socialism, an influential and diverse body of opinion has arisen claiming that a path can be found out of the ecological crisis that does not require the overthrow and supercession of capital. This 'green economics' echoes a number of the economic points made here – that our system suffers from a kind of gigantism, that its values, in particular the espousal of quantity over quality, are severely flawed, that it misallocates resources, promotes inequity and generally has made a botch of the global ecology. But green economics does so on the premise that the system has recuperative powers. It would not be fair to say that the people who espouse it are part of the system,[14] for their critique is severe and they often suffer one sanction or another. But green economics is not really outside the system, either. Its proponents want, rather, to stretch and reorganize the system to realize ecocentric potentials, and they believe that the means are at hand for doing so, so long as one thinks 'small' and in a communitarian way.

We can identify four strands woven into this tendency. The first, ecological economics, represents the ecological wing of mainstream economics: it speaks with an authoritative and technical voice to the entirety of economic relations with nature. Ecological economics comes packaged as a professional association with a refereed journal. As a recent quasi-official volume asks:

> Can we ... reorganize our society rapidly enough to avoid a catastrophic overshoot? Can we be humble enough to acknowledge the huge uncertainties involved and protect ourselves from their most dire consequences? Can we effectively develop policies to deal with the tricky issues of wealth distribution, population prudence, international trade, and energy supply in a world where the simple palliative of 'more growth' is no longer an option? Can we modify our systems of governance at international, national, and local levels to be better adapted to these and new and more difficult challenges?[15]

Clearly, ecological economics is uninterested in social transformation, and accepts the potentials of the present system to absorb the crisis, that is, to 'adapt'. To this means, which has in effect become an end, ecological economists employ a great variety of instrumental measures, from 'incentive-based' regulations (such as the above-discussed tradable emission credits) to various ecological tariffs and 'natural capital' depletion taxes, as well as mandatory penalties against polluters.

Mainstream ecological economists are relatively unconcerned with the size of economic units. However, there others, clustering about a second strand of green economics, who regard this question as primary. These may roughly be described as neo-Smithian, the Smith in question being the great Adam, father of modern political economy. Adam Smith's advocacy of free markets was in the interest of an end distinctly different from that of today's neo-liberalism. Smith's vision – which in good measure also became Thomas Jefferson's – was of a capitalism of small producers, freely exchanging with each other. He feared and loathed monopolies, and felt that the competitive market of small buyers and sellers (where no single individual could by himself determine prices) would self-regulate to keep these at bay. Smith argued that state intervention, the *bête noire* of neo-liberalism, leads to monopoly and economic gigantism. Neoliberalism, needless to say, has no difficulty at all with these latter ends.

The ambition of neo-Smithian thinking is to restore small, independent capitals to pre-eminence. For this purpose, as David Korten, one of the leading exponents of the view, puts it, Smith's assumption, '*that capital would be rooted in a particular place*,' must be met.[16] Korten's ecological society, the essence of which he describes as 'democratic pluralism', is based upon 'regulated markets', in which government and civil society combine to offset the tendencies of capitalist firms to expand and concentrate, even as these same capitalist firms, now reduced, continue to provide the mainspring of the economy.

Korten has achieved considerable prominence in presenting these views, a number of which parallel those argued here. However, he does so without any concentrated critique of capital itself, nor, significantly, of questions of class, gender or any other category of domination. He would see the primary lesion in philosophical or religious terms, as a suddenly appearing colossal kind of mistake identifiable as the 'Scientific Revolution', whose 'material-ism' stripped life of 'meaning' and crushed the spirit of 'generosity and caring'. Korten regards this grandly:

> Failing to recognize and embrace their responsibility to the whole [human beings] turned their extraordinary abilities to ends ultimately destructive of the whole of life, destroying in a mere 100 years much of the living natural capital it had taken billions of years of evolution to create.[17]

Note the reference to 'natural capital', as though nature had toiled to put the gift of capital into human hands, who then abused their legacy through false science and materialism. Since capital – or class, or the capitalist state – are no big deal, and even, when nature produces them, are good things, Korten has no difficulty in seeing them checked by 'globalizing civil society', which will restrain and effectively domesticate the animal, leading to the neo-Smithian Promised Land. This is essentially an upbeat fairy-tale stand-ing in for history, and if it were true, the world would be a much easier place to change.

It is so short a step from neo-Smithianism to community-based economics as to make one inclined to include them under a single rubric. But to introduce the latter as a third strand of ecological economics is serviceable as a way of indicating the breadth of the community economics movement, which includes, alongside neo-Smithians, followers of E. F. Schumacher, who called for a 'Buddhist economics',[18] or defenders of the 'Commons', grouped about *The Ecologist* magazine, where the emphasis is on small producers from the South or indigenous communities; or major portions of the Green movements, along with social ecologists (see below). The entire community economics tendency has its roots in the anarchist tradition of Proudhon and Kropotkin, who emphasized mutualism as a defence against the forces of modernity and gigantism.[19] As proponents of this point of view are usually hostile to socialism, they oppose public ownership of the means of production and espouse a diverse mixture of economic forms.

Cooperatives are frequently mentioned among the elements of community economics. But the cooperative movement, whether of consumers or, more signficantly, producers, deserves mention as a separate, fourth strand of green economics because of its implications for the organization of labour and the advance of democracy. Because its essence is ownership by producers, the very notion of cooperation cuts into the core of capitalist social relations, replacing hierarchy and control from above with freely associated labour. As Roy Morrison has written:

> Cooperation ... is both *social creativity* – the growth of new lifeways, of neighborhoods and communities – and *economic creativity* – the ways of making a living through the growth of community-based business enterprises ... Such cooperation is a matter of necessity. It is a key response to the crises of modernity. In this sense, the industrial state becomes the catalyst for the creation of its antipode, the dynamic cooperative commonwealth.[20]

Marx at first thought well of cooperatives, speaking of them as:

> a greater victory [for workers, compared to achieving the ten hour workday] of the political economy of labour over the political economy of property ... The value of these great social experiments cannot be over-rated ... they have shown that production on a large scale, and in accord with the behests of modern science, may be carried on without the existence of a class of masters employing a class of hands ... [21]

Cooperatives are properly deemed private, in that they are owned by their workers and not society as a whole. But this meaning needs to be configured against the backdrop of a system that constructs the rules of property. It is here that the limits of green economics come into view. The fact of the matter is that cooperatives are both attractive and, so far as the transformation of society in an ecological direction goes, no more than a very halting and isolated first step. Picking up on Morrison's point, above, we could say that the *principle* of cooperation is only partially realizable within the *institutions* of cooperatives in capitalist society. Actually, a significant portion of the economy, from farmer cooperatives, to credit unions, and even some HMOs, is already in cooperative hands. But this has not stopped the ecological crisis from maturing, just as it matures with unleaded gasoline, recycled newspaper and other worthy palliatives. No doubt, were the entire economy in cooperative hands, matters would be different – but for that to happen, capital itself would have to be shoved aside and replaced, and that is quite another, and revolutionary, matter, which will not come from the existing cooperative movement.

The error of assuming that cooperatives – or community economics, or green capitalism, or any of the reforms in themselves – will stem the crisis arises from confusion about their relation to capital. Capital will tolerate any number of improvements and rationalizations so long as its basic expansion is secured – and indeed, many of the reforms succeed in doing just that, and are encouraged by the state or progressive elements of the bourgeoisie on that account, even if reactionary elements of the class may resist. Thus some cooperatives and green capitalism are allowed or even encouraged to join the club so long as they add modestly to accumulation, or at least keep out of its way.

However, it is this expansion, in the form of the 'gigantic force field', that tears up ecologies – and at the same time, oppresses cooperatives and other forms of green capital. If we examine this 'force field' more closely, we see it as a demand for the growth of profits extended across the entire surface of society. This pressure at first seems transparently obvious, yet on inspection certain puzzling features appear. Profit is obviously a function of price, but prices are fickle and variable, while profits need to be much more structured. How, for example, are the great variety of economic price signals – stock quotes, interest rates, exchange rates, commodity prices and so on – interpreted by economic agents in the capitalist marketplace? Through their monetary amounts, to be sure. But what function of money is involved – money as pure exchangeability, as a commodity itself to be traded, or as the embodiment of value? Clearly, the third: it is value that stalks forth in economic considerations of profitability. Money-as-exchangeability has no substantial existence – it is like writing on water, while money-as-commodity is itself to be traded and cannot stand for anything beyond that. Value, on the other hand, is the active relationship that pervades all transactions of capitalism.

If the force field is extended across the surface of society, then value is, so to speak, implanted throughout that surface to attract the force field; wherever exchange-value is inserted, there arises a commodity. Capitalism is generalized commodity production, and value is the all-pervading vector, the installation and maintenance of which is the actual function of capitalism as such. Profits are the increasing of values (as manifested in money), and values link all elements of capitalism according to profitability; that is, after all, what is meant by the great temple of capitalism known as the Market. As every cooperative manager knows, the *internal* cooperation of freely associated labour is forever hemmed in and compromised by the force field of value expansion embodied in the Market, whether this be expressed in dealings with banks or an unending pressure to exploit labour in order to stay afloat, or through hierarchies or bureaucracies, or any of hundreds of mediations. In Marx's words (written at a later occasion when the limits of cooperatives had become clearer), however well-intentioned they may be, cooperatives within capitalism necessarily reproduce 'the shortcomings of the prevailing system' in forcing workers to become 'their own capitalist … by enabling them to use the means of production for the employment of their own labour', the standards of which are then set by the capitalist Market. Therefore, whether cooperatives like it or not, capital, with all its atomization and competitive pressure, hems them in, and forces them to become like the other capitalist enterprises – as, in the most egregious cases, happens with HMOs or United Airlines, the largest firm with substantial employee ownership.[22]

In every case, the pressure of value must be contended with, and the ecological success of a cooperative, or indeed any economic formation within capitalist society, may be judged strictly by the degree to which this force is neutralized or overcome. But what is the real force of value within capitalism? To return to the previous discussion, it only arises as the world-destroying monstrous form of capital when *human labour* – the productive power essential to all economic activity – is commodified in the wage relationship through the separation, or splitting, of producers from the means of their production. This becomes generalized, hence under capitalism exploitable labour is a ground for all economic activity, green or otherwise, since it determines the general market regulation to which green economics must conform. So long as the main institutions of capital endure to set the basic terms of the market, they continually force the separation of producers, i.e., humanity, from the means of production, including nature, and force labour to be exploited.

Viewed against the reality of capital, community economics seen as an end in itself becomes incoherent. In fact, it does so on logical grounds. For all economic activity is local – in that it involves somebody doing something somewhere – and it is global as well. Even in the most localized instance, say, some youngsters in Southern California picking lemons from the tree in their backyard and making lemonade for sale in front of their house, the final, local act rests upon a deep and widespread foundation. Did lemon trees grow immemorially in what is now San Diego? Are lemon trees, or any food-producing entity, just found in nature, or were they developed over centuries by past labour? Where did the water come from to grow the tree and mix with the lemon juice, and what struggles took place so that it could be delivered so cheaply? And the sugar, what is its history?[23] Was it home-grown, or, more likely, purchased with money, from what source? And the house that becomes the marketplace, how is this owned and built? From local materials?

A pure community, or even 'bioregional' (see below) economy is a fantasy. Strict localism belongs to the aboriginal stages of society: it cannot be reproduced today, and even if it could, it would be an ecological nightmare at present population levels. Imagine the heat losses from a multitude of dispersed sites, the squandering of scarce resources, the needless reproduction of effort, and the cultural impoverishment. This is by no means to be interpreted as a denial of the great value of small-scale and local endeavours: any flourishing ecosystem, after all, functions by differentiated, which is to say particular, activity. It is, rather, an insistence that the local and particular exists in and through the global whole; that there needs to be, in any economy, an interdependence whose walls are not confinable to any township or bioregion; and that, fundamentally, the issue is the relationship of parts to the whole.

Therefore the vision of an ecological society cannot be purely local, and neither can it be a neo-Smithian system of small capitalists. For Smith's reasoning – like that of Jefferson – was strictly contextualized by its gestation in a transitional form of capitalism, primarily agrarian and based on hand-made commodities, before industrialization rewrote the map of society and tore great masses of people away from the earth and from control over their productive activity.[24] Smith's agents of transformation were members of a class of enlightened small landowners, whose freedom of function was given by their control over their land. Only under such circumstances does it make sense even to dream, as David Korten does, 'that capital would be rooted in a particular place'. That was a dream unrealized, as new class formations made accumulation possible on an expanding scale. Today, when to root capital is tantamount to rooting mercury, it is a nostalgic fantasy. And just as Smith's political economy needs to be historicized, so are his basic categories ahistorical and essentialized. Yes, if people have Smith's famous innate propensity to trade and barter, then they should be given capitalist firms to realize this. But since when are the impulses of capitalism directly derived from the innate repertoire of human nature? Since the coming to power of capital, that is all. Why should we submit today to the model of small capital, which, however less murderous than large capital, is still based on the exploitation of labour, that most crucial of ecological insults, and is therefore infected with the virus of capital's cancerous growth?

Do we call, then, for the immediate abolition of money, wage labour and commodity exchanges, along with all market relations and businesses? Absolutely not: measures of this sort recapitulate the Pol Pot or Stalinist solution, and they ride as heavily over humanity and nature as did slavery. They are forms of violence that tear apart ecosystems human and natural alike. An ecocentric people will not need to repress the accumulation of capital because such a people will be free from exploitation, and the drive to accumulate will not arise from the ground of freely associated labour. The problem is to get to that ground, in the course of which present ways of production need to be traversed and transformed and not knocked over. But first it must be envisioned. To create that vision, a radical rejection of capitalist ways is necessary. We should reject, therefore, the phoney tolerance espoused by green economics toward preserving a 'diversity' that gives a substantial role to capitalist firms. One might as well try to raise weasels and chickens in the same pen. In this real world, all forms of capital, including the oxymoronic 'natural capital' that is supposed to rescue us, are swiftly caught up in the flood-tide of accumulation.

My intention is not at all to disparage the virtue of a small economic or community unit. Quite the contrary: as we shall explore in the last chapter, small-size enterprises are an essential part of the path towards an ecological society, as well as the building blocks of that society. There is a question, rather, about perspective: whether the small units are to be capitalist or socialist in orientation, and whether they are seen as ends in themselves or integrated with a more universal vision. For both of these sets of choices, I would argue for the latter position: the units need to be consistently anti-capitalist, and they need to exist in a dialectic with the whole of things. For human beings are not rodents, who live in burrows. Nor are we insects, creatures who thrive at a small scale, because of which they cannot use skeletons or lungs, or any of the organs necessary for larger organisms. Humans are, by nature, large, expansive, universalizing creatures. We need different degrees of realization to express our being, grandeur as well as intimacy, the large grain as well as the fine. We need the equivalent of skeletons to support us, and specialized organs to meet our species' needs. Thus I should think that in an ecologically realized world there would exist significant sectors of large-scale activity, for example, rail and communications systems and power grids, just as world cities would flourish as sites of universality. I hope I may be forgiven for insisting that New York, Paris, London and Tokyo not be taken down in an ecological society, but more fully realized; and that the nightmare cities of global capital – the Jakartas and Mexico Citys – will be restored to similar states of being.

This restoration in its many forms comes back to the question of the emancipation of labour, and not just waged labour, but all compulsive forms of our creativity, including most definitely the alienation of women's household work, and the stifling of children in schools. The fact is that the great bulk of humankind are throttled in their humanity, and overcoming this is far more significant than any tinkering from above with a corrupt economy. This truth is either lost on the ecological economists or mystified out of existence. Any sense of real people, and real popular struggle, are abstracted from mandarin texts such as *An Introduction to Ecological Economics*. Yes, the authors do call for a 'living democracy', which is certainly a good thing. But life is struggle, especially in a class society where antagonisms are built into the social process. Yet for *Ecological Economics*, living democracy is 'a broad

... process to discuss and achieve consensus on these important issues. This is distinct from the polemic and divisive political process that seems to hold sway in many countries today.' Thus we need 'to engage all members of society in a substantive dialogue about the future they desire and the policies and instruments necessary to bring it about'.[25] The image evoked is like one of the official murals that decorate post offices in which the European settlers/invaders are solemnly greeted by the Indians to deliberate on matters of mutual concern. Where sweatshops re-impose slavery within the capitalist system while untold millions of people in the middle are consigned to mall culture and the rat race, consensus is not exactly an illuminating term, and some divisive polemics, well-chosen and coupled with proper action, can do a great deal of good. False reconciliation is not the path out of a world as unjust as this. The demand for justice is the pivot about which labour will be emancipated; it must also be a foundation of overcoming the ecological crisis.

In bringing this section to a close a few words may be added about Herman Daly, in my view the best of the mainstream ecological economists. Daly, formerly with the World Bank and a student of Georgescu-Roegen, has done more than anyone to question the pathological growth inherent in the system. He has held firmly, in the teeth of elite opinion to the contrary, to the thesis of limits to growth and attempted to redefine economics accordingly. Nor has Daly hesitated to call for fundamental change, or to use strong, non-technocratic language in doing so.[26] I would see Daly as a bridge-builder between the established thought, the folly of which he appreciates keenly, and the more radical approach chosen here.

To this end, Daly has gone a considerable way (beyond, say, David Korten) toward a basic critique of capital. He was not afraid to advocate a maximum wage, and caught the expectable amount of scorn for his troubles.[27] He is willing to use Marx's framework for use- and exchange-value and the circulation process underlying capital formation.[28] And he has a keen awareness of the dehumanization of labour endemic to the capitalist system, and calls for widespread worker ownership as a remedy. He has even shown flexibility on the question of socialism, being an admirer of Karl Polanyi and Michael Harrington, who opened his eyes to the democratic potentials within socialism.

But these insights do not translate into praxis, especially on the all-important subject of labour. Yes, Daly would have worker ownership, but kept firmly within a capitalist market. His sensitivity to the predicament of labour is vitiated by an odd reading of history, in which the opposition between capital and labour is seen as the 'dominant situation of the *past* ... [when it] was supposed that the interests of labor and management were in conflict more than they were in harmony. This was true when capital treated labor as a commodity ... It is much less true today' – a startling insight. As a result, 'the goal should be to increase communications between labor and management so that the situation would be improved for both'. Daly here repeats the ideology of Fordism, which has been scrapped since the crises of the 1970s, and was basically a mystification to begin with.

More pointedly, Daly does not believe in it, either. For example, he – and Cobb – would 'insist that [trade policy] be accompanied by greatly increased competitiveness among American producers'. For the purposes of competitiveness, of course, capital has to treat labour just as it always has, namely, as a commodity whose cost is to be ruthlessly driven down – or shifted to the dirt-cheap overseas sources provided by globalization. In any case, the day when capital ceases treating labour as a commodity will be the dawning of a new, socialist era. In the meanwhile, Daly stays with the *ancien régime*, unable to cross the bridge he is building. He does 'not want to see the renewal of labour militancy directed toward increasing its share of the pie over against capital and the general public' (as though the workforce were not the general public). On the other hand, neither would he and Cobb 'encourage continued interest in global domination', for which we may all offer a modest round of gratitude.[29]

Ecophilosophies

An 'ecophilosophy' represents a comprehensive orienting statement that combines the understanding of our relation to nature, the dynamics of the ecological crisis, and the guidelines for rebuilding society in an ecological direction. These positions are not simply contained in texts, but inform social movements as well. They have practical and political implications which need to be cursorily addressed here. I will try to avoid needless repetition of points already made, and focus instead on ecophilosophies as principles of social transformation, that is, what society are they envisioning?

Deep Ecology

Since capitalism is the regime of the ego, and holds 'Man' over all things, including, certainly, nature, the deep-ecological principle of decentring humanity would seem to possess an innate resonance with the anti-capitalist project. But nothing of the sort transpires. These two sides are the furthest removed of all those to be considered: between actually existing socialism and actually existing deep ecology there is a radical barrier. There is considerable responsibility for this from the socialist side, which we will examine in the next chapter, but there is also considerable responsibility from the deep ecological side.

Actually, there is one deep ecologist, the most famous and influential of all, who has recognized the potential rapprochement with socialism. Arne Naess, the Norwegian philosopher who more or less sired the project, writes that 'it is still clear that some of the most valuable workers for ecological goals come from the socialist camps'.[30] But Naess is clearly an exceptional figure – exceptional in his range of interests, sense of justice and openness, and also in being from a European nation where anti-communism and neoliberal ideology have not stifled the political intelligence with hatred of socialism. In the USA, very few people influenced by deep ecology bother to read Naess, or would attend to statements such as the above. The deep ecological position, rather, has been assumed by the philosophically and/ or spiritually minded, who tend to keep a measured distance from the messy world of struggle,[31] along with defenders of wilderness and untrammelled nature. Many virtuous souls here, but no internal connection with the critique of capitalism or the emancipation of labour. These are the kind of folks who tend to fall in line behind the fatuous pronouncement that green politics is 'neither left nor right, but ahead' – a mere slogan that leads to the question of what being 'ahead' constitutes (see below), while forgetting that in the real world, that which does not confront the system becomes its instrument. In any case, the deep ecology ecophilosophy is far too loose to form itself into a coherent movement, and almost by definition excludes the formation of parties or any organized assertion of power. Indeed, what kind of a society can be formulated out of so flaccid a doctrine as would hold that:

Our first principle [with respect to resource conservation] is to encourage agencies, legislators, property owners and managers to consider flowing with rather than forcing natural process. Second, in facing practical situations we favor working within the minority tradition, in the local community, especially the bioregion.[32]

There are also certain less than virtuous souls attracted to deep ecology. The flaw in deep ecology derives from its effort to decentre humanity within nature, a measure that can easily go too far and split us away from wild nature, allowing us to forget that 'nature', as we employ the concept, is a social construction before it is anything else. This passes very easily into the splitting away of unwanted people.

· One of the more disgraceful impacts of the deep ecological perspective on policy is the habit, in preserving 'wilderness', of erasing the people who lived there from time immemorial, so much a part of nature that they had no separate word for it, and certainly no word for wilderness. Now comes an estranged creature who sees wilderness all around, whose power derives from his estrangement, who forgets that human beings are natural creatures, and who, in preserving wilderness, expels lesser humans. In the turbulent climate of contemporary ecopolitics, this is complicated by the needs of the US State Department and the World Bank to shore up their shaky legitimacy. In order to counter criticisms of their role in the ecological crisis, these institutions often make aid packages conditional on preserving wild areas – which then have added value as sites for ecotourism, a favoured way of recycling the economic surplus. So deep ecology comes home as the strategy of advanced capitalist elites, for whom nature is what looks good on calendars.

In the meanwhile, in the decade 1986–96, more than three million people were displaced by development and conservation projects. This policy began not with deep ecology, but with the nineteenth-century conservation movement. In the USA, this was very much tied up with getting rid of Indians. Our enjoyment of the great national park system, for instance, needs to be tempered with the recollection that 300 Shoshones were killed in the development of Yosemite, by no means an isolated case. Deep ecology, border politics, the genocide of indigenous peoples and ecotourism are all, then, part of the same package. This trap is loaded because of the pressing population crisis, which makes it easy to rationalize exclusion. The trait is by no means confined to deep ecology, but haunts the environmental movement at large, which has not covered itself with glory on questions such as immigration, often allying with reactionaries in a deluded and cryptically racist quest to keep our borders 'clean'. Certain exponents of deep ecology have disgraced themselves and the movement yet further by suggesting that pandemics such as AIDS are nature's, that is, 'Gaia's', way of ridding itself of the pestilential species *Homo sapiens*. So far as I know, they never apply the same reasoning to themselves or family members when they get sick. We shall pick up this thread in the final section of the present chapter.[33]

Bioregionalism

The appeal of this doctrine, which connects some of the principles of community economics with the back-to-the-land movement, is obvious. Bioregionalism represents a specifically ecological rendition of the contemporary movement toward the break-up of nation-states. Where separatists typically define themselves in terms of distinct nations subsumed within the larger political entity, bioregionalists take this a step further, grounding – literally – themselves in the ecological preconditions of nationhood, that of the *place* shared by a people. This, however, is not merely location, but the concrete ecological workings of a part of the earth: the flows of watersheds, the lie of the hills, the kinds of soils, the biota that inhabit a bioregion, regarded as the organic substrate of a revealed community, human-scale and dedicated to living gently on the earth and not over it. From this perspective, the bioregion is the essential ground within which the principles of sustainability and its reliance on ecological technology and economics may be applied.

Certainly, an emphasis on place in any realized ecophilosophy is essential. It would be impossible to construct any adequate notion of an integral ecosystem without such a ground. It might be added that as someone who has chosen to live in the Catskill Mountains and Hudson Valley of New York State, and who has had good relationships with people in the back-to-the-land movement, I personally speak with a great deal of affection for this point of view. Nevertheless, the attempt to extend it to bioregionalism as an ecophilosophy is to be challenged and rejected, because the idea is incapable of guiding social transformation.

Some of these difficulties may be seen in an essay by the bioregionalist

Kirkpatrick Sale, who is led to posit a regime of *self-sufficiency* for the bio-region. A consistent bioregionalist has to do so in order to establish his view as an ecophilosophy. What comes, however, with the 'territory' is the need to define boundaries. Of this, Sale has the following to say:

> Ultimately, the task of determining the appropriate bioregional boundaries – and how seriously to take them – will always be left up to the inhabitants of the area. One can see this fairly clearly in the case of the Indian peoples who first settled the North American continent. Because they lived off the land, they distributed themselves to a remarkable degree along the lines of what we now recognize as bioregions.[34]

There are three major problems with this statement.

First, what is an 'area'? The term is vague in itself, but cannot remain that way if boundaries of the bioregion need to be decided, as must be the case if there is to be a 'self' to be self-sufficent about. But who is to decide who lives where? Can this conceivably be done without conflict, given the differential suitability of different regions for productive development? And who is to resolve the anticipated conflicts, which will involve major expropri-ation? The land where I live is part of the watershed for New York City. Are the members of the Catskill Mountain Bioregion to declare that the city can go dry, and are they prepared to go to war to preserve the integrity of the bioregion?

Second, the Indian peoples lived bioregionally because only about 6–10 million of them inhabited the now United States at the time of the European invasion. Today's vastly greater population exists not in simple relation to place but in an interdependent grid. Remember, too, that the Indians fell into bitter warfare as their territory became destabilized by the European intrusion.

Third, and most important by far, the Indian's bioregional life-world was predicated on holding land in common – in other words, it was a primitive communism. The genocidal wars with the invaders had a great deal to do with the latter's capitalism, which required the alienation of land as property, something the Indians would rather die than submit to (which is pretty much what happened). Capitalism has definitely not changed in this respect, and no coherent project of bioregionalism can survive if productive land remains a commodity, to be owned by absentees, hoarded, rented out, concentrated in fewer and fewer hands and generally exploited. Sale is fully

aware of the plight of the Indians, but ignores the implications of transforming capitalism. He writes that bioregional institution-building 'can be
safely left to people who live there, providing only that they have undertaken
the job of honing their bioregional sensibilities and making acute their
bioregional consciousness' (p. 476) – a pretty gross understatement of what
history shows to be the need to transform society in a 'communist' direction,
without which a people simply cannot democratically control their bioregion. And if they rose up to take such control, how much imagination
does it take to see what would be the response of the capitalist state?

Even if these problems could miraculously be ironed out, retaining Sale's
autarkic concept of a bioregion would be impossible. He calls for self-
sufficient regions, each developing the energy of its peculiar ecology – 'wind
in the Great Plains; water in New England; wood in the Northwest' (p.
482). But how on earth are these resources to be made sufficient? I would
be surprised to learn that the rivers of New England could supply more
than a tenth of its energy needs, and as for wood in the Northwest (where
there is more hydropower, though again not enough), how will Sale answer
to the environmentalists – or the economists, or any sane person – if, say,
Seattle is converted to forest-destroying and smoke-spewing wood-burning
stoves? Of course, an ecological society would have greatly enhanced energy
efficiency and reduced needs, but there is something slapdash in these
prescriptions, which seem deduced from a naturalized ideology rather than
grounded in reality.

'Self-sufficiency,' adds Sale, 'before I am badly misunderstood, is not the
same thing as isolation, nor does it preclude all kinds of trade at all times.
It does not require connections with the outside, but within strict limits –
the connections must be nondependent, nonmonetary and noninjurious –
it allows them' (p. 483). We should not misunderstand badly, or at all, but
the understanding is hard. No required connections between bioregions?
Suppose your daughter lives in the next one (or worse, the one beyond
that) and you want to visit. Can you phone her, and whom do you pay for
the purpose? Are there to be no roads, or rail systems, or aeroplane travel
for the purpose? Are people only to walk between bioregions on trails
through the brush, as the other means would require some monetary intercourse?

We need take this no further. A strict bioregionalism dissolves in a flood
of contradiction, because in it, nature is abstracted from history. In itself

it cannot arrive at the transformation of the whole of society needed to resolve the crisis.

Ecofeminism

Ecofeminism is a powerful ecophilosophy grounded in the two great struggles of women's liberation and ecological justice. However, it is uncertain as a social movement. As an ecophilosophy it theorizes the thematic we have drawn as the gendered bifurcation of nature. This began with the control over women's bodies and labour, and is at the root of patriarchy and class. The splits between classes, between genders, and between 'Man' and nature are to undergo distinct paths of development and intertwine into complex patterns. They enter the history of capitalism at its foundations – in the reduction of nature to inert resources; in the valorization of cold abstraction and the identification of this masculine trait with what is truly human; and in the super-exploitation of women, beginning with unwaged domestic labour and extending to cheapened wage labour in the periphery and fodder for the sex industries. In the strange brew that is capitalist culture, money becomes the hieroglyph for the phallus, the signifier of power and the laurel of competition – and the race is on.

It follows that capitalist domination always entails gender domination, and that the enmity to nature we are tracking is integrally related to its gendered bifurcation. Therefore any path out of capitalism must also be ecofeminist. Logically, ecofeminism should also be anti-capitalist, as capital and its state hold the reins of power by means of which women and ecologies are degraded. Indeed, a substantial body of ecofeminist theory and practice meets this condition.[35] But ecofeminism, like feminism proper, need not be anti-capitalist. Other ecofeminists take a kind of refuge in an unmediated relationship to nature, that is, they can *essentialize* women's closeness to nature and build from there, submerging history into nature in the process. The 'eternal feminine' results: archetypally maternal, close to the earth, and, in its further reaches, the source of Goddess-based spiritualities.[36]

This variant of ecofeminism is closer to the category of feminist separatism. Because essentialism takes its object outside history, there can at best be a weak, imitative reconnection of what had been split off. The holding and provisioning functions assigned to a historically degraded femininity cannot be recovered for the transformation of capitalist/patriarchal society. Essentialist feminisms, whether eco- or not, remain therefore essentially bourgeois in orientation. Their place is in the comforts of the New Age Growth Centre, rather than on the barricades of struggle. And the prevalence of this point of view keeps ecofeminism from becoming a coherent social movement.

Social Ecology

This doctrine, the last ecophilosophy to be considered, builds on the central insight that ecological problems have to be seen as social problems, and specifically as the outcome of hierarchies. In contrast to deep ecology, bioregionalism and essentialist ecofeminism, social ecology is intrinsically radical: it begins with social critique, and follows this through to the en-visioning of a political transformation.

Why, then, is this not a book within the social ecology tradition? The reason, as I see it, is partly theoretical, partly a function of how political movements have played themselves out. The theoretical distinction has to do with the fact that social ecology has tended to regard hierarchy in-itself both as a kind of original sin and as the efficient cause of the ecological crisis. The particular path traced in the present work, which begins with gender domination and moves to class, and then, eventually, to capital, is eschewed in favour of a blanket condemnation of any human relationship in which person *a* has authority over person *b*. This forgets that there are rational forms of authority such as the teacher–student relationship, which are grounded in the very human-natural fact that our young are born helpless into the world, and need the transmission of culture if they are to become human. What makes a hierarchy worth overthrowing is its character of *domination*, where this signifies an expropriation of human power for the purposes of self-aggrandizement. Dominative relationships need to be con-trasted to those relationships of differential authority that are reciprocal and mutual (so that the student can look forward to becoming a teacher herself some day). What this means in practice is that hierarchies and authorities have to be concretely examined to see whether they are *just* or not; and this in turn requires that they be assessed in terms of the specific alienations of human creative power that occur in different historical set-tings. For this purpose the notions of gender and class, which connect real individuals to history and nature, are very apt, as is the idea of production as the defining characteristic of human nature.

These rather abstract points are given substance in terms of the actual political contours of an ecophilosophy such as social ecology. Social ecology continues the anarchist project, a tradition with quite a few noble souls on its roster, and also some scoundrels, whose principal point of action has been the defence of community and the attack on state power.[37] Anarchism incorporates spontaneity and direct action along with communitarian values, and developed in the nineteenth century as an alternative to Marxian socialism, which it continues to oppose. Since the revelations of twentieth-century socialism's potential for centralism, bureaucracy and authoritarianism, and its subsequent collapse (to be discussed in the next chapter), anarchism has gained a renewed hold on the left. An influential strand has been evident in the post-Seattle emergence of new movements against globalization, in whose demonstrations it has taken a leading role. This current emphasizes direct action, which is a necessary component to any radical ecopolitics, but not a sufficient one, as it leaves unspoken the question of building an ecological society beyond capital.

Social ecology is less concerned as a movement with direct action than with an appropriation of the communitarian values inherent in anarchism. These have also become integral to the various green movements, within which anarchism, and specifically its social ecological form, have played a vital role. But the rejection of socialist and Marxian ways of approaching the ecological crisis sacrifices too much. In its formative period, social ecology tended to play down the goal of taking on the capitalist world system, in all its massive obdurateness and penetration of life-worlds. Anarchists and social ecologists generally profess to be anti-capitalist, but they do not analyse capitalism to its root in the domination of labour. Similarly, they correctly emphasize the need to overcome the domination sedimented into the state, but they overlook the fact (chiefly from hostility to Marxism, I fear) that the prime function of the state is to secure the class system, indeed, that the two structures, class and state, are each absolutely dependent on the other, so that we cannot address the one without the other. Thus if the state is a primary problem, so is the class system, and avoiding confrontation with this latter – which means, in practice, avoiding giving central importance to the emancipation of labour – tends to vitiate the anarchist reading of things and to lose concreteness.

Having said this much, it remains to be emphasized that these difficulties do not in my view amount to an antagonistic contradiction between the positions of social ecology, or indeed, of any anarchist formation, and those argued here. Whatever begins with radical rejection of the given order combines it with the affirmation of freedom for all creatures,[38] and takes upon itself a humility that recognizes the shortcomings of all movements in relation to the task before us, and is positioned to contend with the ecological crisis. Within these boundaries the active contestation of ideas goes forward. In truth, we are all groping toward a transformative vision deeper and wider than any yet subsumed under the labels of past struggles. Therefore, one enemy we should all be able to agree upon is sectarianism.

To some degree these problems were embodied by Murray Bookchin, who conjugated anarchism with ecological awareness in the 1960s, and emerged from that fruitful decade with social ecology in hand. Charismatic as well as brilliant, but also unrelentingly dogmatic and sectarian, Bookchin both created social ecology and led it into a cul-de-sac. There were structural reasons for this that extended far beyond any individual failing. When Bookchin first announced social ecology – indeed, when the environmental movements both radical and liberal got going – we were on the cusp between the affluent, expansive and Fordist capitalism of 1945–70, and the neoliberal era that rages today. Bookchin launched social ecology with *Post-Scarcity Anarchism* in 1970, and both the title and the date of that work are revealing. The extent of the ecological crisis had not been felt, which enabled a relatively easy sense of Utopianism. Neither the collapse of Soviet communism nor globalization had set capital so firmly as the brutal overlord of the world. Today things are dreadfully clearer, and it has moved social ecology in an increasingly anti-capitalist direction, while the emerging direction of 'what has to be done' is sweeping all the ecophilosophies towards a new radical synthesis.[39]

Democracy, Populism and Fascism

'Democracy' is the favourite way of organizing humankind for everyone to the left of General Pinochet and the Olympic Organizing Committee. No word is dearer to the ideologues of the regime, who were given to hail our side as the democracies in the holy war against communism, and set up institutions such as the National Endowment for Democracy to superintend the transition of developing countries into the camp of the West. Countries such as Indonesia and Guatemala in the time of the Generals were hailed as democracies (sometimes qualified as 'fledgling'), as has been Nicaragua in the post-Sandinista years, despite an appalling loss of freedom and participation. And today, the latest spasm of capital's global reach, the Free Trade Agreement of the Americas, is legitimated with the promise that it will cement the rule of democracy in the Western hemisphere. Democracy as preached by the establishment is a regime where elites rule on behalf of capital using an electoral mechanism that affords some legitimacy, while permitting a limited degree of lower-class participation along with a check on rampant corruption. The model derives from deep within the history of capitalism, inasmuch as freed citizens were necessary to sell their labour power on its markets. The freedom, as we have seen, has had to be always contained, whence democracy in its bourgeois form has been intrinsically constrictive on the lower classes while offering a means to power open to men of property.

If we regard the ideology of democracy with more than a little scepticism, however, it is only to fight for the true meaning of the notion, since the perpetual struggle for freedom that it encapsulates is nothing less than our coming into full species-powers – which is to say, the power of men and women *beyond* the bourgeois notion of property. The struggle for substantive as against ideological democracy is therefore the necessary precondition for overcoming the ecological crisis, simply because this requires achieving a just society.

In his 2000 Green Party campaign for the presidency, Ralph Nader cited the Ciceronian statement that 'freedom is participation in power' as the most fundamental principle of politics. I would agree, with this qualification: that we be clear that power here means the restoration of our species-potential for creative transformation. And because this is universalizing, democracy is the exercising of power in a universalizing direction – and the building of those institutional forms that enable this to happen. Democracy is to be built by the people themselves, and it is always a work in progress. It points beyond where we are, and never settles for the given.

The fulfilment of democracy is not getting more people to vote, although such an outcome would be more democratic than what we have today insofar as it signifies rising hopes of participation. Nor is it giving voters better parties to vote for. Although, this, too, is a turn on the road, it is limited by the fact that within the confinements of the given state, the power expressed in the polling booths is by definition stunted. If popular agitation built a more powerful electoral foundation, say, by achieving proportional representation so that smaller parties could meaningfully participate, then we could say that democratic power had been advanced, because power had to some further extent built its own base – but we would not rest at that level, either. By the same reasoning, worker ownership of corporations would be a relative democratization, yet so long as the firm has to play by the rules of the capitalist market, this remains self-defeating.

Because the compass of democracy points to the mobilization of our species power, full democracy will not happen without the overcoming of capitalism. Yet such a demand scarcely appears on today's parched political landscape. What we generally see are stunted derivatives, as in the vague identification of people of good will as 'progressive'. The question is: progressing towards what? Towards a virtuous citizenry placing checks on corporate power, who then stand about until startled by the next head of the hydra? Towards the gratification of an alternative 'lifestyle' caught up in capital's consumerist regime? Or does it progress beyond the limits of the given? Our progressivism fails not because of its inability to spell out what the 'beyond' may be, but through its indifference to the question, because of which it settles into the ecodestructive system on the ground.

Progressivism today is largely defined as *populism*. As the word suggests, for populism, the political agent is the 'People', considered as one gigantic person rising up and becoming the subject of its own history. Populism is a compelling political construction, with an immediate appeal. It fills each individual who accepts its terms with the power of historical agency, and because it personalizes history, it offers a cogent and instantly graspable narrative. If the People is afflicted, then another kind of person, the personification of arbitrary and corrupt power, is doing the afflicting. A morality play is invoked. There is an injustice, a villain, and a hero-in-waiting: the People, set to rise up and smite its oppressor, or at the very least to demand fairness. The model resonates across a great range of circumstances and historical moments. It animated peasant rebellions in the Middle Ages, the *sans-culottes* in the French Revolution, Luddites and Chartists in nineteenth-century England, and in the later nineteenth century, in America, took the name of populism itself and became a substantial force. Populist movements

in America have made notable contributions wherever corrupt and alienating economic power has oppressed large blocs of people – farmers in the
Plains and the South, small businessmen victimized by banks, urban workers
afflicted by layoffs. Populist movements were behind William Jennings Bryan
and his 'Cross of Gold' agitation, and they have periodically resurfaced
until the present, when the evils of globalization, striking home across a
great variety of settings, have provoked resistance. The Greens are proud
to be progressive populists, and the heterogeneous character of their demands, ranging from environmental protection to prison reform, changes
in drug policy, and community economics, are readily assimilable to the
populist narrative. In Ralph Nader they gained a recognized champion of
populism, a man who has fought to redress the grievances of ordinary
citizens and consumers victimized by corporate greed.

But populism's 'People' does not exist except as a rallying point, beyond
which it tends to fragment. After all, not all people are oppressed, for the
oppressors are human beings, too. Nor do the oppressed exist as a homogeneous mass, for oppression has constructed significant lines of division.
Would that these could be erased with a slogan! Yes, workers and small
businessmen can go to a rally and feel united; even, let us imagine, blacks
and whites, and Latinos and Asians can do so – or, taking it to another level
of particularity, blacks of African-American extraction and of Caribbean
extraction, or farmers and consumers, or wherever the fault lines have been
laid down. But this does not make them a 'People' once the event is over,
nor will they become so until the hard and patient work has been done to
find the lines of division and build counter-institutions to overcome the class
and state structures that institutionalize oppression. Populism can itself be
no more than a point of entry into the building of movements that address
the structures that fragment a people. Unless it is surpassed, everyone will
go home to his or her particular problem and things will go no further.

Or they may go badly. Populism, by personalizing oppression, becomes
a mythology whose evocative power welds together a divided people into a
unified body: such is populism's evocative power. But there are serious
pitfalls. For one, the populist myth encourages the idea that there was a kind
of 'golden age' before the Bad Oppressor entered the scene and made life
miserable for the People. These days the corporation, especially because it
achieved spurious personhood thanks to a nineteenth-century interpretation
of the 14th Amendment, is exceptionally well situated for the role of villain.

It is an easy matter to proceed from this to construct the myth that somehow we were in good hands before 1865, when corporate greed entered the world – and that this blissful condition will be restored if only corporate power can be checked. No matter that the notion of a golden pre-corporate age is not true: the idea is convenient to the legend of a happy era of small capitals sought by the neo-Smithians, and so a wishful illusion is perpetrated.[40]

There is a more ominous flaw to populism's mythos. Populism that remains merely itself is bound to fail because it cannot address the realities of power. What happens then to the myth? The answer, unhappily too often, is that its personalization turns malignant and persecutory. Sinister conspiracies are alleged to explain the persistence of corporate and financial power; or, in another turn of the screw, the blame is shifted on to alien others, of different colour or ethnicity. This is the stuff of racism, which in actual history has been intertwined with populisms gone bad. Rural populism of the turn of the twentieth century failed when its militancy lost the thread of socialism; with this, it became virulently racist against blacks.[41] Progressive populists are reluctant to associate their cause with Father Coughlin, but the demagogic priest who dominated the airwaves of the 1930s was an authentic populist who took hold of massive rage against capitalism, turned it into a mythologized crusade against banks and then, when he lost the contest for power, turned rightward into anti-Semitism and fascism.[42] Today, these kinds of racist exclusion become especially likely in the context of conflicts over immigration afflicting both the USA and Europe.

The result reawakens the great nightmare of the last century: fascism, most of all in its Nazi form. The special relevance of this painful association arises from the fact that Nazism was both a populism and a self-professedly ecological movement.[43] It goes without saying that the Nazis were never a 'progressive' movement, quite the contrary. Emerging in the wake of a ferocious crisis of accumulation, they did criticize big business and call themselves National Socialists, because socialism had prestige in those days. But the Nazi project was a kind of populism precisely directed against actual socialism, which was countered with an organic ideology that sought a mythicized union of the Germanic people, workers included, with the soil. It was an ecology of merging, which became an ecology of splitting. This kind of unification is all too reminiscent of the nature mysticism still fashionable in certain ecological circles, especially the deep ecological reduction of human beings to the status of just another species in the 'web of life'. Biological reduction fosters racist thought, which is, intellectually speaking, a demented effort to find sub-speciation within humankind. Everyone serious about matters ecological should familiarize themselves with the sayings of Hitler, or of Heinrich Himmler, leader of the SS, about the 'decent' attitude of Germans towards animals, whence the master race should be trusted with the 'human animals' under its care, such as Slavs – trusted, too, to remove the verminous animals such as Jews, Gypsies and homosexuals.[44] This is a degenerate ecophilosophy, beyond doubt, but an ecophilosophy nonetheless, and calls attention to the fact that the degeneration is inherent in whatever denies the value of the specifically human within (and not over) the manifold of nature.

No one should be so naïve as to believe that this way of thinking is a matter only for historians to study. It is most doubtful that progressive populism will turn rightward; its fate lies more in absorption back into the capitalist mainstream. But there are other sources of a malignant ecofascism. A grim far-right presence often recurs within green movements under the umbrella of falsely unified ecological thought. Considerable evidence of this has already appeared in England and Northern Europe, even in the great Seattle protests of 1999, when contingents of anti-Semitic skinheads made an appearance. We should recall, too, that organicist thinkers such as Rudolf Bahro, following Heidegger, betrayed an affinity for Nazi ideology, and that a founding German Green and author of the best-selling 1975 work, *A Planet is Plundered*, Herbert Gruhl, did likewise. Indeed, Gruhl left the party to found an alternative because it had 'given up its concern for ecology in favour of a leftist ideology of emancipation'. Gruhl, it is well to recall, was the originator of the phrase, noted above, that Greens are 'neither left nor right, but ahead'.[45]

Neo-fascist ecological thought comes in many varieties, the common feature of which is to take some aspect of the ecological crisis and, under the guise of being 'neither left nor right, but ahead', move in fact rightward. The instigation is usually population pressure and conflicts over immigration, the context of which are persistently uneven stretches of prosperity (as between the former East Germany and the remainder, or between Southern California and Baja, Mexico), and more basically, the shocking breakdown of large swathes of the world under the chaotic conditions of capital. Presently, ecofascism is limited to a small number of elite intellectuals, just as street-fighting fascists are confined to small groups of radically disaffected youth. But there should be no underestimation of the potential of these movements.

Fascism is an inherent breakdown pattern of capitalism. To say, 'it can't happen here', is to misread the explosive tensions built into the capitalist system. All it takes is a certain degree of crisis, and fascism may be imposed as a revolution from above to install an authoritarian regime in order to preserve the main workings of the system. Regressive ideologies and racism are then introduced as ways of re-establishing legitimacy and displacing conflict. So much was learned in the last century; what we are poised to learn in this one are the fascist potentials in a capitalist system facing crisis of an ecological kind. We may imagine this in the context of pandemics, or terrorist-induced breakdown, or famine, or global warming, or ozone depletion, of the inevitable reckoning as shrinking petroleum supplies become uneconomical to extract and replacements remain insufficient, or as any consequence of non-linear ecosystemic breakdown on a world scale – consider only the gruesome prospect of bovine spongiform encephalopathy and its possible sequelae.[46]

The actual path of the unfolding crisis is not a matter of collapsing ecosystems, but will be drawn as the ongoing interaction of this with political responses. The possibilities are numerous, and need not be speculated upon here. What we should bear in mind, however, is that although fascism may be introduced violently from above to save the system of accumulation, it necessarily introduces more problems than it solves. A fascist order will be more ecodestructive than the liberal one it replaces – because it is further from the democratic realization of human power that is the essential condition for ecological rationality, and because, as a manifestation of this, it builds unbearable and explosive tensions into society. The installation of ecofascism on a national, and eventually global, scale may in fact be the trigger that sets into motion the cascading avalanche that will bring an end to nature's peculiar experiment with a species on whom was bestowed the power to direct evolution.

It is a fate we can choose to defy, for the sake of this very power. But if we succeed in doing so, it can only be through a creative transformation of our existence. Populism and social ecology, green politics, community economics, ecofeminism, bioregionalism, cooperatives – the entire mass of ideologies and movements, coming from below, overlapping, interpenetrating and set going as progressive responses to the crisis – have been tried. They have discovered much, and taught us much, but nothing so much as the need to go further. Today, the streets are full of a new generation of activists, raging against globalization run amok. They have discovered what they are against. But what are they to be *for*? It is time to see if this can be given the name of ecosocialism.

Notes

1. For good surveys, see Tokar 1997; Karliner 1997; Athanasiou 1996.

2. And to the composition of a book on the ecological crisis which combines New Age insight with faith in capitalism: Gore 2000.

3. In the dismay over Bush II's barbaric administration, nostalgia for Clinton-Gore is understandable. Yet the Justice Department under Clinton/Gore reduced by some 30 per cent effective prosecution of environmental crime compared to that of the first Bush administration. Dr Sidney Wolfe, perhaps the most knowledgeable individual on the subject, reports (personal communication) that the Food and Drug Administration and Occupational Safety and Health Administration, chief watchdogs protecting the health of the American citizenry, sank under Clinton to the lowest level of morale and competency that he had witnessed in his 29 years of studying these agencies. See also Cockburn and St Clair 2000. Is it better to have fakers and con men in office, or a frank reactionary who at least strips away the veil of illusion about capital?

4. Breyer 1979. This was published under the title of 'Analyzing regulatory failure, mismatches, less restrictive alternatives and reform', in the *Harvard Law Review*. For a discussion, see Tokar 1997: 35–45.

5. That anyone would believe this scheme capable of containing global warming is testimony to the intense brainwashing that goes on these days. Of course the jargon of tradable permits uses all the latest buzzwords of the rationality that would allow business to have its cake and eat it as well. And it is a fine idea, except for two problems: that it cannot work, especially for global warming; and that if it did work, it only perpetuates the kind of world that gives us the ecological crisis in the first place. As for the first, the notion presupposes a rational marketplace of nations in which rich developed ones pay poor developing ones for the right to emit greenhouse gases. But this kind of market requires an orderly world society of cooperating nations – exactly what globalization has made impossible. More, the fact that the trading of emission credits keeps the 'developing' nations from in fact developing has not been lost on countries such as India and China. As for the second point, the scheme cements the existing system in place, further strengthening irresponsible finance capital, making the rich richer, and, as Brian Tokar has written, giving the 'largest "players" … substantial control over the whole "game"' (1997: 41). The marketing of pollution will drive down the cost of the credits and give incentive to cheating rather than reducing emissions. 'There is little doubt', Tokar continues, 'that an international market in "pollution rights" would widen existing inequalities among nations and increase the dominance of those best able to shift their assets from country to country based on the daily fluctuation of financial markets … the potential for unaccountable manipulation of industrial policy would easily compound the disruptions already caused by often reckless international traders in stocks, bonds and currencies' (ibid.: 42) See also Bader 1997: 102–5.

6. A word about solid waste. There is no doubt that the crisis would be worse if we did nothing about garbage, just as it would be worse if lead were still in gasoline. But the crisis already factors in these palliations, which set certain rates of ecosystem decay, slowing it to the extent we now see without altering the dynamics an iota. In the case of waste management, the large corporations that run the show provide another source of accumulation, exploitation of labour, criminality and concentration – and another kind of industrial setting, the recycling plant. '[M]ost of the recycling plants [that do New York City's work] are owned by big waste companies, and the few that are not will probably wind up being absorbed,' reports the *New York Times* (Stewart 2000: B1). The workers are 'a legion of low-paid workers, including a high percentage of immigrants', who do work that is 'sometimes boring and sometimes dangerous', as a man from Senegal, who works endless hours so he can send money back to his family, put it. In fact, the plant seems a regular Satanic mill, as the fantastic detritus of consumer society is moved on conveyer belts past the workers, who have to concentrate intently, and 'all day … grab and flip. The stuff is thrown into holes, where it falls into heaps', to be collected and resold on a very volatile market. But what good does it really do, besides making more money from exploited labour? 'The dirty secret of recycling is the waste. A third of the trash dumped at the plant is not salvageable, and is hauled to private landfills' – where the environment is subjected to the unsavoury mix. New York is, as can be imagined, the worst case, where only 2,400 tonnes of the 13,000 generated each and every day are recycled, 800 tonnes of which ends up in landfills anyway. But even the more ecologically sane cities only approach 50 per cent recyclability, scarcely reassuring when one looks at the Wal-Marts, etc., springing up all over the landscape, spewing forth garbage-to-be.

7. Manning 1996 offers a paean to the New Energy movement. I would not want to rule out all the energy fixes discussed with breathless enthusiasm by Manning, but I would not bet the future of civilization on them, either. One matter persistently raised by this kind of reasoning is the economics of gathering, storing and distributing the energy. Yes, there may be 'space energy', but how is one to collect it? No doubt the energy of even a small black hole would suffice to keep us going to eternity, but that and a dollar will buy a copy of the *New York Times*.

8. A recent, horrific finding: the Associated Press reported on 10 July 2000, that the US Fish and Wildlife Service estimated that 40,000,000 birds a year are killed by crashing into the 77,000 microwave transmission towers that dotted the American landscape at that time, with more on the way every day. So much for this 'ecologically benign' technology (not to mention the effects of electromagnetic fields from transformers, cell phones, and so on).

9. For an excellent discussion of the environmental load of the information economy, see Huws 1999.

10. See Sarkar 1999: 93–139 for a thorough discussion of the material limits to growth. Sarkar may be overly pessimistic, but his reasoning remains fundamentally sound.

11. Lovins 1977.

12. For a recent survey of the overall fossil fuel picture, with an emphasis on building a hydrogen-based economy (viz. note 10, above), see Dunn 2001.

13. Lappé et al. 1998. As organic produce grows in popularity, capital tries to take it over, with deleterious consequences.

14. Though they often have secure and desirable jobs, as in academia. But then, so does the author of this work.

15. Costanza et al. 1997: 5. Of the book's five authors, Robert Costanza and John Cumberland are associated with the University of Maryland; Herman Daly (see below) and Robert Goodland have been connected with the World Bank; while the fifth, Richard Norgaard, is at UC Berkeley, and the author of *Development Betrayed* (Norgaard 1994), a work that approaches the crisis from the standpoint of a 'coevolutionary' paradigm. A related approach with considerable historical depth, and closer to the perspective offered here, may be found in Martinez-Alier 1987.

16. Korten 1996: 187. Another neo-Smithian is Paul Hawken, author of *The Ecology of Commerce* (Hawken 1993). For my thoughts about Hawken, see Kovel 1999.

17. Korten 2000.

18. Schumacher's Buddhist view of labour includes that it must 'give a man a chance to utilise and develop his faculties', also that work not be separated from leisure, as the two are both sides of the living process. The emphasis is on work as an expression of life and the purification of character – actually rather close to Marx's views, especially in the early philosophical writings and the theory of alienation. However, Schumacher gives no concrete understanding of class struggle, nor of agency in general, nor does he have a theory of capital as such, nor, it follows, of what it would take to get beyond capital. Schumacher 1973: 50–9.

19. *The Ecologist* 1993; Proudhon 1969; Kropotkin 1975.

20. Morrison 1995: 151. Italics in original.

21. Karl Marx, 'Inaugural Address of the Working Men's International Association' (Marx 1978d [1864]). It is worth noting that Marx wrote in a letter to Engels at the time that the speech was difficult to 'frame ... so that our view should appear in a form acceptable from the present standpoint of the workers' movement ...' (p. 512), an acknowledgement that revolutionary hopes had waned from 1848, when the more militant *Communist Manifesto* was written.

22. Marx 1967b: 440. The closest exception is the Mondragon system of cooperatives of northern Spain, perhaps the greatest success of the movement – although it is fair to say that, given the system constraints to which it is exposed, Mondragon has probably reached its limits, without in any way threatening the overall capitalist regime. Morrison 1991.

23. Mintz 1995.

24. 'Smith's solution could not survive the changed circumstances of the transition to industrial capitalism' (McNally 1993: 46).

25. Costanza et al. 1997: 177, 180. The authors also mangle their representation of Marx, limiting his contribution to the ownership and allocation of physical resources, and blaming the 'labour theory of value that neglected nature's contributions' for the ecological devastation wrought by communist societies. It is hard to imagine a grosser distortion.

26. In Daly and Cobb 1994: 21, the following appears, after a statement of respect for academic standards: 'But at a deeper level of our being we find it hard to suppress the cry of anguish, the scream of horror – the wild words required to express wild realities. We human beings are being led to a *dead* end – all too literally. We are living by an ideology of death and accordingly we are destroying our own humanity and killing the planet.'

27. Daly 1991.

28. Daly 1996: 39.

29. Daly and Cobb 1994: 299, 370. Italics added.

30. Naess 1989: 157.

31. For a comprehensive survey, see Zimmerman 1994, a work uncontaminated by the actual world.

32. Devall and Sessions 1985: 145.

33. Stille 2000. See also Cronon 1996; Hecht and Cockburn 1990: 269–76 has a discussion of the expulsions from Yosemite.

34. Sale 1996: 477.

35. As in Mies 1998; Shiva 1988; Salleh 1997.

36. Compare for example, the arguments of Eisler 1988, which make an effort to bring historical understanding to bear, but end by substituting New Age slogans and postulating the existence of a 'Goddess', a notion that replaces male domination with a female-centred hierarchy.

37. For a history, see Woodcock 1962.

38. Humans cannot be free unless they affirm the self-determination of all creatures. This essentially Buddhist insight is the ground of the animal rights movement, which must be integral to any fully thought through ecopolitics and philosophy. Needless to say, the problem is greatly complicated by the fact that one creature's 'nature' will often consist of eating another creature.

39. Bookchin 1970. Bookchin's *chef d'oeuvre* is *The Ecology of Freedom* (Bookchin 1982). I have discussed this complicated figure in some detail in Kovel 1997b. See also Light 1998 (in which my essay is reprinted), as well as Watson 1996. An inkling of the problems with Bookchin's approach, which, aside from being rigidly anti-Marxist, is also rigidly anti-spiritual and highly Eurocentric, may be sensed by the fact that the only political path he can envision is that of 'libertarian municipalism', a confederation of social-ecologic small cities that is supposed to revolutionize society from below. Individuals greatly influenced by Bookchin, yet who have proven capable of moving social ecology along an anti-capitalist road, include John Clark and Brian Tokar. See Clark 1984, 1997; see also the Symposium on the latter, with comments by myself, Kate Soper and Mary Mellor, and Clark's reply in Kovel et al. 1998; Tokar 1992.

40. The first volume of Marx's *Capital* appeared in 1867, before the appearance of large corporations and the 14th Amendment; what on earth could he have been writing about?

41. Sheasby 2000. We should not forget that the origins of the Ku Klux Klan lay similarly in rural discontent.

42. For a summary of Coughlin and further references, see Kovel 1997a.

43. Bramwell 1989 offers an overview of Nazi–Green connections.

44. Himmler, addressing *Einsatzgruppen*, or mobile killing teams, in Poland, 1943: 'We Germans, who are the only people in the world who have a decent attitude to animals, will also adopt a decent attitude to these human animals, but it is a crime against our own blood to worry about them and to bring them ideals.' Quoted in Fest 1970: 115.

45. Biehl and Staudenmaier 1995. See also the excellent website http://www.savanne.ch/right-left.html.

46. Rampton and Stauber 1997.

8 Prefiguration

The Bruderhof

There are, in the eastern USA as well as the Dakotas, adjacent Canada and England, communities of Christian followers of Jakob Hutter (d. 1536), founder of the pacifist branch of the Anabaptists. This offshoot of the Radical Reformation, having endured the persecutions attendant upon their kind, found its way to the New World, where it built agricultural communes and prospered. In the twentieth century, a similar branch arose in Germany under the leadership of Eberhard and Emmy Arnold, first as a Christian pacifist collective, then as a Hutterite intentional community. Persecuted by the Nazis, they fled to Paraguay and built an agricultural commune. In the 1950s they came to the USA, where, under the name of 'Bruderhof', they settled in Rifton, a town in New York's Hudson River Valley. By now, the Bruderhof (a Hutterite term for 'community of brethren') had separated from the original Hutterites, who found them too much in the world. The worldliness of the Bruderhof included a shift from agricultural to industrial production, with an associated embrace of technology. They entered the business of making high-value learning aids for schools and disability centres. While the commodities so produced never captured more than a small share of this market, the realized profit was considerable and enabled the community to grow. Once a Bruderhof community reaches a certain size, say 300–400, it 'hives', dividing and forming a new unit elsewhere. In this way, there have now arisen six Bruderhofs in the USA and two more in England, linked by dedicated phone lines, so that all eight communities can be placed in instant contact with each other simply by picking up a receiver and pressing a button. They have their own publishing house as well, Plough Books, through which their ideas can be disseminated, and I am also told that they possess a small fleet of aircraft, bought with the profits from their business.[1]

There are a considerable number of interesting things to be said about the Bruderhof – whom, it should be added, I have visited on a number of occasions, and worked with on several projects.

First, the Bruderhof thrive in the capitalist market. They make fine and useful objects, using sophisticated machinery, computers and a functioning distribution and sales network, including catalogues, trucks, and so on. In short, they are successfully integrated into the economy.

Second, Bruderhof are radically non-capitalist. The 'value' added on to and extracted from their learning aids derives from the capitalist market at large. Surplus value from the point of production does not figure in this picture. No value is added from their own labour, for the plain reason that the Bruderhof are communists. In the enterprises from which their money is made, they are all paid the same amount: nothing. Nor is there any hierarchy within the factory; there is division of labour, of course, but no boss. The plant managers have no particular authority beyond their differentiated task. A vistor to the plant is greeted with a starkly different scene from what obtains in the standard capitalist workplace. Workers self-direct, come and go at different hours, punch no time-clocks. Time is not bound, nor is work dominated by considerations of productivity. Octogenarians and seven-year-old children work side by side as they please, sharing in the labour. There is no contradiction between this relatively indifferent productivity and the profitability of their factories, because the Bruderhof are not driven to accumulate and increase market share, but are content with sufficient incremental profit to meet their needs, which is made possible by the technology at their disposal. Work is driven by the desire to make fine objects and the larger ends to which it is put.

Third, being communists, the Bruderhof hold 'all things in common'. Beyond a few minor personal possessions, they have no individual property – no cars, no DVD players, no designer jeans, no subscriptions to *Self* and *Connoisseur* magazines. The community takes care of all their needs with its collective profits: communal meals, education and health care, for there are schools on the premises for the young, and Bruderhof physicians to care for most problems. What has to be done outside, such as tuition for advanced study[2] – say, of their doctors – is likewise paid for by the revenues of their factories. By the same token, the material needs of the Bruderhof are considerably lighter than the typical American, both because they share in most things – including the ownership of a few motor vehicles for going here and there – and because everything about their world radically denies the culture of consumerism. Thus the ecological load imposed by the Bruderhof is substantially less than that of the population at large, and if we could somehow figure out a way to get all the people of the industrialized nations to live so lightly on the earth, there would be no crisis of anywhere near the present scale to worry about.

If the Bruderhof are any example, we can affirm that neither industrialization nor technology can be the efficient causes of the ecological crisis. They are immersed in both and consume lightly, showing no compulsion to grow. The reason is the social organization of labour, which under these communistic conditions causes the withering of capital's rage to accumulate.

But these findings open up new questions. What are the conditions, both inner and outer, that enable so radical a shift to occur? What does this imply for markets in an ecologically sane society? And what does this say about socialism? Can we in fact get all the people to live this way? Should we?

As for the first question, there is no mystery. The Bruderhof are deeply Christian, which they interpret as Christian–communist. The 'holding all things in common' derives not from Karl Marx, but from the Biblical record of the first Christians, Acts 2: 44–45: 'And all that believed were together, and had all things common; And sold their possessions and goods, and parted them to all men, as every man had need.' No matter that it has been perennially betrayed, the notion of communism remains foundational for Christianity. It has a long and intricate history, within which Marx himself (who included in his best-known definition of communism, the phrase 'to each according to need') belongs.[3] The Bruderhof are simply being orthodox when they affirm communism. However, it needs to be added that they take this quite a distance. For they not only practise Christian communism, but preach it with a vengeance, and this makes them of special interest to us.

There is probably no more militant group on the left today than these descendants of the Radical Reformation. They have gone on pilgrimages against the death penalty, have sent their children in solidarity to blockaded Cuba and Iraq, and have become spiritual counsellors to Mumia Abu-Jamal. The theme of these activisms is always to counter a persecution, as Jesus was persecuted, and as they themselves have been. That is the Christian logos playing itself out in historical actuality, creating a new history to which their communism integrally belongs. Communism for the Bruderhof is not an economic or a political doctrine but one aspect of a universalizing spiritual force. The community does not tell others to be communists because they believe in its economic or even social superiority, but because being communist is part of the 'good news' they wish to spread as Christians. It is an integral element of a spiritual totality. They do not want people to be communists for the sake of communism; they want them to be as Jesus, for which end communism is an essential practice.

We would say, then, that the Bruderhof have found a way to offset the capitalist market by inserting a spiritual moment into their worldly practice. Markets, the economists tell us, are powerful signalling systems, generating the prices that serve to tie together all economic agents. But this assumes that all agents are equivalently tuned to prices and monetary values and that they all obey the same logic and reason – or in terms of our discussion, that they are not Bruderhof. For when the market into which all economic actors are inserted issues the signal 'maximize profit and market share!' these economic actors do not hear the command, as they are marching to a different drum, and their practical faculties no longer resonate to the force field of capital. They simply do not 'value' their business that much. I have been told by Bruderhof that if it ever came down to a choice – if, for example, their political activity required that they all go to jail, or if the pursuit of their enterprise became too contradictory for whatever reason – then they would give up the business gladly. I am sure this is true. For Bruderhof, the meaning of productivity, and the labour arrangements necessary for this to be maximized, are only dimly lit points on the screen of a world-view where faith shines more brightly. The Bruderhof are an *intentional* community, and intentions, properly understood, can be material forces.

It must be that an important reason cooperatives, organic farms, and so on succumb to capital's force field is the lack of an offsetting belief-system that enables them to renounce profitability. But this needs to be taken to another plane, if only to avoid the conclusion that our cooperatives need to convert to radical Christianity in order to enter the promised land of ecosocialism. Such is clearly not the case: first, because an ecosocialist society must be fully democratic, and not the province of any religious interpretation; and more specifically, because the Bruderhof are not actually ecological in their orientation. They neither espouse particularly ecological concerns, nor is their practice compatible with ecocentrism, especially in the sphere of gender, where a highly patriarchal structure clashes with the values of ecological transformation.[4] Although the spiritual dimension of things is to play a very fundamental role in the process, ecosocialism cannot be religious, not the least because religion is a kind of binding of spirit that tends to foreclose the opening to ecological transformation.

But that is not the main point here, which is that the Bruderhof go further than the ordinary cooperative in resisting the force field of the capitalist market bcause they are an 'intentional' community. Therefore the generation of some kind of collective 'intention' that can withstand the power of capital's force field will be necessary for creating an ecosocialist society, and it must be the 'moral equivalent' of the Bruderhof's all-encompassing belief. When the Bruderhof resisted the blandishments of the market, they were saying that the commodities they made meant something radically different from what bourgeois society would impose. Instead of the set of signals generated by the market, Bruderhof respond to a whole set of qualitative relations inserted into the meaning of the commodity. Further, these meanings were part of a reconfiguration of their *needs*. This is another way of stating what the *use-value* of the commodity became to them, for use-value is a universe of meanings pertaining to the satisfaction of needs and the wants that manifest needs. This applies not just to the commodities the Bruderhof make, but also to the productive relations in which they engage in order to make them – inasmuch as costs of production are themselves prices of commodities: the machines, the energy to run the machines, the inputs of materials, and, most important, the labour expended in making their 'goods'. For the Bruderhof, the entirety of their production is subsumed into a schema of use-value directed toward providing the means of going forth as Christ. That, in a word, is their 'intention'.

Intentions are deployments of values, about which a brief amplification would be in order. Use-values stand at the juncture of a more original form of value and the kinds of value inherent in an economy. This original, or *intrinsic* value, may be thought of as the primary appropriation of the world for each person, in two senses: it is the way we first come to appreciate things and relationships in childhood; and it is, throughout life, the value given to reality irrespective of what we do to reality. It is the sense of the world conveyed in words like 'wonder', 'awe' or simply the quiet appreciation of everyday reality without regard for what can be made out of it –

including, of course, the making of money. Intrinsic values apply to the spiritual side of things, and also to what is playful, and are manifestations of an attitude we might call an 'active receptivity' towards nature.

Use-values represent the form of value relevant to the application of labour to nature, or production, whether this be done for pure utility or as an exchangeable commodity. Use-values signify a more 'transformatively active' relation to nature, the kind of transformation being different in the case of utility and exchange. Clearly, use-value is necessary for human life; and one might venture to say that a realized, ecologically integral life can be carried out through a rich interplay of use-value-as-utility with intrinsic value, in other words, through a combined receptive and transformative relation to nature.

Commodity production expands human capability but, by introducing the germ of exchange, also becomes that serpent in the edenic arrangement noted above.[5] With this shift, nature shifts from being 'for-itself' (which implies being for us insofar as we are part of nature) to a state of objectification within the framework of an economy. The matter does not stop here, but depends upon the way that the economy and the society within which it is embedded deploys the different kinds of value. Since use-value now implies the presence of an exchange-value, it will be in a relationship with that exchange-value. Exchange-value, like use-value, entails a mental registration. Although it does not exist as such in nature, it exists in the mind of a natural creature, where, like any idea, it can have various valencies and intensities. Thus some people are very attached to exchange-value, so that one could say that they 'value exchange-value'. Indeed, exchange-value can have use-value – for what else is money but the usefulness of exchange? Use-values also stand between intrinsic values and exchange-value, and express varying degrees of estrangement from nature. Certain use-values are in a position of differentiation, where they are close to, and seek to restore, intrinsic values, while others are alien, or as we say, split from intrinsic value, as in the use-value of money.

Ecological politics can be translated into a framework of values. The Bruderhof care very little for exchange-value, opting instead for a radically Christian intrinsic value. The economy has its laws; but whether those laws are obeyed depends on the subjective balance within individuals, which in turn depends upon their social relations. This can be sketched as a kind of coefficient between the two kinds of economic value. If we call use-value uv, and exchange-value xv, then the coefficient, uv/xv, expresses in a rough sort of way the balance of forces disposing toward acceptance and rejection of the capitalist force field. I say 'rough' not because these elements are indeterminate, but because they are qualitative and profoundly political. They exist not as something we can measure and put on a graph, but as collective practices and sets of meanings, which have been struggled over and command in varying degrees the loyalties of people. When we say more, or less, with respect to use – and exchange – values, we mean it in the sense of 'more fully realized'. From this angle, capitalism comprises that society that sees to it that xv>>uv, so that people internalize the signals of the market and obey them as gospel; and furthermore, that the use-values of commodities are configured to the needs of exchange- and surplus-value, and not to those of nature's intrinsic value, nor to that of a fulfilled human nature, whence we get sports utility vehicles, caffeinated soft drinks, Roundup Ready soy beans, Huey helicopters, submission to globalization – and coordinatively, the loss of contact with nature and its reduction to mere matter and energy.

The 'usefulness' of this kind of formulation derives from its potential to pry off the heavy stone laid over the possibilities of transforming capital, thereby opening the field to a wider and more differentiated range of action. Under normal capitalist conditions, exchange-value prevails and use-values are subordinated and degraded, both as they stand and as they are constantly multiplied to subserve endless, wasteful and destructive commodities. Only consider, for example, the indifference with which people throw things out once they are 'used': the spectre of Styrofoam cups (even at gatherings of ecologically active groups); the shelves of Toys 'R Us groaning with plastic items awaiting their batteries and the swift transfer to the dump. Like the passage from the straight razor endlessly sharpened to the bag full of throwaway razors, life itself has become disposable. My grandfather repaired watches, one of hundreds, perhaps thousands, of his kind in New York City. Now his successors are as rare as snow leopards, and they work on items of conspicuous consumption while I wonder whether to throw away the Casio and buy another because the strap has broken. What is cost effective? This has become the 'to be or not to be' question of capitalism, and in the search for surplus value it drives sensuously creative labour out of the market and replaces hand-craft with automated technical prowess.

In a liberated and ecologically sane world, use-values would take on a character independent of exchange-value, not to rule but to serve the needs of human nature and nature. They would, in other words, be shifted in the direction of intrinsic value. There is no necessary reason why this could not happen – although it cannot happen without a social transformation that expands democracy, allows the great range of human powers to be expressed and consolidated, and incorporates the great, countervailing intentions necessary to nullify capital's force field. Were there enough ecological militants about, organized according to coherent praxes that were not mere voluntarisms, but linked across a great international theatre of action, well then, the capitalist order could be surpassed. It would not stand one day if enough of the people said no! in thunder to it. Of course there is a big hedge here: if *enough* people decide, including soldiers and police, who are people, too.

Ecosocialism now reveals itself as a struggle for use-value – and through a realized use-value, for intrinsic value. This means it is a struggle for the qualitative side of things: not just the hours worked and the pay per hour and benefits, but the control over work and its product, and of what is beyond mere necessity – a control that eventuates in the creation and integration of new ecosystems, and also incorporates subjectivity, beauty, pleasure and the spiritual. These demands were part of the labour tradition, as workers asked for not just bread but roses, too. We would take it to the limit of its implications: the ecosocialist demand is not just for the material things – bread – on one side, and the aesthetic things – roses – on the other. It regards both bread and roses from the same perspective of enhanced and realized use-values – or better yet, as post-economic intrinsic values: bread and the making of bread to become aspects of a singular ecosystemic process into which a universe of meaning is condensed – for what has more resonance than the 'staff of life'? And roses are not external pretty things; they, too, have to be grown by labour. They, too, have a universe of meaning, closed to the eye dulled by exchange, a universe of terror and beauty to the eye opened:

> Oh Rose thou art sick.
> The invisible worm,
> That flies in the night
> In the howling storm:
> Has found out thy bed

Of crimson joy:
And his dark secret love
Does thy life destroy.[6]

Socialism

If we wish to restore the intrinsic value of nature in this sad world, we have to break down capital and the power of its exchange-value, thereby freeing use-values and opening up the differentiation with intrinsic value. But the consistent demand for the liberation of use-value from the clutches of exchange leads inexorably to that one use-value into which is condensed the core of capital: labour power. This is the sticking point, and it makes no sense at all to evade it.

Ecosocialism is more than socialism as traditionally known, but it is definitely socialism as well. Capital is the efficient cause of the crisis afflicting ecologies, but the *sine qua non* of capital, the one feature that defines its dynamic above all others, is the commodification of labour power and its reduction to abstract social labour for sale on the market. If one prefers another line of explanation for the ecological crisis, so be it, and this consideration does not hold. But if capital is truly the enemy of nature, then we do not overcome it without the liberation of labour. This demand, which is the core of socialism, eco- or otherwise, comes down to the following: undoing the separation of the producers from the means of production. And this means a basic change in property relations so that the earth, viewed as the source of all use-values and all ecosystems, is appropriated by the 'associated producers'. Otherwise there is no overcoming of separation. With the overcoming of separation, the use-value of labour ceases to be subordinated to exchange-value: labour would be freed from the chains of capital and human power would become freed from false addictive needs and able to resume its potentials.

There is much more to ecosocialism than this, but we need to dwell on the fundamental theme, as its implications are significantly different from the standard complex of green politics. Greens in the USA, for example, have 'ten key values', each meritorious. Yet none raises this demand, except derivatively, and in practical fact almost all Greens would reject it in favour of a populist position.[7] We have already pointed out that this leaves capital in the driver's seat, with all that implies. Now the goal of socialism itself needs to be confronted, and first of all, the taboo that has descended upon its name, at least in the USA.

I think I should be a rich man if given a dollar for every time someone has helpfully pointed out that it's not good form to use the word socialism in political discourse, unless, of course, one wants to rouse the audience against an enemy. People, I have been told on countless occasions, turn off at the sound of that word, with its triple association of economic failure, political repression and environmental blight. Ecosocialism, it is said, will never get to first base so long as it remains associated with the disgraced socialist tradition.

It is important to deal with these objections head-on, and neither finesse them by trying to think of another word for the same thing,[8] nor dismiss them by pointing to the anti-communist blight on the political intelligence. For the fact is that the nations who called themselves 'socialist' in the past century did display all three of those defects, and the fact also remains that as a result of the epochal collapse of the Soviet system, along with the tremendous setbacks in other societies that either called themselves socialist or had the name given to them, the morale of the socialist cause has taken one blow after another, and has pretty well declined to vanishing point over the past decade.

There are a number of questions to be tackled here, chiefly whether the societies in question were actually socialist, why their failings took place, and whether a fully realized socialist society would fall into the same abyss.

As for the first of these, one must unequivocally say that 'actually existing socialism' never passed over the threshold of restoring to the producers control over the means of production. In other words it did not live up to the stirring words of the *Communist Manifesto*, that the goal is for society to become 'an association in which the free development of each is the condition for the free development of all'.[9] It is essential that we not confuse the conventional definition of socialism, that it consists of *public ownership* of the means of production, with the true definition, that it consists of a *free association of producers*. The latter implies the former, no doubt, but the converse is definitely not necessarily so. A free association implies the fullest extension of democracy, with a public sphere and public ownership that is genuinely collective and in which each person makes a difference. But the word 'public' is tricky, and can signify another kind of alienation, namely, that of the state, or the Party, or the Leader, or whoever gets substituted for the producers and owns and/or controls the means of production in their stead. It is this latter turn of events that became the fate of socialisms past.

The notion of a free association of producers is indisputably the keystone of Marx's conception of socialism. It can be demonstrated as much as one likes from a study of Marx's life and work – just as it can be demonstrated to have not been the case for the 'actually existing socialisms', chiefly the USSR and its satellites in Eastern Europe, or China, or Vietnam, North Korea, and, with varying degrees of exactitude, for the socialisms of Latin America, Cuba and Nicaragua.[10] These latter all relied on some kind of alienating substitute 'public', generally speaking the Party–State, as the active force directing the revolution. There is as little doubt about the two sides of this proposition – of what Marx actually intended, and of what actually happened in socialism – as about the phases of the moon, and yet the error of identifying these failed experiments with Marx's concept of socialism still persists.

We need to ask why they all seemed to fail this way and whether this general failing was not in itself an indictment of the core socialist notion; and, consequently, whether there is any chance of building a socialism along the lines of a free association of producers, and with ecological rationality. Several characteristics stand out among those societies that made – and failed to realize – socialist revolutions. First of all, they were all in peripheral and dependent status among the capitalist powers. This meant that they started with two strikes against them: they were economically weak to begin with and unable to meet even the basic needs of their people; and they had to face the hostility of the stronger adversary from the moment of the inception of revolutionary power. To these may be added the third strike that put these ventures out so far as the realization of socialism is concerned: they all, each and every one, lacked democratic traditions and the institutions of civil society that fostered such traditions.

In the gestation of a revolution, there is first the pre-revolutionary period, with a build-up of tension, a delegitimation of the established authority, and the growth of a revolutionizing movement. Next comes the revolutionary moment as such, aiming at seizure of state power, with greater or lesser degrees of violence and the introduction of contradictions that have to be handled further on. Finally, the transformation of society begins; this is the revolution proper, an inevitably extended period of struggle. On day one after the moment of triumph, all that has been achieved is a new state apparatus: no small accomplishment given the importance of the state as an instrument of coercion and direction, yet with no necessary effect on society itself. To be more exact, any effect depends upon the character of the revolutionary movement, a fact of great importance for us. To the extent that the movement is conspiratorial, or cut off from the development of society, its triumph will find society an inert mass requiring leadership from above; to the extent that broad strata of the population participate in the revolutionary process, so that it becomes a kind of gigantic school, so will the triumph become the acceleration of an organic (in the terms employed here, ecosystemically integral) development in which the democratic potentials of socialism can be released.

The actually existing socialisms came to exist by virtue of the corruption and weakness of their *ancien régimes*, often accelerated by war – or, as in the case of the Soviet satellites, because of the proximity of these regimes to a powerful centre of influence. Thus the first two stages of the revolution were, however bloody and contested, open for the winning. But in all cases, the third and essential stage of social transformation was foreclosed by an ensemble of forces that, however distinct from country to country, shared a common inaptitude for the democratizing motion of socialism.

In Russia, where there was virtually no democratic heritage, the Tsarist police forced anti-democratic, conspiratorial patterns on the Bolsheviks, who took power – despite their name, which means 'majority' – as a distinct minority. The revolution fell into their lap thanks to the Great War, which also, however, further crippled society. Then, in a counter-revolution of immense savagery, greatly abetted by Western intervention and invasion, the extraordinary needs of 'war communism', carried on in a situation of maximum chaos, put the seal of authoritarianism on the process. Lenin and Trotsky resorted to terror as an instrument and blocked the free development of labour, shutting down the workers' councils, or 'Soviets', and crippling the unions. At the same time, they espoused the emulation of capitalist efficiency and productivism as a means of survival. Is it any wonder, then, that socialism failed to take hold – or that the stage was set for Stalin's barbarism?[11]

In China, where again there was effectively zero democratic heritage, a much more extended period of internal development of the movement took place prior to the triumph. However, this was inordinately marked by warfare. Massacres of the Communist Party in 1927 set the stage for more than twenty years of guerrilla war, the militarization deepening with the Japanese invasion and the Long March. Bitter memories of humiliation and penetration by imperialism in this most ancient – and once pre-eminent – society created a burning desire to catch up with the capitalists. The state that emerged from this cauldron bore much more resemblence to the centralized bureaucracy that had ruled China for two millennia than it did to a socialist democracy. Terrible struggles with Russia and the USA, along with the imperial status granted to Mao Zedong, only hardened its authoritarian tendencies. Given the impulsive grandiosity of the latter, the result became the horrors of the Great Leap Forward, with its associated famine, and the Cultural Revolution. Despite certain remarkable and brilliant advances, especially in the countryside, is it any wonder, again, that socialism failed to take hold – or that the stage was set for Deng Xiaoping's capitalist road?[12]

Similar considerations held for Vietnam, hardened by generations of colonialism, US invasion and post-war punitiveness by the superpower. In Cuba, yoked with centuries of dependency, the limiting factors took the shape of being scissored between superpowers; for Nicaragua, it was an even greater underdevelopment, and an incomplete revolution with a sudden dénouement that left great chunks of the bourgeoisie intact, while exposing the revolution to the vengeance of Big Brother to the North; for the Eastern Europeans, it was revolution imposed from above and the constant shadow of Stalinist Russia. In case after case, the elementary conditions for socialist development in the period after revolutionary victory were either not present or crushed.

This should not be interpreted as a blanket rejection of the accomplishments of these regimes, for socialism is not a switch one turns on and off, and part-way toward a socialist ethos is still some way forward. The people of the former USSR, curently facing social disintegration on a scale unparalleled for a nation not invaded in war, have just cause to look back with pride on the cultural achievements, full employment and solidarity of the Soviet era, as well as their heroics against Nazism. First-hand experience with Cuba and Nicaragua has convinced me, as it has many others, that what was being germinated there remains of inestimable value to the future of humanity, if value be measured in terms of dignity and generosity instead of money.[13]

The Nicaraguan revolution had to be slaughtered, according to Oxfam, because it posed 'the threat of a good example' to other nations in the USA's sphere of influence. As for Cuba, all of its empty shelves do not nullify the fact that it offers resources of education and health care that would make most of the people of the South believe they were in heaven were they to wake up there one day. Nor should it be forgotten that Cuba is the first, and still the only, country to have adopted organic agriculture on a national scale – no doubt out of harsh necessity thanks to the US blockade and Soviet collapse, but nonetheless feasible because there was no agribusiness there to stay in the way of rational planning.[14]

Still, part-way toward socialism is not far enough; not only were these models not exportable, but they were primed to self-destruct. They resembled less a breakthrough than a rubber band stretched to the point of recoil. The vectors pulling actually existing socialism back included the social and cultural forces sedimented into the psyche by generations of patriarchy and autocracy. However, these would never have had effect without the failure of the productive system to transcend the *ancien régime*, and, specifically, to overcome capitalism. The actually existing socialisms did not, of course, reproduce the capitalist structures of the West. Instead, they rearranged capital to introduce other engines of accumulation, notably using the state and political means rather than economic incentives as in traditional capitalism. This ended up by proving that old-fashioned markets work better than centralized state control for purposes of accumulation. One may be forgiven for not hailing this as the greatest of discoveries. The 'bottom line' – if we may borrow appropriately here from capital's lexicon – remained accumulation; and the presupposition of accumulation remained, as ever, the hierarchical division of labour and the extraction of surplus value through exploitation. There can be no mystery as to why this fatal contradiction forced the state under actually existing socialism to be specially coercive and non-democratic, or why a new type of bureaucratic ruling class arose by virtue of control over the state apparatus – or why the workers secretly, and eventually openly, longed for good old-fashioned liberal capitalism, whose wage mechanism creates more opportunities, whose state can afford to provide certain limited democratic rights, and where the more fluid productive system churns out a much greater amount of higher quality goods. After all, if one is going to live under capitalism, one might as well do it properly.[15]

The basic contradictions of the state capitalism that was called actually existing socialism had complex ecological effects, although the end result was worse than that under market capitalism. To be more exact, its effects were intensively worse, and extensively less so, owing to poorer overall productivity. These were, it should be repeated, end results; on the way to that end, the actually existing socialisms did grapple with the ecological question in an interesting way. It is scarcely appreciated, for example, that in the first decade of the Soviet system, a great deal of attention was paid to conservation, and an effort was made to integrate production with natural laws and limits. This impulse was grounded in a pre-revolutionary environmental movement, and a tradition of radical innovation that accompanied the early years of Bolshevism and included a great deal of concern about ecology. It was nourished by radical innovators such as Aleksandr Bogdanov, whose *Proletkul't* movement attempted to open Russian culture to democratic impulses; and supported to a degree by none other than Lenin, who, as Arran Gare writes, 'interpreted Marxism in such a way as to acknowledge the limitations of the environment, [and] of the existence of dynamics within nature with which humanity must accord.'[16]

But there were countervailing forces at work in all the major figures of Bolshevism, and in the doctrine itself. Despite his ecological insights, Lenin harshly attacked Bogdanov in his 1908 *Materialism and Empirio-Criticism* for an alleged 'idealism'. To this, Lenin opposed a sharply dualistic materialism, rather similar to the Cartesian separation of matter and consciousness, and perfectly tooled, like Cartesianism, to the active working over of dead, dull matter by the human hand.[17] A function of this was to overcome the national 'backwardness' and sloth, that dreamy, vodka-soaked, impractical immersion in Mother Russia that had haunted its intelligentsia,[18] and in so doing, to move full speed ahead into industrialization and modernity. From this angle, Russia's modern history is dominated by a messianic ambition and ambivalence towards the West. Bolshevism incorporated features of both. A ferocious drive to catch up with the West shaped its world-view from the start, and was accelerated by the severe crisis of the early years. The tendency was especially pronounced in Lenin's brilliant associate, Leon Trotsky, architect and commander of the Red Army during the counter-revolution, and a cosmopolite and modernizer *par excellence*. Although he was a resolute atheist, Trotsky's worship of technology was of idolatrous proportions. This was expressed in a rhapsodic paean to Communist Man after the Soviet triumph, in which Trotsky allowed himself to fantasize about a future of rearranged rivers and mountains, where the human body itself would be reshaped into that of a Superman who conquers death, the great entropic leveller. In the Soviet Utopia, a heroic Bolshevism redeems fallen humanity.[19]

The gruesome outcome is well known, but bears brief reflection. After Stalin's accession to power in 1927, persistent economic stagnation triggered a second revolution, now from above. Whatever democratic impulses had endured through the early period of the Bolshevik regime were jettisoned, and the entire might of Soviet society was concentrated on building the forces of production for all-out accumulation. The result was utter top-down control, maximum subordination of human beings to the production process, the surplus being taken by the state, willingness to let millions die for the larger purpose, the deification of the ruler and the party–state to mobilize messianic forms of legitimacy, profound cynicism and mendacity, and, last but certainly not least, a reign of terror to eliminate the remnants of opposition. In this regime, Trotsky's musings were given an official imprimatur even as he himself was driven out and eventually murdered. 'Within a few years all the maps of the USSR will have to be revised', wrote one Stalinist planner, while another opined that the conservation of nature for its own sake 'reeks of ancient cults of nature's deification', and a third proclaimed the goal of 'a profound rearrangement of the entire living world ... All living nature will live, thrive and die at none other than the will of man and according to his plans.' Still another called for eliminating all references to 'plant communities' in biology books. In other words, as Stalinism developed, the very notion of ecology came under attack, in addition to ecologies.[20] This was the framework that spawned Lysenko's official doctrine that acquired characteristics can be inherited, and that did in fact set about to rearrange the Russian map, diverting rivers, creating cities overnight, building colossal hydroelectric plants, and so transforming the land that what took three hundred years under capitalism was accomplished in one generation.

Were Stalin's monstrosity still with us, it would win the gold medal for enmity to nature – and indeed there was an element of outright hostility to nature in Stalinism beyond what obtains under market capitalism, even after Stalin passed and the regime ceased using terror. That Stalinism did not survive owes something, moreover, to its radically anti-ecological character. Choked with pollution, beset with declining agricultural yields and haunted by nightmares like the virtual disappearance of the Aral Sea, the Soviet system lacked internal correctives and was hurled down into an chasm of ecocatastrophe. In good measure, this lack of adaptability lay in a rigid, self-perpetuating bureaucratic regime fixedly programmed on the goal of accumulation. As inefficiencies proliferated and the internal market withered for lack of consumable goods, accumulation became increasingly difficult. A chief response to this crisis was a heightened exploitation of nature. Ecological concerns kept being shelved, a vicious cycle set in, and, abetted by US policy, collapse was only a matter of time.

Our Marx

How does one assess this in relation to the ecological potentials of socialism? To some, the answer is straightforward: because the USSR was fundamentally non-socialist, there can be no relation. The Soviets, it is said, broke with socialism from the moment they put the clamps on labour and started the emulation of capital. Given the way of the world, the rest was foreordained: gigantism, bureaucratic state capitalism, the stifling of democracy – all contributed to a radically anti-ecological regime that would have likely executed Marx had he shown up in Moscow in 1935. From this angle, the extreme enmity toward nature that marked Stalinism is an example of how a noble ideal, once perverted, can turn into its opposite, as Satan, once the favoured son of God, became God's greatest enemy.

But this is too simple: it smacks of consolation, not a facing of reality. For the truth is that almost the entire socialist tradition, including those branches of it unburdened by Stalinism, has largely been unable to appropriate an ecological attitude. There have been a few important individual exceptions, such as Rosa Luxemburg and William Morris, and a strong recent effort to correct things, but these hopeful signs do not relieve us of the necessity of accounting for what has been on the whole a significant lapse. Despite all the recognition of the fact that there is a global crisis of nature for which capital is primarily responsible, the fact remains that minding nature still tends to strike the typical socialist as an afterthought, both in the sense that nature does not come immediately to the socialist mind, and that the caring for nature is something added on to existing socialist doctrine rather than integral to it. An integral appreciation of nature's intrinsic value is not at the existential heart of socialism, nor does nature command a passion comparable to that reserved for the emancipation of labour. This is accompanied by a somewhat naive faith in the ecological capacities of a working class defined by generations of capitalist production. To the characteristically socialist way of thinking, labour, once freed from the prison-house of capital, will unproblematically proceed to rearrange production in an ecologically sane way.

Here is an example from *Against the Market*, by David McNally, an otherwise estimable work that argues for a full socialism grounded in the emancipation of labour. After showing convincingly how the 'socialist economy does possess an inbuilt drive to increase the efficiency of production: the impetus to maximize free, disposable time', McNally continues with the observation that just as capital increases people's needs but 'restricts their opportunities to realize them', so will socialism liberate 'this *positive side of capital's self-expansion* from the alienation and exploitation associated with it'. He elaborates: 'Three things follow from this. First, the reduction of necessary social labour *cannot be at the expense of the range of human satisfactions*. On the contrary, the productivity gains brought about by the development of the forces of production would in all probability be distributed in two ways … by *increasing the social output to raise consumption levels* … and, after that, by reducing necessary social labour.' The second and third principles are that this reduction in social labour 'could not be at the expense of the conditions of work itself' or of 'the natural and social environment outside the workplace'.[21]

This finesses a serious contradiction between raising consumption levels and protecting 'the natural … environment outside the workplace'. Are workers – not just in the industrial West, but also in China, India, Indonesia, and so on, as required by the internationalist ethos of socialism – to have more cars, even ecologically better cars, without further deterioration of ecologies? Questions like this scarcely arise in socialist discourse, which, however much it may surpass capital morally and economically, has significant trouble going beyond capital's fatal addiction to growth.

McNally claims there is a *positive side of capital's self-expansion* that can be liberated. But this is ecologically quite dubious. One expects gases to self-expand. But humans, being organisms in ecosystems, can only *self*-expand to the detriment of the ecosystem, and/or as a sign of its degeneration, the way algal blooms signify that a pond is disintegrating ecosystemically. As alienation and exploitation are overcome, therefore, we would expect human life not to expand, but rather to develop ever more subtle, inter-related, mutually recognizing, beautiful and spiritually fulfilled ways of being. We should seek not to become larger within socialism, but more *realized*. Bach did not quantitatively expand music, making it louder and more insistent like degenerate forms of rock music that mirror capitalist relations; he rather saw more deeply into its possibilities and realized them. So would it be expected for an ecological society, where the ideal of growth as such simply needs to be scrapped. *Sufficiency* makes more sense, building a world where nobody is hungry or cold or lacks health care or succour in old age. This can be done at a fraction of the current world output, and would create the ground for ecological realization.

Sufficiency is a better term than the ecological buzzword, sustainability, as the latter leaves ambiguous the question of whether what is to be sustained is the existing system or not. But in either case, humanity needs to greatly reduce its load on planetary ecosystems. The customary response of environmentalism is to think of restraining consumption. But such a focus is repressive, requiring some combination of market forces, as by making petroleum more expensive to discourage purchase of gas-guzzlers and eventually cars themselves; along with coercion, as by rationing or exacting legal sanctions like prison. Measures of this sort may be necessary in the short term, but they are never desirable, and get us no closer to an ecological socialism, which builds on the liberation of labour sought by 'first-epoch' socialism and seeks the restoration of intrinsic value by liberated producers.

Actual socialism was ill-formed by history for this task. Forged at the moment of industrialization, its transformative impulse tended to remain within the terms of the industrialized domination of nature. Thus it continued to manifest the technological optimism of the industrial world-view, and its associated logic of productivism – all of which fed into the mania for growth. The belief in unlimited technical progress has been beaten back in certain quarters by a host of disasters, from nuclear waste to resistant bacteria, but these setbacks barely touch the core of socialist optimism, that its historical mission is to perfect the industrial system and not overcome it. The productivist logic is grounded in a view of nature that regards the natural world as an 'environment', and from the standpoint of its utility as a force of production. It is at that point that socialism all too often shares with capitalism a reduction of nature to resources – and, co-ordinatively, a sluggishness in recognizing ourselves in nature and nature in ourselves. When McNally says that socialism 'cannot be at the expense of the range of human satisfaction', then he is failing to recognize that these satisfactions can be problematic with respect to nature when they have been historically shaped by the domination of nature; and more, that the industrial tools and techniques that pass into the hands of the workers after the revolution are also a sediment of that history. Therefore, unless the socialist revolution also undoes the domination of nature, which is to say, becomes ecosocialist, its satisfactions – and the needs and use-values in which they are grounded – are going to tend to reproduce the domination of nature. Simply overcoming the power of exchange-value can be no more than a necessary condition for this. From another angle, there can be no ecosocialist environmentalism as such, since to the ecological world-view the notion of nature as an environment outside us will wither away.

Recognition of ourselves in nature and nature in ourselves, in other words subjective as well as objective participation in ecosystems, is the essential condition for overcoming the domination of nature, and its pathologies of instrumental production and addictive consumption. For an example, we may turn to Rosa Luxemburg, mentioned above as one of the few socialists who showed what might be called an authentically 'ecocentric way of being'. I mean this existentially, for Luxemburg was not ecologically oriented in her views of what socialism ought to be (unlike William Morris, whose thought was consciously ecocentric, albeit without using that term).[22] But what she did evince – and this is connected with her gender – was a capacity to express a *fellow-feeling* for non-human creatures that is quite exceptional in the Marxist tradition. Witnessing the beating of a buffalo from her prison where she was kept while protesting the war, Luxemburg wrote the following in a letter:

> the one that was bleeding, all the while looked ahead with an expression on its black face and its soft black eyes like that of a weeping child who has been severely punished and who does not know why, what for, who does not know how to escape the torment and the brutality ... I stood facing the animal and it looked at me: tears were running from my eyes – they were *his* tears. One cannot quiver any more painfully over one's dearest brother's sorrow than I quivered in my impotence over this silent anguish ... Oh! My poor buffalo! My poor beloved brother! We both stand here so powerless and spiritless and are united only in pain, in powerlessness and in longing.[23]

Such an ethos in itself does not ecosocialism make – that would require what Luxemburg did not do, namely, develop a consciously ecological line in her socialist practice. Nor does it imply a fundamentalist position on animal rights, which forgets that all creatures, however they may be recognized, are still differentiated and that we make use of other creatures within our human nature. Nor, it is scarcely necessary to add, does this imply a deep ecological affirmation of 'wilderness' that splits the wild away from the human and would just as soon dispense with the latter; nor, to go yet further down the track of nihilism, would it consist of the kind of deep ecological attack on industrialism infamously associated with Theodore Kasczynski, the Unabomber. To overcome the limits of actually existing socialism requires, rather, a synthesis in which humanity is restored to ecosystemic differentiation with nature. To follow the example of Luxemburg, it would connect existential fellow-feeling with a sense of justice, and build from there. In other words, the option of traditional socialism for the travails of labour needs to be matched by, and dialectically interwoven with, an equivalent existential option for nature. The wounds of one must be felt with the same passion for justice as those of the other. Our very being needs to be turned towards nature, not as an afterthought nor as an instrumental necessity for production, but as a sensuously lived reality. And this needs to be grounded in specifically ecological relations of production lest it become a purely voluntaristic slogan.

As for Karl Marx himself, we find a bewildering array of opinions concerning his ecological *bona fides*. From one side there is a fairly robust tradition alleging that Marx essentially shared the enmity towards nature evinced by the Bolsheviks, or at the least set them on their profoundly anti-ecological path. In this view, which may be termed the 'Promethean' interpretation, the founder of historical materialism is tasked with enough elements of the domination of nature to justify the often-made identification with the god who gave humankind fire, and whose temerity was punished by Zeus by being chained to a rock, where he suffered the assaults of an eagle on his liver. The substance of the indictment holds Marx to have been an advocate of technological determinism, of productivism, of the ideology of progress, and of hostility to rural life and primitivism – in sum, as an unreconstructed apostle of the Enlightenment in its rankest industrial form.[24]

An opposing point of view, recently argued by Marxists such as John Bellamy Foster and Paul Burkett, energetically contests the indictment, and holds that Marx, far from being Promethean, was a main originator of the ecological world-view. Building their argument from Marx's materialist foundations, his scientific affinity with Darwin, and his conception of the 'metabolic rift' between humanity and nature, Foster and Burkett consider the original Marxian canon as the true and sufficient guide to save nature from capitalism.[25]

To enter the substance of this debate would distract us from the thread of the present argument. But we may say the following: that it is foolish to reduce the subtlety of so profoundly dialectical a thinker to any label or singular interpretation. A close reading will show Marx to be no Promethean.[26] But he was no god of any kind, either, only the best interpreter humanity has ever had of its own historical emerging; and this great virtue sprang from the integration of a passion for justice with intellectual power and dialectical gift. However superior it might be, Marx's thought, being a human product, remains time-bound and incomplete. For this reason it becomes most realized when most free, or to use his own expression, 'ruthlessly critical of everything existing'.[27] This would include, needless to say, being critical of itself. Therefore Marxism today can have no greater goal than the criticism of Marx in the light of that history to which he had not been exposed, namely, of the ecological crisis.

Here it needs to be observed that, however Marx may not have been Promethean, there remains in his work a foreshortening of the intrinsic value of nature. Yes, humanity is part of nature for Marx. But it is the active part, the part that makes things happen, while nature becomes that which is acted upon. Except for a few entrancing anticipations, chiefly in the *Manuscripts* of 1844, nature to Marx appears directly as use-value, and not as what use-value leaves behind, namely, recognition of nature in and for itself.[28]

In Marx, nature is, so to speak, subjected to labour from the start. This side of things may be inferred from his conception of labour, which involves an entirely *active* relationship to what has become a kind of natural substratum.

Now there are two ways of not being active. There is *passivity*, with its implication of inertia; and it is from this condition that Marx sought to free the alienated realities of labour under the domination of capital. But there is also *receptivity*, which is not passive and inert at all, but another kind of activity; and it is this side of things that Marx – and, by and large, the socialist tradition – failed to see. When Rosa Luxemburg felt for the buffalo she was being receptive to its anguish. There was recognition there, which meant a taking in of the buffalo's being, and its re-awakening inside her. Is this the female position? Well, yes, so long as we keep in mind that it is the constructed and relegated female position, at once the source of women's strength and the measure of their downfall in male-dominated society.

Full receptivity is of both identity and difference. The world is taken in, but never fused with the self. This is a knack of language, which represents the given, but as imaginative signifier that never stays still. To recapture the receptive moment in labour, therefore, requires an active opening of being. This does not simply absorb the world and register it subjectively. It opens being to the world as prelude to the transformation of the world; and it links the making of poems and songs to the making of solar ovens. It is a *ful-filling*, which is essential both to the freeing of labour and to the ecological trans-forming of labour, so that labour may transform reality in an ecologically integral way. The opening of the self to the world engages the sensuous imagination and our full being. Absent the receptive moment in labour, the self is closed, impacted inside itself, and isolated from others and from nature.

We return to the anti-ecological moment enshrined by capital: the way of the ego. This is the secret to the riddle of growth and the mania of consumption. These twin compulsions of the reigning order are expressions of an impeded motion between inner and outer world. Occluded and incapable of a full life, the human being compulsively turns to grinding out commodities without end, and, just as wantonly, consuming them. The insertion of exchange-value is that invisible barrier caging in the capitalist ego, a film of abstraction reinforced with the titanic power of the capitalist state and cultural apparatus.

That is why these must be taken down, and why labour must be really, truly freed. But it becomes free in order to transform production eco-logically. The recovery of intrinsic value proceeds through a struggle for use-value, a struggle in which the goal is embedded in the path.

Ecological Production

Nature does not produce anything. Rather, it evolves new forms that interact with each other in ensembles we call ecosystems, which become the loci of further evolution. As it turned out on earth, this led to a creature who introduced production into nature, and then economies, class economies and capitalism, which, spreading cancerously, generates our ecological crisis. Production is therefore nature's formativity as expressed through human nature.

What distinguishes production from natural evolution lies in the dimension of consciousness as shaped by language and social organization. Human beings work with a mental image of nature; we represent the section of nature before us – itself virtually always modified by previous labour – then act upon it to transform it according to an envisioned end. In every instance, some prearranged configuration of nature-as-transformed-by-labour is imaginatively appropriated, then rendered according to a plan. Production is therefore inherently temporalizing and incorporates the future; that is why we call it pro-duction, to make with a view ahead.

Humans do not choose whether to produce, but there are numberless ways of producing. Capital is one such organization of production that violates ecosystemic integrity through the interposition of exchange-value as an instrument of exploitation. Each such moment is a cutting of the specific interconnectedness that defines an integral ecosystem.

The hope of socialism is to overcome exploitation and bring down the regime of exchange-value. Ecosocialism develops this further through the realization of use-values and the appropriation of intrinsic value. From the angle of production, this means building ecosystemic integrity. As an integral is a whole, ecological production has as its overriding condition the creation of wholeness.[29] Ecosystems are not to be regarded in the way of commodities, as countable and isolable things. They are, rather, mutually constitutive, interacting with and transforming each other. That is why the notion of an 'environment' sits ill with an ecological world-view. There is no 'outside' in nature, where all beings inhabit and co-determine each other, and where subtle force fields interpenetrate reality and can be registered in consciousness. Similarly, producing ecosystemic integrity connects form through all dimensions, temporal as well as spatial. Past being is integral to present being regarded ecologically – as against capital's fetish of the new. And there is no being intrinsically alien to ecological production, except capital itself, the creator of alienated labour, and strangers and false boundary lines.

A considerable number of interwoven patterns are involved here, some of which are presumed to be more prominent than others in the concrete instance.

The *process* of ecological production is aligned with the product, thus, the making of a thing becomes part of the thing made. Since the end of production is satisfaction and pleasure, as in a finely made meal or garment, pleasure would obtain for the cooking of the meal or the designing and making of the garment. These processual pleasures are generally reserved for hobbies under capitalism; in a society organized around ecological production, they would compose the fabric of everyday life.

For this to happen, labour has to be freely chosen and developed, in other words, with a fully realized use-value as against its reduction to labour power. At first and for some time, this is a matter of shifting the coefficient uv/xv in the direction of the numerator in order to build anti-capitalist intentions. Since use- and exchange-value are not immediately comparable, this involves the dialectical 'negation of the negation': exchange is negated through a withdrawal from capitalist values; in this context, realization of use-value ensues, further delegitimizing capital and furthering the rupture. The 'Food Not Bombs' projects in cities such as San Francisco and New York have been examples of this, and the fact that this seemingly innocent activity has brought down severe repression upon itself is a sign of just how subversive the notion is.[30]

Mutual recognition is required for the process as well as the product, such being the condition of ecosystemic integrity. The most important implication of this is that it rules out hierarchical and exploitative relations of labour, and fosters democratization at all levels of production, and, *mutatis mutandis*, all of society.

Production stays within the entropic relations of natural evolution, in which the inputs of ambient solar radiation are able to subserve the creation of order. Because the 'closed' system within which the Second Law applies is the earth + surrounding cosmos, nature provides a certain space for creating lower entropy from the binding of solar energy – a space, however, that requires distinct limits if it is to be sustained. It is precisely the aim of ecological production to incorporate limits into functioning ecosystems, in stark contrast to capital. Therefore it goes without saying that ecological production makes use of all modes of conservation and renewable energy. An additional implication of living within the entropic law is that direct human labour would replace, as far as possible, the consumption of the low entropy of past aeons sedimented into fossil fuels, the release of which markedly increases entropy to destabilizing levels. But the 'as far as possible' is defined through the active interposition of human agency into nature. Instead of living passively and, indeed, parasitically from the negentropy stored in fossil fuels, humanity now will live more directly and receptively embedded in nature, hence more sensuously, too, with an overcoming of the ancient division of labour between head and hand and an enhancement of craft. From another angle, the fulfilling of a use-value/ecosystem is accompanied, at the level of the subject, by a quantum of satisfaction, joy and aesthetic realization. All this is summed up in the notion of 'virtue',[31] and it comprises the coming together of dialectical ensembles within a free human being.

'Limits to growth' are to be predicated on a reorientation of human need made possible by enhanced receptivity. Clearly, highly developed production need not be dependent on destabilizing inputs of energy. Singing songs is certainly productive, and creating them even more so. Even interpreting dreams is productive, because it introduces a new configuration into the human ecosystem. So the ways in which time is passed become integrally related to the form of production, and what is perceived as necessary. By regarding limits to growth in terms of altered needs, we still address the question of 'sustainability'. But we treat it non-technocratically and in connection with the basic organization of labour and the question of satisfaction, in other words, from a qualitative standpoint.

Such considerations apply to the question of technology, once it is no longer seen as a 'technical' problem, subjugated to considerations of profit and efficiency. The making and using of technology in ecological production is directed, rather, towards the making of ecosystems and participation within ecosystems. The enhancement of use-values and the corresponding restructuring of needs becomes now the social regulator of technology rather than, as under capital, the conversion of time into surplus value and money. We would expect considerable areas of technological overlapping between capitalist and ecological production. One would, for instance, use sophisticated medical imaging in each case, and this one application implies the whole edifice of informational and electronic science. But it makes a world of difference whether a technology is incorporated into medical profiteering, or used to care for the organismic aspect of a human ecosystem. Capital would have technology isolated from the manifold of social relations of which it is but an element. But ecological production includes theory as well, and has as its deepest consideration the fullest range of interconnections. Therefore to begin seeing a machine or a technique as fully participant in the life of ecosystems is to begin removing it from exchange and restoring a realized use-value. This is what is called familiarly in ecological discourse as 'appropriate technology', and indeed it is a technology enabling us to appropriate nature in human ways.

If we take the notion of human ecosystems seriously we are led fully to incorporate consciousness into them. Fullness here implies the development of the receptive mode of being. It entails a consciousness of nature as such, according to the principle that the interconnections of a human ecosystem include subjective recognition as an element – not alongside, but integrally related to physical connections.[32] An organic farm is not simply a collection of organisms; it is those organisms interrelated in a universe of meaningful recognition through the farmer. This does not make the farmer a lord over the farm, or the gardener mistress of the garden. It means that the farm, and the garden – and the whole universe to which they connect – are integral to the human self who produces through them. A relative of mine could catch fish with his bare hands. This feat required a contact with the fish that went beyond the coarsely physical, along with a kind of mutual recognition between human and animal. Such recognition could, if it were realized in production, extend to the entire universe as a fully active and alive consciousness.

The relative in question was male, and the function of recognition is as open to individual men as to women. Nevertheless, the systematic development of an ecological consciousness across our civilization depends on overcoming the barriers between humanity and nature, which, as we have seen, requires overcoming the dualism imposed by woman = nature/ man = reason; and for this, patriarchy itself needs be overcome. I am certain that at least 95 per cent of readers would identify Rosa Luxemburg's account of seeing herself in the suffering buffalo as the work of a woman, without knowing the gender of its author in advance. Men are simply not socialized to feel that way, while women are by and large socialized to limit themselves to feeling this way. That a woman such as Luxemburg would escape the constraints of intellectual suppression placed upon her gender is not an astounding finding, needless to say. But under the dominant gender system such occurrences, no matter how frequent, remain individual exceptions to a dualism that must be overcome if we are to survive.

To build ecological production, then, means restoring the ecosystemic capacity for interrelatedness and mutual recognition, most elementally, to restore nature as a source of wonder and be open to nature. The grandeur of the untrammelled world is an essential aspect of this, but not its whole. Wilderness, recall, is a constructed category with its own use-value, while actual nature, whether experienced in the Grand Canyon or in the intaking of a breath, is always directly 'at hand', even if scarcely realized. A man can visit the Grand Canyon and remain preoccupied by his stock quotes; another sees a tree, as Blake put it, as only a green thing in the way. But trees still abound, and each is a wonder, as is a blade of grass, or a paramecium.[33] To be open to nature means being receptive to ecosystemic being without the fear of annihilation that is the legacy of the male ego. The masculine construction of being interprets receptivity as the castrated condition of the female. Receptivity is read as passivity, with the symbolic threat of being swallowed up by the world-mother. Gaia is a Medusa or a Harpy to the ego. The terror induces severe death anxiety with associated mental repression, distancing, reduction of nature and counter-aggression, along with compulsive production and consumption: in this way human nature is *restricted* to tearing nature apart and aggressively rebuilding it at ever greater distances. The ensemble enables separation and is the core attitude of the domination of nature as it surfaces into productivism with a fierce energy, an attitude which has so permeated the capitalist (and state capitalist) mentality as to be read as an axiom.

The larger and practical virtue embedded here is an expansion of the immemorial role assigned to women, that of providing and caring for life. The profound rationality inherent in this role is both downgraded and split off in nature's gendered bifurcation. Overcoming this gives to production a specifically ecological form. The functions of receiving, provisioning and holding, once sequestered in a lower social level, now prevail, and in so doing, move to become the regulating principles of production. Ecological production, therefore, goes beyond the virtues of formal distributive equality to women, or their access to previously male preserves such as strenuous athletics. It also negates the lowliness of what had been sequestered as 'woman's work', and transforms this, while realizing use-values associated with it.[34]

If past being is integral to present being in ecological production, so is future being. An important political principle now emerges – one that applies to the production of use-values for the sustenance of life, and also to the production of ways beyond capital. The potential for the given to contain the lineaments of what is to be may be called *prefiguration*. It is intrinsic to ecological production, rendering the *provisioning* of ecofeminism as the *previsioning* of a Utopian moment.

The prefigurative praxes that are to overcome capital in an ecosocialist way are at once very remote and exactly at hand. They are remote insofar as the entire regime of capital stands in the way of their realization, and they are at hand insofar as a moment toward the future exists embedded in every point of the social organism where a need arises. Many instances are bound to wither – it is, after all, very difficult to imagine any ecosocialist inspiration arising from a trip to Wal-Mart beyond rage at the given order; others will propagate, but not very far, like hauling recyclable junk mail to the dump; still others will propagate, perhaps even to a transformative extent, but take a wrong turn, like that of fascism; finally, there will arise those who move in an ecosocialist way. It goes without saying that in the real world there can be no neat categorization capable of covering all possibilities. If everything has a prefigurative potential, then prefiguration will be scattered over the entire, disorderly surface of the world. This fact generates another principle of ecosocialist politics: it is, besides being prefigurative and building upon the transformative potentials of found configurations of events, also *interstitial*, in that its agency can be found almost anywhere.

This is a blessing, because it signifies that there is no privileged agent of ecosocialist transformation, but it also imposes a great responsibility. For as they now exist, instances of ecological production are both scattered and mainly entrapped like irritants in the pores of capital. The task is to free them and connect them, so that their inherent potential may be realized. We cannot rest in this until ecological production has become an ecological *mode* of production. When this happens, for which an extensive struggle must be anticipated, the power to regulate society will be in ecosocialist hands.

Notes

1. Zablocki 1971. A great deal of information is also available through Plough publications.

2. All youths are required to live away for two years following graduation from high school, either at college or in supervised settings doing good works. Following this, the

individual must decide him- or herself whether to return and re-enter the community as an adult. From what I have been told, about three-quarters decide to do so.

3. The phrase is from his 'Critique of the Gotha Program', Marx 1978e: 531. The literature on this subject is vast. See Cort 1988. For Marx himself, see Miranda 1974.

4. Bruderhof are very strongly homophobic, for example, having gone out of their way to try to close gay bars in their vicinity, and refusing to join coalitions against the death penalty in which gay rights groups participate. Within the commune, although women have a definite voice, there is also distinct inequality, for example, in dress code, where the men can wear what they please while the women must wear traditional calico. Furthermore, divorce is forbidden. Moreover, the moral authority of the community devolves from the paternal voice of the Arnold family. There are signs that the generation coming up may see things differently, and it will be interesting to follow this development. But in general, it seems to be harder for radical religions to give up patriarchal than class domination.

5. Could this be the hidden meaning of the Fall? One should not be too hasty, for an archaic pre-economic life of pure utilization is not free of aggression or ambivalence, although it does lack expansive and cancerous implications.

6. 'The Sick Rose,' from 'Songs of Experience,' in Blake 1977: 123.

7. The values are grassroots democracy, social justice, ecological wisdom, non-violence, decentralization, community-based economics and economic justice, feminism, respect for diversity, personal and global responsibility, and future-focus and sustainability. The closest relative to socialism, economic justice, goes no further than the call for protecting workers' rights and a mixture of economic forms, including 'independently owned companies' – in short, it stays within the perspective criticized in the previous chapter.

8. Well into the last century, American socialists used the term 'cooperative commonwealth'. No doubt that's a good way of putting socialism, but then, does one call what we have in mind an 'eco-cooperative commonwealth?' Whatever the short-term tactical gains of such circumlocutions, it is clear that they gain nothing overall. If the word socialism is in that much disfavour, then the fact had better be confronted and not evaded.

9. Marx 1978c: 491.

10. For Marx, see Draper 1977, et seq.; for a magisterial account of the failings of the Soviet bloc, see Mészáros 1996; for a general survey of the whole socialist tradition in this light, see Bronner 1990.

11. Figes 1997.

12. Hinton 1967; Meisner 1996.

13. I tried to put some of this in writing. See Kovel 1988.

14. Rosset and Benjamin 1994.

15. Of course, what they got after socialism's breakdown was a special version of capitalism, overseen by the IMF and the US Treasury, where the rapid sell-off of state assets was used to finance accumulation in its most ruthless and uncontrolled form. Russia's domestic output has fallen by about half since the collapse of the USSR, and while this has limited the effects of pollution, there has been virtually no effort to improve the dismal record of the Soviet years with respect to the environment. In many parts of the economy, even exchange-value has broken down, and payments in barter – or no payments at all – have been the case. In May 2000, Russian President Vladimir

Putin, in his effort to reinstate the iron hand while pleasing transnational capital, dissolved Russia's State Committee on Ecology as well as the Forest Service, whereupon the World Bank approved another billion dollars in loans. Thus 'the worst of both worlds' could be the title of the latest chapter in the sufferings of Russia.

16. Gare 1996b: 266, 211–28. At its height early in the revolution, *Proletkul't* had 400,000 members, published 20 journals, and drew in great numbers of artists and intellectuals. Material on Bogdanov can be found in Martinez-Alier 1987 as well as Gare. Martinez-Alier also writes extensively about Sergey Podolinsky, a nineteenth-century engineer who pioneered the integration of thermodynamic and Marxist theory, and can be seen as the progenitor of ecological economics. Gare's treatment of the Soviets is very extensive: see pp. 233–80, *passim*. A shorter and more accessible version of the argument may be found in Gare 1996a. Similar considerations pertained to Communist China. Although the manifest ideology was highly productivist in accordance with first-epoch socialist values and in contrast to the ecocentric philosophy of traditional China, still, 'until recently it has had a far better record than traditional China in relation to environmental problems. The Communists, at least when Mao Ze Dong ruled, did much to reforest the country, to conserve resources and to improve the environment in other ways' (Gare 1996b: 36). In support of this, Gare cites Orleans and Suttmeier 1970 and Geping and Lee 1984.

17. Lenin 1967. Nothing if not complex, Lenin veered away from this in his later philosophical writings, notably his reading of Hegel's *Logic* (Lenin 1976). It is safe to say, however, that it was the cruder and more mechanistic side of Lenin's ambivalence that sedimented into Soviet practice.

18. Classically depicted in Goncharov's novel *Oblomov*, about a man who could not get out of bed. Lenin would frequently inveigh to his followers against the dangers of succumbing to 'oblomovism'.

19. 'Man, who will learn how to move rivers and mountains, how to build people's palaces on the peaks of Mont Blanc and at the bottom of the Atlantic, will not only be able to add to his own life richness, brilliance and intensity, but also a dynamic quality of the highest degree. The shell of life will hardly have time to form before it will be burst open again under the pressure of new technical and cultural inventions and achievements ... Emancipated man will want to attain a greater equilibrium in the work of his organs and a more proportional developing and wearing out of his tissues, in order to reduce the fear of death ... [he will] raise himself to a new plane, to create a higher social biologic type, or if you please, a superman' (Trotsky 1960: 253).

20. Gare 1996b: 267–9.

21. McNally 1993: 206–8. Italics added.

22. The great British socialist thought in terms of a production that incorporated craft and the aesthetic dimension, thereby envisioning an emancipation of use-value. See especially the Utopian novel *News From Nowhere* (Morris 1993).

23. Bronner 1981: 75. Italics in original.

24. The list of plaintiffs in the case ranges from members of the socialist and Marxist traditions, such as Ted Benton and Rainer Grundmann (who is for the Promethean attitude), to anarchist/social ecologists such as John Clark, to ecocentric philosophers such as Robyn Eckersley. See Benton 1996 for a survey from the Marxist side; also Clark 1984; Eckersley 1992. There is an associated question, of Marx's relation to Engels, and of Engels himself on these matters. This is an important issue, which cannot,

however, be taken up here. The cover of the paperback edition of Bertell Ollman's *Alienation* (Ollman 1971) shows an illustration from 1842, when Marx was all of 24, directly depicting him as Prometheus. Marx's later physical afflictions, such as his boils, reinforced the association. See Wheen 2000.

25. See Burkett 1999; Foster 2000. For my assessment of Foster's book, see Kovel 2001.

26. Parsons 1977 provides a good anthology of relevant passages. For an earlier contribution of mine on this theme, see Kovel 1995.

27. From a youthful letter to Arnold Ruge. Marx 1978a.

28. Marx's most important statement about use-value appears in the little-read *Theories of Surplus Value*, (Marx 1971: 296–7), where we learn that the terms of value 'originally express nothing but the use-value of things for people, those qualities which make them useful or agreeable etc. to people. It is in the nature of things that "value", "valeur", "Wert" can have no other etymological origin. Use-value expresses the natural relationship between things and men, in fact the existence of things for men. *Exchange-value*, as the result of the social development which created it, was later superimposed on the word value, which was synonymous with use-value. It [exchange=value] is the *social existence* of things. [There follows an etymological passage, viz: 'Sanskrit – Wer means cover, protect, consequently respect honour and love, cherish...' etc, and then:] The value of a thing is, in fact, its own *virtus* [virtue], while its exchange-value is quite independent of its material properties.' Italics in original. I am indebted to Walt Sheasby for pointing out this passage, which clearly reveals that for Marx use-value is embedded in natural ecologies, but at the same time, that he sees no need to differentiate use-value from any notion of intrinsic value in nature. That is, a term belonging to economic discourse suffices to embrace the entirety of what nature means to humans.

29. Enrique Leff has made an important contribution to this concept in his *Green Production* (Leff 1995). However, the subjective elements developed here are not incorporated in his approach, nor does he set the goal of overcoming capital.

30. The linkage between use- and exchange-values needs to be kept in mind, as many cases of enhanced use-value exist whose outcome need not be inherently ecological. Thus fine and enhanced use-values occur regularly within a regime of exchange, as in the production of luxury goods, while at the other end, we find collapsing states of production, in which both forms of value deteriorate. A current example is the former USSR, where demoralized workmanship abounds, creating 'accidents waiting to happen' (viz., the submarine Kursk) while at the same time exchange-functions have also broken down for great blocks of the population, many of whom have had to resort to barter and other circuitous means in order to survive, rather than, as would obtain for a functioning ecological society, to develop beyond exchange.

31. See Note 28.

32. Two recent works that do this theme justice are Kidner 2000; Fisher 2001.

33. Even a garden slug, though here I must confess a certain barrier of recognition.

34. Mellor 1997.

9 Ecosocialism

If we imagine that decrees are all that is needed to get away from competition, we shall never get away from it. And if we go so far as to propose
to abolish competition while retaining wages, we shall be proposing
nonsense by royal decree. But nations do not proceed by royal decree.
Before framing such ordinances, they must at least have changed from
top to bottom the conditions of their industrial and political existence,
and consequently their whole manner of being. (Marx, *The Poverty of
Philosophy*[1])

Revolutions become feasible when a people decides that their present social
arrangements are intolerable, when they believe that they can achieve a
better alternative, and when the balance of forces between them and that
of the system is tipped in their favour. None of these conditions is close to
being met at present for the ecosocialist revolution, which would seem to
make the exercise upon which we are about to embark academic. But the
present is one thing, and the future another. If the argument that capital
is incorrigibly ecodestructive and expansive proves to be true, then it is only
a question of time before the issues raised here achieve explosive urgency.
And considering what is at stake and how rapidly events can change under
such circumstances, it is most definitely high time to take up the question
of ecosocialism as a living process – to consider what its vision of society
may be and what kind of path there may be towards its achievement.

The present chapter is the most practical and yet also the most speculative of this work. Beaten down by the great defeats of Utopian and
socialist ideals, few today even bother to think about the kinds of society
that could replace the present with one of ecological rationality, and most
of that speculation is within a green paradigm limited by an insufficient
appreciation of the regime of capital and of the depths needed for real

change. Instead, Greens tend to imagine an orderly extension of community, accompanied by the use of instruments that have been specifically created to keep the present system going, such as parliamentary elections and various tax policies. Such measures make transformative sense, however, only if seen as prefigurations of something more radical – something by definition not immediately on the horizon. It will be our job here to begin the process of drawing in this not-yet-seen. The only certainty is that the result will at most be a rough and schematic model of what actually might emerge.

However uncertain the end point, the first two steps on the path are clearly laid out, and are within the reach of every conscientious person. These are that people ruthlessly criticize the capitalist system 'from top to bottom', and that they include in this a consistent attack on the widespread belief that there can be no alternative to it. If one believes that capital is not only basically unjust but radically unsustainable as well, the prime obligation is to spread the news, just as one should feel obliged to tell the inhabitants of a structurally unsound house doomed to collapse of what awaits them unless they take drastic measures. To continue the analogy, for the critique to matter it needs to be combined with an attack on the false idea that we are, so to speak, trapped in this house, with no hope of fixing it or getting out.

The belief that there can be no alternative to capital is ubiquitous – and no wonder, given how wonderfully convenient the idea is to the ruling ideology.[2] That, however, does not keep it from being nonsense, and a failure of vision and political will. Whether or not the vision of ecosocialism offered here has merit, the notion that there is no other way of organizing an advanced society other than capital does not follow. Nothing lasts for ever, and what is humanly made can theoretically be unmade. Of course it could be the case that the job of changing it is too hard and capital is as far as humanity can go, in which instance we must simply accept our fate stoically and try to palliate the results. But we don't know this and *cannot* know this. There is no proving it one way or the other, and only inertia, fear of change or opportunism can explain the belief in so shabby an idea as that there can be no alternative to capital for organizing society.

Logic alone neither persuades nor gives hope; something more solid and material is required, a combination of the dawning insight of just how incapable capital is of resolving the crisis, along with some spark that breaks through the crust of inert despair and cynicism by means of which we have adapted to the system. At some point – it has to happen if capital is the efficient cause – the realization will dawn that all the sound ideas for, say, regulating the chemical industries, or preserving forest ecosystems, or doing something serious about species-extinctions, or global warming, or whatever point of ecosystemic disintegration is of concern, are not going to be realized by appealing to local changes in themselves, or the Democratic Party, or the Environmental Protection Agency, or the courts, or the foundations, or ecophilosophies, or changes in consciousness – for the overriding reason that we are living under a regime that controls the state and the economy, and will have to be overcome at its root if we are to save the future.

Relentless criticism can delegitimate the system and release people into struggle. And as struggle develops, victories that are no more than incremental by their own terms – stopping a meeting of the IMF, the hopes stirred forth by a campaign such as Ralph Nader's in 2000 – can have a symbolic effect far greater than their external result, and constitute points of rupture with capital. This rupture is not a set of facts added to our knowledge of the world, but a change in our relation to the world. Its effects are dynamic, not incremental, and like all genuine insights it changes the balance of forces and can propagate very swiftly. Thus the release from inertia can trigger a rapid cascade of changes, so that it could be said that the forces pressing towards radical change need not be linear and incremental, but can be exponential in character. In this way, conscientious and radical criticism of the given, even in advance of having blueprints for an alternative, can be a material force, because it can seize the mind of the masses of people. There is no greater responsibility for intellectuals.

In what follows, there will be neither blueprints nor omniscience, although I will be laying out certain hypothetical situations as a way of framing ideas. The overall task can be stated simply enough: if an ecological mode of production is the goal, what sort of practical steps can be defined to get us there? What might an ecosocialist society look like? How are the grand but abstract terms of basic change to be expressed as functions of lived life? And how can the path towards an ecosocialism that is not sharply defined incorporate the goal towards which it moves?

Ecological Ensembles and the Modelling of Ecosocialist Development

If ecological politics is to be prefigurative and interstitial, then it must begin with what is at hand, and according to its potential for realizing integral ecosystems. Let us call any such unit an ecological ensemble. It consists of a human ecosystem viewed from the standpoint of its potential for ecological production. What we look for is the growth and interconnection of ecological ensembles, from islands within the capitalist sea, to a kind of archipelago that further coheres, finally, into a continent of ecosocialism.

The notion of ecological ensembles is deliberately cast widely, thus any of the following would qualify:

- an organic farm
- an affinity group engaging in direct action against the World Bank
- a small community credit union
- a performed cultural work, engaging an audience
- an intentional community
- a political party
- a classroom, or a child within it
- the Du Pont corporation
- a neighbourhood in Manhattan – or Manhattan itself, or New York State, or the USA.

At its end, this list seems to become a *reductio ad absurdum*. It is preposterous, many would say, to think of Du Pont, or the USA, in the same breath as an organic farm in terms of their potential for ecosocialism. And what does a child have in common with any of these? One might as well put the World Bank on the list along with the affinity group stopping traffic in an effort to bring the Bank to heel.

Well, yes, one might as well, since the World Bank, too, is an ecosystem, insofar as the human world is that sub-set of nature whose ecosystemic being is given through production, and since all production contains some moment pressing toward universality. In this respect a child, more particularly a child in relation to its human and sensuous world, is certainly an ecosystem, as is any organized portion of the human world. It follows that even the bleakest capitalist enterprise has some ecosocialist potential. However, the judgement of bleakness applied to such an enterprise means, in effect, that its development has left the path of ecosystemic wholeness for the alternative and cancerous form of capitalist accumulation. As this is the case for DuPont and the World Bank, we may say that they are ecological ensembles with a very low internal ecosocialist potential, confined, say, to a pledge taken by the former to cut its greenhouse gas emissions, or in the case of the Bank, by the conscientious impulses of some staff members, all of which are hemmed in and tamed by the powerful force field of capital that they exist to serve, and therefore become mainly used for greenwashing and public relations. Nor will this potential develop spontaneously; it will develop only after very strenuous and protracted action taken against these institutions. Action of the sort is provided by the affinity group, by reason of which we would say that this kind of ecological ensemble has a high ecosocialist potential; indeed, that it is not just active, but *activating* – although it must be added that this potential exists at present as a loosely configured set of points scattered relatively harmlessly over the political landscape.

The general model of ecosocialist development is to foster the activating potentials of ensembles in order to catalyse the emergence of others so as to draw together those points into ever more dynamic bodies. The praxis by which this takes place is *dialectical*, that is, it comprises the active bringing and holding together of negations, as when the affinity group confronts the World Bank, or when a person confronts a painful truth. Negation in political confrontation defines what it means to struggle, and it has multiple aspects: the group offers itself as a counter-institution, more internally democratic and with enhanced ecocentric potentials; it offers direct critique of the Bank and seeks to educate others in the same, thereby bringing a painful truth to bear; and finally, it seeks to shut down the Bank, at least for a while, by blocking access to its meeting. The development of a human ecosystem depends greatly on the degree of recognition it appropriates, in this case the degree of understanding the affinity group holds of the Bank (and the police, politicians, media, and so on, who support the bank); and also of the fidelity, internal coherence, and so forth, of the group – in short, its capacity to stay together in dialectical activity throughout the period of confrontation. And the longer and more sustained the confrontation, the more developed the dialectic, the more mobilized the holding together (this being the insertion point of ecofeminist values into ecosocialist practice), and the more integral the ecosystem so produced.

The model can be applied to ensembles engaged in economic activity, such as the credit union, where the coefficient of use-value over exchange-value, uv/xv, can be expanded. Community enterprises of this sort object-ively tend to keep capital local and away from being leached into the great pool of ecodestruction; at the same time, they subjectively tend to detach people from capital's force field and induce ever-widening degrees of eco-logical production.[3] Two broad types of function differentiate themselves from this matrix, and, remaining differentiated, continually stay in contact: those having to do with the production, proper, of ecological use-values, as, for example, in the growing of food according to organic principles; and those having to do with the activation, or transforming of labour itself, the maker of all use-values as it engages nature. It may be said of activating groups such as the affinity group that their production becomes one of ecosocialist possibilities. This is seen prefiguratively in their theoretical production, which starts from the present level and achieves a fuller and more radical understanding from the struggle itself. Needless to say, this distinction must not be regarded too rigidly, for in fact the process described is equally possible within groups, and indeed, within individuals. As struggle develops, activation is spead across the whole social field, and gradually comes to define a new set of orienting principles that will coalesce into a 'party-like' formation. In this way there arises, interwoven in combinations presently impossible to predict, growing islands of relatively ecological production, along with the emergence, along other dimensions, of a guiding political spirit embodied in nascent organizations, whose work enables the bringing of productive ensembles together and strengthening their resolve. All of this is presumed to be played out against the backdrop of a gathering realization that capital is the efficient cause of the ecological crisis.

The next step to be imagined in this development is the emergence of more formal organizations, taking the shape of micro-communities serving the combined functions of *resistance* to capital, *production* of an ecological/socialist alternative to it, and mutual interconnection of their semi-auto-nomous sites through the vision of a common goal. To weave one possibility, the affinity group at some point 'settles in', constructing its ties now along more formally productive lines and drawing their lives more closely together around this. We can think of these along the lines of the Bruderhof dis-cussed in the previous chapter, with an anti-capitalist intention formed out of the combined withdrawal of value from exchange and its replacement with transformed use-value production. As we saw with that religious commune, a powerful spiritual movement is necessary to neutralize capital's force field and provide the protective umbrella to permit ecosystemic development. It is akin to the greenhouse that allows young plants to grow during the winter, allowing certain radiation in, and holding it in so that the young shoots may be protected from the cold. There is no reason why this cannot be Christian, although it would have to be a post-patriarchal Christianity in order to realize the goals of ecological production. By the same reasoning, there is no need that it be Christian at all, or religious, either, so long as it is post-patriarchal and post-capitalist, and spiritually attuned to the logic of ecological production. Spiritualities arise prior to their religious construction. They are formed from the striving of human being beyond the given, and there is ample resource within those forms of being that negate the domination of nature to give content to an emergent ecological spirituality – including, it should be emphatically added, from within the socialist tradition itself, which had a glorious spirituality when it had genuine claims on the Utopian imagination.[4] Nor need this spirituality be proclaimed as such. In a time saturated with New Age huckstering, that spirituality is best which does not announce itself, and truest to the extent that ego is transcended in a greater cause.[5]

Such a development will undoubtedly be highly uneven. Certain areas – for example, organic agriculture or permaculture – are favoured in terms of being able to produce ecologically realized use-values; thus for them, the numerator of the coefficient uv/xv can be increased relatively independently, raising the potential to break loose of capital. Other areas – for example, the emergent anti-globalization movements – are relatively more able to diminish the denominator, exchange-value, through political practice, thus achieving the same general effect. Clearly, however, the processes in either case can go only so far before becoming snared by the force field – the organic farmer by the brutal intrusion of market forces, which impose debt, competition and the need to exploit labour; the affinity group member, who is most typically a student, by the need to make a living, with all its attendant compromises, as well as by the powerful forces of state repression.

Practices that in the same motion enhance use-values and diminish exchange-values are the ideal in terms of ecosocialist potential. Needless to say, the student radical can then go on to law school and study to become a defender of the people and earth; just so, the organic farmer can find him/herself 'naturally' positioned to adopt Green political values and to organize accordingly – and in all such cases the possibility exists for unified ecosocialist practice to emerge collectively as this happens. But there are also types of activity yet closer to the ideal, where both aspects of the uv/ xv coefficient can change directly in relation to each other – for example, education. As current educational policy in the US grinds down the living child into an interchangeable part for the great capitalist machine, the possibility of resistance immediately arises for teachers of conscience. By organizing against the system and criticizing its educational policy, one necessarily protests the regime of exchange inasmuch as education under capitalism moves toward standardization, quantification and the treatment of children as passive containers to be shaped into docile workers and consumers. But it also requires reshaping one's practice as an educator, toward a model that, whatever its particular shape, regards the child as an active, self-determining being who lives through mutual recognition. In this way the teaching process becomes the production of ecosystemic use-values even as its political arm attacks the rule of exchange-value. Note, too, that this can occur in advance of an explicit assault on capital, being located rather at the point of capital's penetration into life-worlds.[6]

A highly salient example applies to the alternative media community, situated at the Archimedean point of capitalist legitimation and control. Here prefigurations of the new society in the form of the 'Indymedia' centres have recently arisen, as collectives of radical media activists in the cities visited by anti-globalization protests. Initially set up to document the protests in ways denied by corporate media, the independent centres tended to stay on after the waves of street protests receded. Their way having been prepared by a generation of media activists, the centres manifest a flexible and open structure, a democratic rendering of the use-values of new technologies such as the Internet, and a continual involvement in wider struggle. They grow and gather into national and international collectives, forming nodes on a growing web unified by an increasingly anti-capitalist vision. The same force that binds together the movement for democratic media also keeps it ecosystemic, that is democratically communitarian, and to that degree unwilling to compromise with the powers that be. In this way the spontaneously developing collective evolves into a *community of resistance*, one defined by praxis rather than place, and, in contrast to the plan of traditional Green theory, cosmopolitan to the core.[7]

It is essential to not get carried away by these successes. Media workers occupy one end of the spectrum of labour favourably configured for the spinning off of ecosocialist possibilities. However, the emancipation of labour requires that the entire international division of labour be overcome, and this is a problem the difficulty of which can scarcely be overestimated. Capital's domination of labour is predicated on separating workers from the means of production, and also from each other. This is the foundation of its triumph, and has become sedimented into the labour movement itself, which, being dependent upon jobs within existing capitalist workplaces, often shares with capital a resistance to environmental protection, or is divided nationally or regionally, North and South having many separate agendas. But the problem is equivalently that of existing environmentalism, with its single-issue focus on protecting natural habitats without concern for labour. The entire impasse cries out for the synthesis of an ecological production in which there is no contradiction between labour and nature, and creative work for all. But that is the goal, and a long way off; our job in the here and now is to develop prefigurative ensembles for it. The best candidates would be autonomous zones of production within which eco-centric potentials can be developed. At present, these appear drastically Utopian and out of reach for most industries. For auto workers, say, to build productive communities, as radical media workers are doing, is a fantasy under present conditions. Not only does it encounter the crippling blows suffered by the labour movements over generations, it must also face the globalized productive system in which motor vehicles today are virtually made everywhere, with labour so divided that nobody outside the inner circles of the corporation can even track its path.

In sum, the current potential of organized labour to reclaim its use value is low, and the international division of labour may be the most backward point of prefiguration. Yet even here, significant openings exist to bring along ecosystemic development. Three can be noted, two of them tendencies, the third a necessary possibility.

First, we might remind ourselves again of the Bruderhof, who survive rather well in a heavily industrialized market thanks to their communistic mode of social organization, which blunts the effects of capital's force field. Such a model can be duplicated widely through a limited portion of the industrial system. No, it will not presently include the making of automobiles, passenger planes, missiles, telecommunication networks, and so on. But this leaves a considerable amount of industrial production open to the incursions of developing ecological ensembles, so long as these are protected from the force field through a heightened anti-capitalist intentionality. That is what has been missing by and large from the much-touted green business movement, which accordingly has succumbed time and again to the nefarious effects of the market. There is nothing wrong with 'green enterprise', therefore, so long as it does not sink into 'green capitalism', with its accompaniment of exploiting labour, competition for market share, and so forth.

This tells us little about the great mass of proletarians whose labour holds up the capitalist world. However, even here there have been significant stirrings, as the class struggle has become internationalized in the face of globalization, and even begun to take on an ecological consciousness. In the first six months of 2000, huge strikes, some of general proportions, broke out across the globe: Nigeria, South Africa, South Korea, India, Uruguay and Argentina, to cite only the most massive. What makes this significant in terms of our argument is that the strikes represent points of rebellion against *globalized* capital, mainly as administered by the IMF, though carried out by national bourgeoisies.[8] This introduces a universalizing moment into labour politics, drawing the eyes of labour to wider horizons – within each nation (in India, for example, the strikers, 20 million strong, included farmers and factory workers), between nations, and, critically, toward an ecological inclusion of nature. When the instrument of capital is less the individual firm attempting to maximize value-extraction and cut costs than the boundary-dissolving instruments of globalization, then grounds for a genuinely globalized resistance are also in place. For the IMF, World Bank and WTO put their pressure on whole nations, and a nation in this context comprises territory along with the society upon it. It is globalization's destiny to break boundaries, but this means also that global capital's regime cannot legitmate itself as did the classical nation-state, leaving the realm of nature open for recovery by oppositional forces. When the forests as well as the hospitals and trade unions are subjected to capital's onslaught, resistance begins to encompass nature as well as labour.

In fact, labour's most cherished values are already immanently ecocentric. When working people sing 'Solidarity forever', they express humanity's deepest wishes for wholeness. The notion of a 'union' itself prefigures solidarity, as a process of coming together, a joining of working people into a larger entity. Solidarity is as much a subjective experience as it is an objective connection. Subjectively, solidarity corresponds to a partial dissolving of the harsh separateness imposed by egoic being, replacing it by joining into a collectivity, appropriating a previously suppressed power, and achieving historical agency. If, under capital, all that is solid melts into air, with the self-organization of labour, what been alienated achieves effective solidity, that is, ecosystemic integrity. The mutual receptivity it engages is one of the most intense and ennobling experiences that human beings can undergo.

Whether this can be extended depends on a third development not yet on the horizon, but necessary if ecosocialism is to move forward. We have spoken of the activating potentials aroused in ecological ensembles. At first, these are scattered and, given the present intellectual climate, remote from an anti-capitalist orientation, much less the further development into a demand for socialism. As these develop into communities of resistance, their activating potentials can come together into the germ of a consciously 'Ecosocialist Party', an organization that takes it upon itself, from country to country, and transnationally as well, consciously to organize the struggle.

The Ecosocialist Party and its Victory

Two models of party-building dominated the last century: the parliamentary parties of the bourgeois democracies and the 'vanguard' Leninist party of the Bolshevik tradition. Neither model can suit the ecosocialist project, which cannot be voted into power, and dies immediately if internal democracy is not made integral to its growth, as proved the case with Leninism. Leninist parties succeeded in installing first-epoch socialism chiefly because they were configured to the largely pre-capitalist societies in which the revolutions succeeded. Those capitalisms vanquished by first-epoch socialism were either imperial offshoots of metropolitan capital, or backward regimes grafted on to a largely precapitalist society. They encompassed neither the internal penetration nor the external global reach of capital's present order, both of which radically change the revolutionary project.

Modern capitalism legitimates itself by invoking 'democratic values'. This is spurious, as we have seen, but, however unfulfilled, it is a real promise that rests upon a definite foundation. By fragmenting life-worlds and traditional hierarchies, capital sets humanity loose into an unfree freedom of formal liberty and stunted development. The uneasy balance is kept going in capitalist institutions, which bind it for purposes of accumulation. To go beyond capital, one begins, then, with the betrayed promise of freedom and builds from there. It follows that the means of transformation have to be as free as the ends. That is why vanguardism, where the party is separate from as well as ahead of the people, is a non-starter in today's climate. Only a freely evolving praxis of participation can mobilize the imagination and bring together the innumerable points at which anti-capitalist struggle originates. And only a 'party-like' formation that postulates a goal common to all struggles without constraining them from above can organize this into 'solidarity solidified' and press toward power. Thus the party is formed from its own dialectic; it is a 'holding together' both objectively and subjectively – the former being the provision of material conditions, the latter being the attunement to intersubjective and relational nuance, all subsumed into the practical notion that dialectic is a matter of artfulness and subtlety.

Though open to individuals, the ecosocialist party should be grounded in communities of resistance. Delegation from such communities will supply the cadre of party activists as such, and the assembly that is its strategic and deliberative body. The party is to be internally funded through contributions by members, structured in such a way that no alienating force can take financial control. The delegates and such administrative bodies as may arise within this structure are to rotate on a regular basis and to be subject to recall. Further, the deliberations of the assembly, indeed all the activities of the party except certain tactical questions (for example, the details of a direct action), are to be open and transparent. Let the world see clearly what the party stands for – if this is worthwhile, it will only draw in more participants; if not, one needs to find out sooner rather than later.

The various green parties that have arisen across the world (as of this writing, in some 80 countries) are an important movement in this direction. Experience has shown, however, that by defining themselves as a progressive populism within the framework of bourgeois democracy, greens are solidifying as a kind of intermediate formation that stops considerably short of what is needed for transformation.[9] Green activists continue to make valuable contributions, but their parties lack a prefigurative vision surpassing the given society. As a result, green parties tend to lapse into narrow reformism and anarchic bickering. And when they have achieved some state power, as in Europe, greens have proven loyal to capital, giving it a shield of ecological responsibility.

One sign of the limits of green politics as currently practised has been a severe inability to reach out to communities of non-European origin. Frequently chastised for their lily-white make-up, greens regularly inveigh against the problem and resolve to do better. Yet little changes. The reason cuts to the core of the green dilemma: the parochial values intrinsic to their localism. Unless the notion of community is advanced in a universalizing way, it loses transformative power and, despite good intentions, drifts towards ethnocentricity. Therefore the greens' inertia on questions such as immigration and prison reform, and their general inability to appeal with more than token gestures to blacks and Latinos, are no oversight. These are manifestations of an inability to see beyond capital itself that all too often renders green politics, to choose an unfashionable but vivid term, petty-bourgeois.

With anti-capitalism the point of reference, one sees the whole of society, as well as its concrete workings. The ecological crisis and imperial expansion now appear as distinct and deeply connected manifestations of the same dynamic – invasive, cancerous growth tearing up nature and humanity. Today's buzzword, 'globalization', is imperialism's currently prime manifestation. But the history of empire is a narrative of the creation of peoples and the races themselves, including the subalterns who inhabit the South. From this perspective, a politics against and beyond capital needs to be as firmly rooted in overcoming racism as in ecological mending. The two themes intersect directly in the 'environmental justice' movement, grounded in the defence against capitalist penetration and pollution by communities of colour, and often led by women.[10]

Ecosocialism will be international or it will be nothing. And when its history is written, a starting point will be noted as 1 January 1994 – the day that NAFTA went into effect and the EZLN (Zapatista Army for National Liberation) launched a revolution of the oppressed in Chiapas, Mexico. The Zapatistas provide perhaps the first model of a revolutionary movement on a bioregional scale. Despite constant harassment by an army vastly superior in firepower, the Zapatistas retain a kind of ecosystemic integrity. They form a society within a state and without a state, productively united in resistance. What Marx said of the Paris Commune, that it lived the idea of the 'dictatorship of the proletariat', could be said, therefore, of the Zapatista path, with the wider lesson that there can be no single way valid for all peoples, but rather a multiplicity of ways defined by concrete societies, joined in common opposition to global capital.[11]

Another variant, more defined and less embattled, is the town of Gaviotas in the Colombian highlands. Here, beginning in 1971, one of the harshest environments on earth has been transformed by creative labour using ecologically rational technology. On what was once a blighted and arid plain, the soil toxic with naturally occurring aluminium, today stands a reforestation project larger than all the rest of Colombia's projects combined, some 6 million trees, a source of resin and musical instruments. These and other commodities are produced outside capitalist circuits, and without a capitalist state – in other words, with enhanced use-values and reduced exchange-value – an island of non-capitalist and ecological production that could become part of an archipelago of anti-capitalist and ecological production.[12]

If, that is, oppositional forces became strong enough, and took the shape, broadly conceived, of an international people's ecosocialist party or effective coalition of similarly constructed bodies. Then one day there could be a furtherance of the pressure on instruments of global capital that began with the great agitations of 1999–2000. James O'Connor has recently imagined something of this sort:

> if you think about it, poverty can be abolished in a few months, assuming the political will and the economic and ecological resources. First step, make poverty abolition the basic goal of international politics. Second step, allocate some billions of dollars of World Bank, IMF, regional development bank, and other monies to the task at hand. Third step, employ these monies, not for human capital or any other kind of capital, but to use local biomass for building homes, schools, and the rest; paying (well) public health and medical technicians, teachers of the 'pedagogy of the oppressed' variety, psychologists of the Fanon-type, planners of the Kerala[13] or Gaviota variety, and organizers of the type presently engaged in the anti-globalist movement (including NGO people of course) ... Then, choose investment projects, not in terms of [Environmental Impact Reports] that seek to minimize damage to local or regional ecologies but rather to maximize ecological values, community values, cultural values, public health values, and so on: a simple reversal of existing capitalist values and investment criteria. Not 'safe food' but 'nourishing food.' Not 'adequate housing' but 'excellent housing.' Not 'mass transport' but 'public transit of different types that are a pleasure to utilize.' Obviously, not 'chemical-laced' agriculture but 'pesticide-

free agronomy.' Not 'food monopolies' but 'farm-to-market global distribution.' The tragedy is that so many people know 'what is to be done,' based
on tens of thousands of local and regional experiments and practices, from
the allocation of water to the production and allocation of steel (in the U.S.
during WWII, for example), yet we can do little to make a world in which
use value subordinates exchange value (and concrete labor subordinates
abstract labor) given the present-day monopoly of power by capital, capital
markets, the capitalist state, and capitalist international agencies. Just suppose the IMF, WB, et al., were reduced to the status of the IHO, ILO, and
other branches of the 'international peoples' state,' while the latter's power
was expanded to the level of the present-day WB and IMF. That would be
something, wouldn't it? The problem of course is not a technical one, a
practical problem, but a political problem, the problem of capitalist power,
in and outside the markets, and no movement can challenge capitalist power
with success without adopting its own political aims and socio-economic
alternatives.[14]

Yes, it would be something. And because a movement of the sort will be
ecosocialist and not populist, it will be infused with a spirit that agitates for
these changes yet regards them prefiguratively and does not settle for them.
This is the reason we postulate a goal far off the present map: because it
offers the hope, vision and energy to transform the present.

If such events as O'Connor envisions were to come to pass, they would
not yet be ecosocialism, but they would form a kind of self-generative and
non-linear dialectic that can rapidly accelerate the motion toward ecosocialism. After all, it is the 'tens of thousands of local and regional
experiments and practices' who would have had to join with communities
of activation to make this possible, and whose power would be accordingly
magnified by it. And being magnified, the Zapatistas, and the Gaviotistas,
and the Indymedia centres that connect them, and the politicized collectives
of farmers from around the world, and the teacher's associations, and the
ecologically radicalized fractions of the labour movement, and the little
Bruderhof-like manufacturing collectives making ecologically sane products
with the aid of local credit unions, and all the ten thousand locally origin-
ating but universally striving community formations – all would come
together in solidarity to make such an event, and, in its aftermath, to press
for further transformation.

There is no point in predicting a scenario according to which this will expand, beyond the condition that it occur in the context of capital's incapability of regulating the ecological crisis. At some time within this span, the communities arising from the process may be imagined to grow to a point of relative autonomy such that they can begin providing material support for activists, with bases of operation and – in the case of those considerable number of communities producing food, wool, hemp, solar technology, and so on – the actual means of subsistence for people engaged in revolutionary struggle. It must also be presumed – a large but feasible order – that these people will have developed the spiritual and psychological strength enabling them to go forward. For there should be no mistake: the struggle for ecosocialism is no technical or voluntaristic process, but a radical transforming of self as well as world to link up in ever-widening and deepening solidarity. Here is where post-patriarchal values will come forward, radicalizing human being itself for the struggle.

Now the movement of events is self-sustaining, rapid and dramatic. Communities of place and of praxis increasingly coalesce to form miniature societies, and these enter into relations with others both inside and outside the national boundary. Capital may be expected to respond with heightened efforts at repression. A heroic phase begins, with much sacrifice. The awesome might of the capital system now encounters a set of factors it has never dealt with before:

- The forces against it are both numerous and dispersed.
- They operate with changed needs, and on the basis of a kind of production capable of sustaining itself with small inputs and labour-intensive technologies; and they have secure bases and 'safe houses' in the intentional communities of resistance, now extending across national boundaries.
- Their many allies in the interstices of the mainstream society are capable of forming support groups and 'underground railroads'.
- As with all successful forms of revolutionary protest, the oppositional forces are capable of shutting down normal production through strikes, boycotts, and mass actions.
- The forces of capital have lost confidence, and are further undermined by support for the revolution within the alternative parties and their various niches in the state. This extends to armies and police. When the

first of these lays down their arms and joins the revolution, the turning
point is reached.

* The behaviour of the revolutionaries is spiritually superior, and the
examples they set are given credibility and persuasiveness by the brute
facts of the crisis and the gathering realization that what is at stake here
is not so much the redistribution of wealth as the sustenance of life
itself.

Thus it could be that in an increasingly hectic period, millions of people
take to the streets, and join together in global solidarity – with each other,
with the communities of resistance, and with their comrades in other
nations – bringing normal social activity to a halt, petitioning the state and
refusing to take 'no' for an answer, and driving capital into ever smaller
pens. With defections mounting and the irreducible fact all around that the
people demand a new beginning in order to save the planetary ecology, the
state apparatus passes into new hands, the expropriators are expropriated,
and the 500-year regime of capital falls.

A Usufructuary of the Earth

From the standpoint of a higher economic form of society, private ownership of the globe by single individuals will appear quite as absurd as
private ownership of one man by another. Even a whole society, a nation,
or even all simultaneously existing societies taken together, are not the
owners of the globe. They are only its possessors, its usufructuaries, and,
like *boni patres familias*, they must hand it down to succeeding generations
in an improved condition.[15]

Thus wrote Karl Marx, in the third volume of *Capital*. The notion of
usufruct is an ancient one, with roots going back to the Code of Ham-
murabi, although the word itself arises in Roman law, where it applied to
ambiguities between masters and slaves with respect to property. It appears
again in Islamic law, and in the legal arrangements of the Aztecs and the
Napoleonic Code – indeed, wherever the notion of property reveals its
inherent contradictions. Interestingly, the Latin word condenses the two
meanings of *use* – as in use-value, and *enjoyment* – as in the gratification
expressed in freely associated labour. As commonly understood today, a

usufructuary relationship is where one uses, enjoys – and through that, improves – another's property, as, for instance, community groups would use, enjoy and improve an abandoned city lot by collectively building a garden there.

Because we are human to the degree that we creatively engage nature, the self is defined through its extensions into the material world. We become who we are by *appropriating* nature, transforming and incorporating it, and it is within this frame that the notion of property logically arises. Therefore a person with no possessions whatsoever is no individual at all, as s/he has no particular grounding in nature. It follows that in an ecologically realized society everyone will have rights of ownership – a place of one's own, decorated according to taste, personal possessions, such as books, clothing, objects of beauty, likewise – and, of special significance, rights of use and ownership over those means of production necessary to express the creativity of human nature. This latter most definitely includes the body – whence the reproductive rights of women are logically secured, along with the rights of free sexual expression.

The notion of property becomes self-contradictory because each in-dividual person emerges in a tissue of social relations, and, in Donne's words, is never an island. Each self is therefore a part of all other selves, and property is inexorably tied into a dialectic with others. This may be imagined as a set of nested circles. At the centre is the self, and here ownership exists in relatively absolute terms, beginning with the body, intrinsically the property of each person. As the circles extend, issues of sharing arise from early childhood on, each potentially resolvable according to the principle that the full self is enhanced more by giving than by taking. For a realized being is generous. The more lightly material possessions weigh upon the self, the more fully can one give, and the richer one be-comes. It is the work of socialism to make this potentiality actual.

The domain of use-value will be the site of contestation. To restore use-value means to take things concretely and sensuously, as befits an authentic relation of ownership – but by the same gesture, lightly, since things are enjoyed for themselves and not as buttresses for a shaky ego. Under capital, as Marx famously saw, what is produced is fetishized by the shroud of exchange-value – made remote and magical. In the fetishized world, nothing is ever really owned, since everything can be exchanged, taken away and abstracted. This stimulates the thirst for possessions that rages under capitalist rule. The unappeasable craving for things – and money to get things – is the necessary underpinning of accumulation and the subjective dynamic of the ecological crisis. The circuits of capitalist society are defined by *having* – and excluding others from having – until we arrive at a society of gated communities inhabited by lonely egos, each split from all and the atomized selves split from nature.[16] They can only be resolved in a society that permits this hunger to wither, and this requires the release of labour from the bondage imposed by exchange value.

Ecosocialist society will be defined by *being*, achieved by giving oneself to others and restoring a receptive relation to nature. Ecosystemic integrity is to be restored across all the nested circles of human participation – the family, the community, the nation, the international community, or, with a leap across the humanity/nature membrane, the planet, and, beyond it, the universe. For capital, property rights of the individual ego are sacrosanct, and become solidified into class structures, whence they succeed in dispossessing masses of people from their inherent ownership of the means to produce creatively. This is only the legal aspect of a regime of fetishized relations. Within ecosocialism, the bounds of the individual ego are surpassed as use-value overcomes exchange-value and opens a way for the realization of intrinsic value. In the new society, the right of an individual freely to appropriate the means of self-expression is paramount. Society is structured to give this primacy by differentiating ownership between individual and collectivity. Although each person – and each family as the extension of personhood into reproduction – has an inalienable right to good housing, the ownership as such of the housing and the land upon which it stands is collective, and granted by the collectivity. In this way, there arise distinct limits on the amount of property individuals can control, both from the standpoint of domestic usage as well as that of the control over productive resources. No person is to be allowed to arrogate such resources, therefore, as would permit the alienation of means of production from another. There will be no such arrangement as now obtains, where well over a billion absolutely landless people, along with several billion more who must sell themselves on the market because they are effectively without control over more than the slenderest threads of property, confront a tiny fraction who own virtually all the wealth-producing world. Extending further out along the nested circles, we find that those things essential for social production are to be shared by all and not owned by the few.

The extension proceeds, as Marx realizes, to the planetary level, and devolves downward from there to govern the particular laws of ecosocialist society. Taken all in all, the earth we inhabit should be regarded not as our collective property but as a wondrous matrix from which we emerge and to which we return. Perhaps it will be easier to dislodge the ruling class from their cancerous ownership if we remind ourselves that this is not done to transfer ownership to 'the people' or some surrogate. Indeed, ownership of the planet is a pathetic illusion. It is plain *hubris* to think that the earth, or nature, can be owned – and stupid to boot, as though one can own that which gives us *being*, and whose becoming we express. The notion of standing over and against the earth in order to own it is central to the domination of nature. A usufructuary is all we can claim with regard to the earth. But this demands that our species proves its worth by using, enjoying and improving the globe that is our home. From that reigning principle can be derived those individual regulations that are to subserve the metabolism between humanity and nature called ecosocialism. No class ownership of the means of production stands at one pole, absolute ownership of one's self as the other – for the self is the earth emerging into consciousness at this one point of individuality; while the institutions of ecosocialist society exist to set going the ways of using, enjoying and improving our common firmament.

The society that emerges from the storm of the revolution will at first be only marginally capable of fulfilling this project. Its highest priority is to set things going in a truly ecosocialist direction and its first goal is to secure the 'free association of producers'. Each term here needs to be respected. The association is *free* because in it people self-determine; hence society must make means of production accessible to all. It is a free *association* because life is collective; therefore the relevant political unit is a collectivity drawn together by mutual productive activity. And it is of *producers*, which is to be taken in the human-natural sense and not economistically. This means that the whole making of the human world is to be taken into account rather than just that which contributes or controls exchange-value. Since a core goal of ecosocialism is the diminution of exchange-value's domain, it valorizes forms of productive activity to the degree that these foster ecosystemic integrity, whether this be the raising of beautiful children, the growing of organic gardens, the playing of excellent string quartets, the cleaning of streets, the making of composting toilets, or the invention of new technologies for turning solar energy into fuel cells.

To secure the association, we need ways of preventing the emergence of alienating agencies. Private ownership of means of production has been shown to be the chief of these under capital, but the Soviets showed that the state can just as well fill this role. And since the gain of state power by the revolution is essential for redirecting society, so must the revolution give high priority to building ways of preventing the state from turning into a monster over society. A key principle is the internal development of true democracy, the absence of which crippled all previous socialisms. That is why alternative party-building in the pre-revolutionary period is important – not to win state power in the here and now, which is out of the question, but to democratize the state insofar as possible, and to train people in the ways of self-governance so that when the revolution is made they will be in a position to sustain democratic development. Another essential principle is the enfranchisement of productive communities, enabling power to flow from the producers – or, since everyone produces and has multiple productive affiliations, from those collectivities that best express their free association and the enhancement of ecosystemic integrity.

As the revolution begins its work, we find that society comprises four fractions. First are those who have engaged in revolutionary practice, either as political agents and/or as members of communities of resistance. Second are those who did not participate actively yet whose productive activity is directly compatible with ecological production – the housewives, nurses, schoolteachers, librarians, technicians, independent farmers, and so on, along with the very old, the very young, the ill, and those on welfare or otherwise marginalized (including many of those in prison). Third are those whose pre-revolutionary practice was given over to capital – the bourgeoisie proper, along with those legions involved in work worthless from an eco-socialist standpoint – the PR men, the car salesmen, the ad executives, the supermodels, the cast of 'Survivor' and like shows, loan sharks, security guards, wealth psychologists, and so on. Finally, we find arrayed between the second and third categories the workers whose activity added surplus value to capitalist commodities, as industrial proletarians, field hands, truck-drivers, and so forth. Many of these latter worked in polluting, ecologically destructive settings; others in industries that have little or no place in an ecologically rational society, for example weapons factories or those making diet sodas. All will have to be provided for and retrained if society is to be rebuilt.

Clearly, it will be no easy matter to reallocate productive activity among so vast an assemblage. The following broad principles may be useful:

- An interim assembly of delegates from the revolutionary communities of resistance constitutes itself as an agency to handle the redistribution of social roles and assets, to make sure that all are provided for out of common stocks, and to exert such force as is necessary to reorganize society. The assembly will convene in widespread locations and send delegations to regional, state, national and international bodies. Each level will have an executive council with rotating leadership, recallable by votes from the level below.
- Productive communities (and now they may be authentically called 'co-operatives'), whether of place or praxis, form the political as well as economic unit of society. The priority of those groups who made the revolution will be to organize others and create paths for the rapid assimilation of other workers to the network of productive communities. This includes all able-bodied people, the ex-perpetrators of capital as well, who – with a few egregiously criminal exceptions – will be allowed to participate in building an ecosocialist world.
- People may join whatever unit they wish (although standards will have to be set, as for health-care providers), and can have associate membership in others – for example, a doctor who is also a father can join his local health service community and have associate membership in the child-rearing community, the community theatre, and so on. The interim assembly will have to devise incentives to make sure that vital functions are maintained. In the initial stages, before ecosocialist values have been fully internalized, these would include differential remuneration, perhaps a factor of three separating the least from most paid.
- In each locality, one such community would directly administer the area of jurisdiction. For example, town government would be considered a collective whose product is the provision of ecologically sound governance – and also an assembly elected by all the inhabitants of that area. Each area, therefore, may have several assemblies – one for adminstration, another for wider spheres of governance.
- Each productive community participates fully as soon as it demonstrates its fidelity to ecosocialist principles. And as it joins, it plays a political role in its local assembly, sending delegates and votes to the next level.

- Two vitally important functions will devolve on to the more central assemblies. The first will be to monitor the degree that communities under its jurisdiction are contributing to ecosystemic integrity, and to give a kind of weight to communities according to their contribution. This supervisory body potentially has considerable power, limited, however, by the fact that it serves at the behest of the productive communities themselves.

- The second function pertains to the general coordination of social activities, the provision of society-wide services like rail systems, the allocation of resources, the reinvestment of the social product, and the harmonization of relations between regions at all levels, including the international. There is no avoiding a state-like function, which must be eventually transferred from the interim assembly and handled at the level of the society as a whole through appropriate and democratically responsive committees. The key to its success – and to that of the system as a whole – lies in the degree to which democracy has become a living presence in society.

Some Questions

What will be the future of markets, and how does this relate to the overcoming of capital? With the revolution's triumph, there will be a rapid transfer of assets to direct producers, and for the majority of enterprises that presumably enter the new epoch as non-ecosocialist, a rapid conversion to ecosocialist production. First of all, this means restoring ecosystemic integrity to the workplace, and to the interrelations with other sites of production. For example, the first change at an auto plant will be worker ownership and control. The new structure will proceed swiftly to redesign its production according to socially developed plans, for example, by beginning a conversion to light-rail transport, or to making super-efficient vehicles, and so on. During the transition, incomes will be guaranteed, using the reserves now in possession of the revolution. This is combined with transforming other sites considered outside the value-producing economy of capital, for example child care, into productive communities, thereby giving reproductive labour a status equivalent to productive labour. At first the old money will be used, though given new conditions of value, namely, according to use and to the degree to which ecosystem integrity is developed and advanced by any particular production. Thus determination of intrinsic value becomes the ultimate standard, rather than abstract labour time.[17] Although no one in ecosocialist society will do without, actual remuneration, and more importantly approval and sense of worth and dignity, comes with the fulfilment of use-values.

Within the new framework, price signals of the capitalist market lose their 'receptors'. This need not rule out a place in ecosocialism for market phenomena – for example, to facilitate the allocation of resources, personal exchanges, and so on. Nor is it forbidden that a person engaged in a small-scale activity may hire others – for example, to help move a household – so long as it is made clear that this is temporary, that no profitable exploitation of labour takes place, and that if the activity becomes sustained and structured, then the labour within it takes on a cooperative and ecocentric form. But a market phenomenon is one thing, and regulation of society by The Market is another. It stands to reason that standards will have to be developed within the society of communities and assemblies to assay the surplus and make decisions about coordination of activity as well as investment in new facilities. But there is no reason beyond capitalist inertia to think that these matters cannot be decided democratically, and in a way that valorizes ecosystemic integrity.[18] Once the ecocentric mode of production is in place, it becomes the 'reason' things stand to, and the capitalist Market loses all but a limited instrumental rationality. With this, the binding of time is undone, and individuals become self-determining agents of ecological integrity.

How is the new society to deal with questions of repression and violence? Specifically, does not the enforcement role give the state a dangerous opportunity to become yet another power over society? In the disorderly transfer that is the likely route to ecosocialism, there will be some violence, perhaps a lot. Almost all of this will be suffered by the revolutionary forces, because the master is always more violent than the subaltern (violence being integral to the master's way), and because the means of ecosocialist struggle should be aligned with its ends. Since violence is the rupturing of ecosystems, it is deeply contrary to ecosocialist values.

It is the situation after the victory, where wounds are fresh and much conflict must be presumed to remain, that stirs fears that the post-revolutionary state might prove repressive and authoritarian. Who is to rule out the possibility beyond a doubt? Nevertheless, measures can be taken that minimize the risk. The necessary condition, even more important than espousing non-violent ideals, is prior development of the democratic sphere. To the degree that people are capable of self-government, so will they turn away from violence and retribution.[19] It is also essential that, wherever else it takes place, the revolution takes place in the USA, or spreads there very rapidly, as the USA is capital's gendarme and will crush any serious threat so long as its own security apparatus remains intact.

In addition, the following principles are important. First, strict standards of governmental openness must be secured, along with active and critical media to serve as watchdog. The exception to this is the interface where public functions intersect with individuals' legitimate needs for privacy, as in medical records or court cases where falsely defamatory testimony can be given. The rule, therefore, is that public functions demand disclosure, while personally private ones demand respect for the rights of individuals not to have their immediate self/property intruded upon. Ecosocialism reverses the constantly expanding penetration of personal space by forms of capitalist surveillance. Important councilar bodies, to which citizens have direct access, need to be established to safeguard this function.

Further, opposition to the death penalty is an important component of any ecosocialist programme and must be strictly adhered to in the post-revolutionary period, especially where the treatment of the vanquished classes is concerned. It needs to be acknowledged that the death penalty is an evil in itself, irrespective of any abuses, because by giving to the state the right to kill, it blocks the path towards transcending violence and denies the realization of human nature. Therefore, there will be no official killing, even of the most repulsive and unreconstructed enemy. In the great majority of cases, unconditional amnesty can be offered to all who agree to enter an ecosocialist path, and take up their positions in a suitable cooperative or community. There will be exceptions, either those who refuse to transfer productive assets, or those whose prior behaviour amounted to crimes against humanity and/or nature. But there are none who cannot be dealt with by incarceration, where the miscreant can have ample opportunity to rethink his or her ways while gazing at flourishing organic farms or street festivals through the bars of the prison window.

In the larger sense, protection against the authoritarian state is a function of the success of ecosocialist production. Ecosocialism will be a great network of productive communities, from agricultural cooperatives, to trans-national scientific teams, to governing assemblies – many varied settings creating the conditions for individual self-realization. To the degree to which this is fulfilled, people become self-governing; and a self-governed people cannot be pushed around by any alien government.

Is there not another level of repression here? Sometimes it sounds as if ecosocialism, with its emphasis on production, will be a gigantic workhouse. Is this not a new kind of Puritanism? The use of the term 'production' can give rise to this impression, but it is highly mistaken. In fact, precisely the opposite is intended. Established religion has tended to reinforce the suffering of the worker under class society. The Puritan mentality went further still: it was integral to the foundations of capital, which it helped secure by turning the body into a machine and the self into an engine of capital's work discipline.

Time-as-money, a core relation of capital, continues the Calvinist project in the form of debt. For the average working family, ravaged by consumer debt, in perpetual panic about affording health care, and only a paycheck or two away from losing the house and the car, individual life becomes a transmission belt in a gigantic factory of accumulation. The Calvinist god that became Puritanism's Hound of Heaven is deployed over a thousand points of surveillance, credit checks and friendly reminders that one's payment is overdue. People can see a face of capital as it appears on the stock market or on television commercials. But they see it with bemused eyes and do not recognize capital as the beast ravenously telling them to pay up.

Ecosocialism explodes this connotation. To emancipate labour is to free humanity from the constraints of work discipline imposed by the clock. Ecosocialism is predicated on eliminating accumulation as the motor of society, and, with this, the hounding of individuals caught up in debt and the rat race. It explodes the time=money equation by restoring the use-value of labour as a free association. Ecosocialism gives production *dignity*, as part of a full life. As realized individuals are self-governing, so are they free from compulsion, including compulsive producing and consuming.

Thus the point of ecosocialism is to overcome toil, not submit to it. In a world of realized use-value, the spheres of work and culture are re-integrated, as in the eighteenth-century Paraguayan Indian communities, organized by Jesuits, which underwent more than a century of autonomous development until empire claimed their territory. As Paolo Lugari, the visionary founder of the Gaviotas community, said of their world: 'Everyone ... was taught to sing or to play a musical instrument. Music was the loom that wove the community together. Music was in schools, at meals, even at work. Musicians accompanied labourers right into the corn and *yerba mate* fields. They'd take turns, some playing, some harvesting. It was a society that lived in constant harmony – literally. It's what we intend to do, right here in this forest.'[20] What the Paraguayans did reminds us of the happy interrelation of play, song and construction in the life of children, as, for example, at a good nursery school. And if we think of this comparison as disparaging to adult work settings, then we have not comprehended the central point of ecosocialism. For children and adults alike have an inherent need to sing, dance and play. To restore use-values is to rebuild the conditions for the expression of human nature as an integral element of caring for nature.

The machinery of capitalist production not only binds the body temporally; it also expresses the life-denying character of male domination. It is Father-power that enforces repression, stifles the flowing of life-forces, and curses production with pain since the expulsion from Eden. The overcoming of male domination also restores to production its intrinsic pleasure. There will be plenty of hard work to do, but hard work freely chosen and collectively carried out is a great joy.

How will ecosocialism be internationalized? Transnational capital flows must be reined in, to release capital's grip on the global economy and open a path for the restoration of use-values and ecocentric production. Needless to say, one does not one-sidedly break down the global capital system; one installs, rather, its alternative, or the pilot projects and prefigurative structures of its alternative, even as the old walls are coming down. A rapid replacement of monetary exchange-value functions with use-value functions will be essential to this.

We have seen (Chapter 6) that money has three functions – enabling exchanges, being a commodity in its own right, and being the repository of value. The goal in the transitional period is to retain the first and bring down the latter two. The effect would be to weaken capitalist institutions while directing money to the creation and free enhancement of use-values. Through subsidization of use-values, therefore, society preserves the functioning core of the economy while gaining time and space for rebuilding it ecologically.

The practical measures would be, first, to cease speculation in currencies as a way of breaking down the function of money as commodity, and redirecting funds on use-values. Alongside this would be the immediate cancellation of the debts of the nations of the South, thereby breaking the back of the value function and enabling ecologically sound development to take over. What is lost in the doing is strictly capital's problem: a vast reservoir of mainly phoney value suddenly evaporates, a grievous blow to the great banks and investment houses. The reservoir, meanwhile, has been opened for use – and some reparations have been made to those upon whose back capitalism has been built. As simple exchange now prevails over exchange-value, the building of use-values becomes the primary goal. The life-blood of comprador elites in the South is rather abruptly drained, and this, along with the immediate shutting down of military aid and other forms of support from the metropolitian capitalist powers, may be expected to lead to their collapse in short order.

With the rise of popular forces, the global society comes together to replace the instruments of capital with those enabling ecosocialism. Re-configuring global trade becomes an immediate priority. We may think of this as a 'World People's Trade Organization' (WPTO), controlled by and responsible to a confederation of popular bodies organized on a global basis, which will set parameters for regulating trade in accordance with the flourishing of ecosystems, while providing at the same time an international forum for the cooperation and unification of peoples.

The degree of control over trade is now proportional to involvement with production – that is, farmers would have a special say over food trade, auto-workers over that of automobiles, while the transport workers who directly carry out the trade would also have a special role corresponding to their function, as would all citizens in their capacity as consumers and 'stakeholders'. A council, elected from and responsible to the people, would take care of overall coordination as well as the setting and collection of tariffs.

A core function of the WPTO would be an alternative calculus of pricing. Where goods are now traded inasmuch as they are profitable to capitalists, goods will become traded according to an 'ecological price' (EP), determined by the difference between actual use-values and fully realized ones, hence, the greater the difference, the higher the tariff. Production along ecological lines, for example organic agriculture, would have low tariffing for purposes of trade. Such production could also receive subsidies generated by tariffs exacted from those producers whose EPs exceed the norm. As an example of those commodities on which a high EP would be set, we could turn first to the automobile industry in its current super-polluting and wantonly wasteful state. Low ecological prices will thus be used as a standard for the transformation of the industries themselves.

Whatever is presently subsumed into the externalization of costs on to the environment – for instance, pollution – would be internalized into the computation of EP. In addition, EP's would be set as a function of the distance traded, inasmuch as ecologically deleterious effects are built into commodities in proportion to this distance (as in fuel costs of transport, the need for extensive packaging, dyestuffs, and so on). In this sense, the WPTO would replace the reckless and environmentally destructive growth of 'free trade' while continuing to provide for the intercourse of peoples and the exchange of goods.

The new system would radically alter the growing crisis of immigration that now besets the world and is associated with much of its racism and neo-fascism. The pressure to migrate is directly related to the differentials in wealth between nations, and, more generally, to the mobility of capital in relation to the fixity of labour. By stopping capital in its tracks, the ecosocialist order knocks out one prime cause of this, while the growing equalization of wealth and the flourishing of once-peripheral societies remove the other. There is simply no societal pressure to migrate when one's home is intact.

Closely related to this, we find the ecosocialist arrangement of global society to be the only rational solution of the population crisis. Whether or not the world's population will level off, or is hopelessly big already, the fact remains that providing optimal conditions for controlling population growth remains a high priority. The core principle is already integral to ecosocialism: giving people, and especially women, control over their lives. A mutually cooperative world society will restore flourishing ecosystemic conditions to life – and as it is in the nature of ecosystems to self-regulate their populations, so will this be the nature of ecosocialist society.

The new order of trade is transitional to a condition in which commodity production withers away. In this condition, now free of money as we know it, use-values are no longer subordinated to exchange-value, but harmonized with intrinsic value. We leave to the citizens of that far-off epoch the details of working out its functions of exchange and distribution. In the interim, the WPTO signifies a dissolution of the imperial system that has held sway since the beginnings of class society. Indeed, it forms the germ of a world society without imposed boundaries. We tend to forget that the lines now drawn on the map are mainly reflections of the expansive dynamic of class structures where an elite exploits the labour of a majority. Aggrandizement is common to this relationship, and empire in all its forms, from direct conquest, to colonialization, to the economic instruments of globalization, is the result. Ecological production cuts the heart out of empire by eliminating the pathological dynamic of growth, and creates the ground for genuine co-operation between nations. Whether the actual boundedness between nations, and with that the very structure of the nation-state, is transformed in the process into a truly global society is a matter for speculation, although it can be said that such a society would not be formless and undifferentiated – quite inconceivable for a realized human nature – but the integral of all the world's eco-communities of place and of praxis, with a corresponding wealth of interrelated cultures.

What are the practical guidelines for today's activists, working at a very great distance from these possibilities? The notions developed here mean that there is no royal road to ecosocialism, nor any privileged agent. It follows that humility and flexibility should guide present politics. The interstitial character of ecosocialist resistance implies a great democracy of protest. Someone who signs a petition against a polluting power plant is a potential ecosocialist, as is someone who decides to garden organically, or work at a community-access cable TV station. The general rule, though, is somewhat different from usual environmentalist assumptions. Where environmentalism seeks first of all to protect external nature from assault, a prefigurative ecosocialism combines this goal with anti-capitalist activity – which implies, as we have seen, anti-imperialist and anti-racist activity, and all that devolves from these. In the great wealth of interstitial openings the general rule is that whatever has promise of breaking down the commodity form is to be explored and developed. This can extend from organizing labour (reconfiguring the use-value of labour power), to building cooperatives (ditto, by a relatively free association of labour), to creating alternative local currencies (undercutting the value-basis of money), to making radical media (undoing the fetishism of commodities). In every instance, the challenge is to build small beach-heads – liberated zones that can become the focal points of resistance and combine into larger ensembles.

For those who decide to democratize the state by building alternative electoral parties, the following rough rules would apply: first, there should be dialogue but no compromise with the established machine parties. To take the USA as an example, the Democratic Party, however many good people may be within it and however lesser an evil it may be compared to the Republicans, remains, as it has for generations, the graveyard of radical politics. The hard work of building alternative political parties therefore has as a first requirement avoidance of co-optation. This requires a continual association of electoral work with movement work, to keep the former from being sucked back into the system. As a corollary, one should be content with losing elections and staying small for some time. A loss by ordinary electoral terms is by no means so from the perspective of ecosocialism, whose gains are measured not in terms of vote counts, but more subtly, as a function of how electoral work contributes to an ecologically worthy building of democratic ensembles. Pandering to win according to the established rules, in a word, all opportunism, is hostile to the cause. One must be fully prepared, rather, to lose, and lose, and lose, in ordinary terms, until victories appear. And that is another reason why movement activities are necessary – so that winning and losing can be seen in qualitative terms, of building ensembles instead of vote counts.

Such electoral victories as do appear are bound to occupy the more local rungs of the political system. This is a good place to begin democratizing the state, within which project, no advance is too small if conscientiously done. At the same time the longer-range goals of ecosocialism need to be brought forward, and for this purpose national campaigns should be carried out. Here the purpose is not at all to win the office, an absurd goal. The intention, rather, is radically to challenge the existing system by the elementary means of exposing its broken promises. Where the standard electoral campaign makes a series of compromises and moves toward the political centre, here the candidate enunciates demands that are lawful, feasible and highly rational so far as the real interests of the people are concerned – for example, winning socialized medicine by making health care a human right, or dismantling the military–industrial complex – but which are not going to be enacted precisely because to do so would fundamentally cut into the power of capital. Moreover, these measures are not to be posed piecemeal, but will apply comprehensively across a great spectrum of social and ecological needs, thereby exposing the fact that it is not one interest group or another that opposes them, but the full weight of the capital common to the corporate order as a whole. Accordingly, the mind of the citizen is drawn to the notion that, as each of these measures is both just and rational, and as there seems to be such a measure for every facet of social existence, then the question needs to be raised as to an alternative society capable of realizing them all. There *should be* such a society – then, *why not* have such a society? – and next, how do we think of such a society, and *what shall be done* to advance it? In other words, one runs not against this Republican or Democrat, each more or less individually the tool of capital, but against the sedimented hopelessness that passes for common sense.

Can there be such a society? Only if we get moving right away. Everything depends on making the building of ecosocialism proceed in advance of ecological breakdown, which at some point will bring all our hopes to an end. If we wait for things to worsen, then the logic of the crisis will see to it that things will get too much worse, so that nothing will save us, either from direct collapse or from its ecofascist precursor. There is no time to lose, and a world to be won.

Notes

1. Marx 1963: 107. I became acquainted with this passage through Mészáros 1996.

2. 'There is no alternative', is often acronymously called 'TINA', is a phrase ascribed to Margaret Thatcher, and useful for rhetorical purposes. I will eschew it/her here, because of the misogynistic implication.

3. See Gunn and Gunn 1991 and Meeker-Lowry 1988 for discussion of how to build local economies in an anti-capitalist direction. Gare 2000 advocates the building of such institutions as a major prefigurative step toward ecosocialism.

4. The British socialists' use of Blake's anthem from *Milton*, 'And did those feet in ancient time/Walk upon England's mountains green?' ending with the immortal words, 'I will not cease from mental fight,/Nor shall my sword sleep in my hand,/ Till we have built Jerusalem,/ In England's green and pleasant land' (Blake 1977: 514), is the best example, especially for how readily it translates into the terms of ecosocialism.

5. Meister Eckhart has a splendid saying, 'Let us pray to God to be rid of "God"', which applies perfectly here. For a general discussion, see Kovel 1998.

6. All 'progressive' education, in my view, follows this model, famously laid out by Paulo Freire (Freire 1970).

7. By August 2000, there were 28 such centres, in places ranging from Los Angeles to the Congo. For the many aspects of the alternative media movement, see Halleck 2001.

8. Moody 2000. For example, the IMF forced the Nigerian government to deregulate and end its $2 billion subsidy of fuel prices, the resultant rise of which precipitated a general strike. In Korea, the strikes were in opposition to draconian working hours imposed by the IMF as a condition for bailing the country out of the financial crisis of 1998. In South Africa, 4 million workers protested IMF-imposed austerity from the mid-1990s. In India, 20 million walked out, in a strike aimed, in the words of one of its leaders, 'against the surrender of the country's economic autonomy before the World Trade Organization and the International Monetary Fund'. Similar patterns were seen in Uruguay and Argentina, as new presidents took office scurrying to impose IMF austerity. See also Moody 1997.

9. Rensenbrink 1999 exemplifies this tendency. For a detailed account of green politics in the USA from an ecofeminist perspective, see Gaard 1998.

10. Faber 1998.

11. Marcos 2001 provides a good introduction. Marx 1978f.

12. Weisman 1998.

13. A state in southern India with a long record of communist adminstrations and remarkable ecological development, including the empowerment of women. See Parayil 2000.

14. O'Connor 2001.

15. Marx 1967b: 776.

16. Prefigured by Marx in the 1844 manuscripts. Marx 1978b.

17. István Mészáros writes: 'the socialist undertaking cannot even begin to realize its fundamental objectives without successfully accomplishing at the same time the shift from the exchange of products ... to the exchange of genuinely *planned* and *self-managed* (as opposed to bureaucratically *planned from above*) productive activities'. Mészáros 1996: 761, italics in text.

18. David McNally summarizes these arguments well: '[w]here labour is communal, and its allocation determined in advance, a certificate or voucher is not money; it is not the mechanism which validates the social character of labour, nor does it transform the latter into the former'. (McNally 1993: 195). For a study of current market contradictions, see Altvater 1993.

19. Gandhi's post-colonial India had a powerful non-violent ideology, but very undemocratic institutions – especially the caste system – as well as the spectre of religious–ethnic nationalism that tore the country apart. Under these circumstances the horrible violence that supervened upon partition was virtually inevitable.

20. Weisman 1998: 10.

Afterword

A work that makes as many claims as *The Enemy of Nature* deserves rounding off with an afterword. But I must confess that I found this no easy task. Over and over I would begin writing this section, then leave off, unsatisfied. The problem was one of tone, finding the proper register to finish off so weighty a subject without seeming heavy. Yet the heaviness would keep returning, until in frustration I thought of dropping the whole passage.

I then recalled something a student had once asked, to the effect of how one could keep from despairing while studying such awful things as the ecological crisis and the ghastly power held by capital over our existence. I had said something perfunctory at the time, but the question continued to flit in and out of my mind, and, as it did, took on a somewhat different value. For the fact was, I did not despair; for whatever reason, I actually found myself in good spirits as I studied the crisis further and devised the ideas that have gone into this work. It didn't make sense at first, given how dreadful is the predicament in which we find ourselves – but there did seem to be a logic to it. And then I thought back to the opening sentence of my Preface, in which I had written of people becoming frozen in their tracks by the dawning realization of capital's radical ecodestructiveness, and it occurred to me that the best tack which my Afterword could take would be to address this dilemma, and try to show in however halting a way that there were grounds for actually being of good cheer within the perspective argued here.

The thesis that drives this work, that capital is both ecodestructive and unreformable, is either true or false. If it is false, then I have been wrong, and the apologists for capital right. But their correctness would require a great sea change in capital, a historic adaptation and overcoming of its evil tendencies. This will be great and good news. For capital will now, having overcome its ecological ordeal, be a better system entirely. It will stand forth not as the enemy, but as nature's friend. Capable of regulating itself, it will be a true friend to humanity as well. The rising tide will lift all boats, and poverty, exploitation and oppression will be things belonging to the dim prehistory of our species. We will have entered a truly golden age.

So there will be plenty to cheer about if the *The Enemy of Nature* turns out to be wrong. But what if I am right, and the choice is either to end capital's reign or face the destruction of our world? Now things seem to get grimmer and more complicated as we turn to face our enemy. But is this really so? What has been proposed here is a line of reasoning to help us come to grips with a great crisis. Whether or not one adopts it – whether or not this book was written in the first place – capital's ecodestruction will take place. All that has been striven for here is to face things squarely – to alter the perception of an impending disaster, to meet it actively instead of passively submitting to the terms of understanding dealt out by the dominant system. And surely it is better actively to comprehend rather than numbly submit to the logic of one's destroyer. Is it not liberating to realize that the mighty capitalist system is at heart a trick played upon us? The delegitimation of its principle of exchange, the revelation of how human possibilities are stunted under its regime – all this opens a path to the intrinsic beauty of the world and lets us join with others of like mind.

If capital is a delusion, then private ownership of the globe is part of that delusion. And once we realize as much, the principle of usufruct will come to apply. Now this tells us to improve and enjoy that which is another's, though it happens to be our home. Why should we wait until after the revolution before doing so? Indeed, the revolution has already begun once this appreciated – and if the principle of usufruct tells us that we should enjoy the earth, should we not also enjoy freeing the earth from bondage?

The great themes of the ecological crisis do not alter our existential position, which remains framed by the fact that each of us is allotted a limited time on the earth and, within it, the opportunity of living as best we can. But it does shape what that best might be, and here, it seems, the great virtue of addressing the crisis appears. For what other generation has been given the chance to transform the relation between humanity and nature, and to heal so ancient a wound? What a fantastic challenge! All creatures must end, and all species. Even the earth, and time and space will vanish. But our creatural destiny is to have a degree of choice over our end. We should not allow the exit to occur under the cold, cruel hand of capital; it is an ending unworthy of the beauty of the world.

> All Human Forms identified even Tree Metal Earth & Stone; all
> Human Forms identified, living going forth & returning wearied
> Into the Planetary lives of Years Months Days & Hours reposing
> And then Awakening into his Bosom in the Life of Immortality.[1]

Note

1. The last lines but one of *Jerusalem* (Blake 1997: 847).

Bibliography

Altvater, E. (1993) *The Future of the Market*, trans. Patrick Camiller, London: Verso.

Aristotle (1947) *Introduction to Aristotle*, ed. R. McKeon, New York: Modern Library.

Arrighi, G. (1994) *The Long Twentieth Century*, London: Verso.

Athanasiou, T. (1996) *Divided Planet*, Boston: Little Brown.

Bader, S. (1997) *Global Spin*, Dartington: Green Books.

Barlow, M. (2000) 'The World Bank must realize water is a basic human right', *Toronto Globe and Mail*, 9 May.

Bass, C. (2000) 'A smile in conflict with itself', *Sacramento Bee*, 28 February: D1.

Bateson, G. (1972) *Notes Toward an Ecology of Mind*, New York: Ballantine Books.

Beckermann, W. (1991) 'Global warming: a sceptical economic assessment', in D. Helm (ed.), *Economic Policy Towards the Environment*, Oxford: Blackwell, pp. 52–85.

Beder, S. (1997) *Global Spin*, Dartington: Green Books.

Benjamin, J. (1988) *The Bonds of Love*, New York: Pantheon.

Benton, T. (ed.) (1996) *The Greening of Marxism*, New York: Guilford.

Bergman, L. (2000) 'U.S. companies tangled in web of drug dollars', *New York Times*, 10 October: A1.

Biehl, J. and P. Staudenmaier (1995) *Ecofascism: Lessons from the German Experience*, Edinburgh and San Francisco: AK Press.

Blake, W. (1977) 'The Sick Rose', from 'Songs of Experience', and *Milton*, in Alicia Ostriker (ed.), *The Complete Poems*, Harmondsworth: Penguin.

Blaut, J. (1993) *The Colonizer's View of the World*, New York: Guilford.

Bookchin, M. (1970) *Post-Scarcity Anarchism*, Palo Alto, CA: Ramparts Press.

— (1982) *The Ecology of Freedom* Palo Alto, CA: Cheshire Books.

Botkin, D. (1990) *Discordant Harmonies*, New York: Oxford University Press.

Bowden, C. (1996) 'While you were sleeping', *Harpers*, December: 44–52.

Bramwell, A. (1989) *Ecology in the Twentieth Century: A History*, New Haven, CT: Yale University Press.

Braudel, F. (1977) *Afterthoughts on Material Civilization and Capitalism*, Baltimore, MD: Johns Hopkins University Press.

Breyer, S. (1979) 'Analyzing regulatory failure, mismatches, less restrictive alternatives and reform', *Harvard Law Review*, 92 (3): 597.

Bronner, S. (1981) *A Revolutionary For Our Times: Rosa Luxemburg*, London: Pluto Press.

— (1990) *Socialism Unbound*, London: Routledge.

Brown, L. and C. Flavin (1999) 'A new economy for a new century', in *State of the World 1999*, New York: W.W. Norton.

Brown, L., C. Flavin and S. Postel (1991) *Saving the Planet*, New York: W.W. Norton.

Brown, P. (1999) 'More refugees flee from environment than warfare', *Guardian Weekly*, 1–7 July: 5.

Brundtland, G. (ed.) (1987) *Our Common Future: The World Commission on the Environment and Development*, Oxford and New York: Oxford University Press.

Burkett, P. (1999) *Marx and Nature*, New York: St. Martin's Press.

Call, W. (2001) 'Accelerating the decomposition of capitalism', *ACERCA Notes*, #8, First Quarter.

Chodorow, N. (1978) *The Reproduction of Mothering*, Berkeley: University of California Press.

Clark, J. (1984) *The Anarchist Moment*, Montreal: Black Rose.

— (1997) 'A social ecology', *Capitalism, Nature, Socialism*, 8 (3): 3–34.

Clastres P. (1977) *Society Against the State*, trans. Robert Hurley, New York: Urizen.

Cockburn, A. and J. St. Clair (2000) *Al Gore: A User's Manual*, New York: Verso.

Colburn, T., D. Dumanoski and J. P. Myers (1996) *Our Stolen Future*, New York: Dutton-Penguin.

Cort, J. (1988) *Christian Socialism*, Maryknoll, NY: Orbis.

Costanza, R., J. Cumberland, H. Daly, R. Goodland and R. Norgaard (1997) *An Introduction to Ecological Economics*, Boca Raton, FL: St. Lucie Press.

Cronon, W. (ed.) (1996) *Contested Ground*, New York: W.W. Norton.

Crossette, B. (2000a) 'In numbers, the heavy now match the starved', *New York Times*, 17 January: A1.

— (2000b) 'Unicef issues report on worldwide violence facing women', *New York Times*, 1 June 1: A15.

Daly, H. (1991) *Steady-State Economics*, Washington, DC: Island Press.

— (1996) *Beyond Growth*, Boston, MD: Beacon Press.

Daly, H. and J. Cobb (1994) *For the Common Good*, Boston, MA: Beacon Press.

Davies, P. (1983) *God and The New Physics*, Harmondsworth: Penguin.

DeBord, G. (1992) *Society of the Spectacle*, New York: Zone Books.

de Brie, C. (2000) 'Crime, the world's biggest free enterprise', *Le Monde Diplomatique*, April.

de Duve, C. (1995) *Vital Dust*, New York: Basic Books.

DeLumeau, J. (1990) *Sin and Fear: Emergence of a Western Guilt Culture 13th–18th Centuries*, trans. Eric Nicholson, New York: St. Martin's Press.

Deogun, N. (1997) 'A Coke and a perm? Soda giant is pushing into unusual locales', *Wall Street Journal*, 5 May: A1.

Devall, B. and G. Sessions (1985) *Deep Ecology*, Salt Lake City, UT: Peregrine Smith Books.

Diamond, S. (1974) *In Search of the Primitive*, New Brunswick, NJ: Transaction Books.

Dobrzynski, J. (1997) 'Big payoffs for executives who fail big', *New York Times*, 21 July: D1.

Draper, H. (1977, 1978, 1985, 1990) *Karl Marx's Theory of Revolution*, 4 vols, New York: Monthly Review Press.

Drexler, K. (1986) *Engines of Creation*, New York: Doubleday.

Dunayevskaya, R. (1973) *Philosophy and Revolution*, New York: Dell.

— (2000) *Marxism and Freedom*, Amherst, NY: Humanity Books.

Dunn, S. (2001) *Hydrogen Futures: Toward a Sustainable Energy System*, Worldwatch Paper 157, Washington, DC: Worldwatch.

Eckersley, R. (1992) *Environmentalism and Political Theory*, Albany, NY: SUNY Press.

The Ecologist (1993) *Whose Common Future? Reclaiming the Commons*, Philadelphia: New Society Publishers.

Editorial (1999) *New York Times*, 29 July.

Ehrenreich, B. and D. English (1974) *Witches, Midwives and Nurses*, London: Compendium.

Eisler, R. (1987) *The Chalice and the Blade*, San Francisco, CA: Harper and Row.

Engels, F. (1940) *Dialectics of Nature*, New York: International Publishers.

— (1972) [1884] *Origins of the Family, Private Property, and the State*, ed. Eleanor Leacock, New York: International Publishers.

— (1987) [1845] *The Condition of the Working Class in England*, ed. Victor Kiernan, Harmondsworth: Penguin.

Epstein, P. (2000) 'Is global warming harmful to health?', *Scientific American*, 283 (2): 50–7.

Faber, D. (ed.) (1998) *The Struggle for Ecological Democracy*, New York: Guilford.

Fagin, D. and M. Lavelle (1996) *Toxic Deception*, Secaucus, NJ: Birch Lane Press.

Farias, V. (1989) *Heidegger and Nazism*, ed. Joseph Margolis and Tom Rockmore, Philadelphia: Temple University Press.

Fest, J. (1970) *The Face of the Third Reich*, New York: Pantheon.

Fiddes, N. (1991) *Meat – A Natural Symbol*, London: Routledge.

Figes, O. (1997) *A People's Tragedy*, London: Pimlico.

Fisher, A. (2001) *Radical Ecopsychology: Psychology in the Service of Life*, Albany, NY: SUNY Press.

Fortey, R. (1997) *Life: An Unauthorized Biography*, London: HarperCollins.

Foster, J. (2000) *Marx's Ecology*, New York: Monthly Review Press.

Frank, A. (1998) *ReORIENT: Global Economy in the Asian Age*, Berkeley: University of California Press.

Freire, P. (1970) *Pedagogy of the Oppressed*, New York: Continuum.

Freud, S. (1931) 'Civilization and its discontents', in Strachey, J. (ed.), *The Standard Edition of the Complete Psychological Works of Sigmund Freud*, London: The Hogarth Press, 21: 59–148.

Freund. P. and G. Martin (1993) *The Ecology of the Automobile*, Montreal: Black Rose Books.

Fumento, M. (1999) 'With frog scare debunked, it isn't easy being green', *Wall Street Journal*, 12 May.

Gaard, G. (1998) *Ecological Politics*, Philadelphia: Temple University Press.

Gardner, G. and B. Halweil (2000) 'Underfed and overfed', Washington, DC: Worldwatch Institute, March.

Gare, A. (1996a) 'Soviet environmentalism: the path not taken', in T. Benton (ed.), *The Greening of Marxism*, New York: Guilford, pp. 111–28.

— (1996b) *Nihilism Inc.*, Sydney: Eco-Logical Press.

— (2000) 'Creating an ecological socialist future', *Capitalism, Nature, Socialism*, 11 (2): 23–40.

Gelbspan, R. (1998) *The Heat is On*, Reading, MA: Perseus Books.

George, S. (1992) *The Debt Boomerang*, London: Pluto.

Georgescu-Roegen, N. (1971) *The Entropy Law and the Economic Process*, Cambridge, MA: Harvard University Press.

Geping, Q. and W. Lee (eds) (1984) *Managing the Environment in China*, Dublin: Tycooley.

Gibbs, L. (1995) *Dying From Dioxin*, Boston, MA: South End Press.

Glacken, C. (1973) *Traces on the Rhodian Shore*, Berkeley: University of California Press.

Glieck, J. (1987) *Chaos*, New York: Penguin.

Goldsmith, E. and C. Henderson (1999) 'The economic costs of climate change', *The Ecologist*, 29 (2).

Gore, A. (2000) *Earth in the Balance*, Boston: Houghton-Mifflin.

Goudie, A. (1991) *The Human Impact on the Natural Environment*, Cambridge, MA: MIT Press.

Gunn, C. and H. Gunn (1991) *Reclaiming Capital*, Ithaca, NY: Cornell University Press.

Halleck, D. (2001) *Hand-Held Visions*, New York: Fordham University Press.

Harvey, D. (1993) *The Condition of Postmodernity*, Oxford: Blackwell.

Hawken, P. (1993) *The Ecology of Commerce*, New York: HarperCollins.

Hecht, S. and A. Cockburn (1990) *The Fate of the Forest*, New York: HarperCollins.

Hegel, G. (1969) *Hegel's Science of Logic*, trans. A. Miller, London: George Allen & Unwin.

Heidegger, M. (1977) 'The question regarding technology', in *Basic Writings*, ed. David Farrell Krell, New York: Harper and Row, pp. 283–317.

Herrnstein R. and C. Murray (1996) *The Bell Curve*, New York: The Free Press.

Hinton, W. (1967) *Fanshen*, New York: Monthly Review Press.

Ho, M. (1998) *Genetic Engineering: Dream or Nightmare?* Bath, UK: Gateway Books.

Hussey, E. (1972) *The Presocratics*, New York: Charles Scribner's Sons.

Huws, U., (1999) 'Material world: the myth of the weightless economy', in L. Panitch and C. Leys (eds), *Socialist Register 1999*, Suffolk: Merlin Press, pp. 29–55.

Jenkins, Jr., H. (1997) 'Who needs R&D when you understand fat?', *Wall Street Journal*, 25 March: A19.

Kanter, R. (1997) 'Show humanity when you show employees the door', *Wall Street Journal*, 21 July: A22.

Karliner, J. (1997) *The Corporate Planet*, San Francisco, CA: Sierra Club.

Kempf, H. (2000) 'Every catastrophe has a silver lining', *Guardian Weekly*, 20–26 January: 30.

Kidner, D. (2000) *Nature and Psyche*, Albany: SUNY Press.

Korten, D. (1996) 'The mythic victory of market capitalism', in J. Mander and E. Goldsmith (eds), *The Case Against the Global Economy*, San Francisco, CA: Sierra Club Books, pp. 183–91.

— (2000) 'The FEASTA annual lecture', Dublin, Ireland, 4 July.

Kovel, J. (1981) *The Age of Desire*, New York: Random House.

— (1984) *White Racism*, 2dn edn, New York: Columbia University Press.

— (1988) *In Nicaragua*, London: Free Association Books.

— (1995) 'Ecological Marxism and dialectic', *Capitalism, Nature, Socialism*, 6 (4): 31–50.

— (1997a) 'Bad news for fast food', *Z*, September: 26–31.

— (1997b) *Red Hunting in the Promised Land*, 2nd edn, London: Cassell.

— (1997c) 'Negating Bookchin', *Capitalism, Nature, Socialism*, 8(1): 3–36.

— (1998a) 'Dialectic as praxis', *Science and Society*, 62(3): 474–82.

— (1998b) *History and Spirit*, 2nd edn, Warner, NH: Essential Books.

— (1999) 'The justifiers', *Capitalism, Nature, Socialism*, 10 (3): 3–36.

— (2001) 'A materialism worthy of nature', *Capitalism, Nature, Socialism*, 12 (2).

Kovel, J., K. Soper, M. Mellor and J. Clark (1998) 'John Clark's "A social ecology": comments/reply', in *Capitalism, Nature, Socialism*, 9 (1): 25–46.

Kropotkin, P. (1902) *Mutual Aid*, London: Heinemann.

— (1975) *The Essential Kropotkin*, ed. E. Capouy and K. Tompkins, New York: Liveright.

Kurzman, D. (1987) *A Killing Wind: Inside Union Carbide and the Bhopal Catastrophe*, New York: McGraw-Hill.

Lappé, F., J. Collins and P. Rosset (1998) *World Hunger: Twelve Myths*, 2nd edn, New York: Grove Press.

Leff, E. (1995) *Green Production*, New York: Guilford.

Leiss, W. (1972) *The Domination of Nature*, Boston, MA: Beacon Press.

Lenin, V. (1967) *Materialism and Empirio-Criticism*, Moscow: Progress Publishers.

— (1976) *Philosophical Notebooks*, Moscow: Progress Publishers.

Lepkowski, W. (1994) 'Ten years later: Bhopal', *Chemical & Engineering News*, 19 December: 8–18.

Levins, R. and R. Lewontin (1985) *The Dialectical Biologist*, Cambridge, MA: Harvard University Press.

Lichtman, R. (1982) *The Production of Desire*, New York: The Free Press.

Light, A. (ed.) (1998) *Social Ecology After Bookchin*, New York: Guilford.

Lovelock, J. (1979) *Gaia: A New Look at Life on Earth*, Oxford: Oxford University Press.

Lovins, A. (1977) *Soft Energy Paths*, San Francisco, CA: Friends of the Earth International.

Manning, J. (1996) *The Coming of the Energy Revolution*, Garden City Park, New York: Avery.

Margulis, L. (1998) *Symbiotic Planet*, New York: Basic Books.

Marsh, G. P. (1965) [1864] *Man and Nature*, ed. D. Lowenthal, Cambridge, MA: Belknap Press.

Martinez-Alier, J. (1987) *Ecological Economics*, Oxford: Blackwell.

Marx, K. (1963) [1847] *The Poverty of Philosophy*, New York: International Publishers.

— (1964) [1858] *Pre-Capitalist Economic Formations*, trans. Jack Cohen, ed. E. J. Hobsbawm, New York: International Publishers.

— (1967a) [1867] *Capital, Vol. I*, ed. Frederick Engels, New York: International Publishers.

— (1967b) [1894] *Capital Vol. 3*, ed. Frederick Engels, New York: International Publishers.

— (1971) [1863] *Theories of Surplus Value Vol. III*, Moscow: Progress Publishers.

— (1973) [1858] *Grundrisse*, trans. and ed. Martin Nicolaus, Harmondsworth: Penguin.

— (1978a) [1843] Letter to Arnold Ruge, September 1843, in Tucker 1978, p. 13.

— (1978b) [1844] *Economic and Philosophic Manuscripts of 1844*, in Tucker 1978, pp. 66–125.

Marx, K. and F. Engels (1978c) [1848] *The Communist Manifesto*, in Tucker 1978, pp. 469–500.

— (1978d) [1864] 'Inaugural address of the Working Men's International Association', in Tucker 1978, pp. 517–18.

— (1978e) [1875] 'Critique of the Gotha Program', in Tucker 1978, pp. 525–41.

— (1978f) [1871] *The Civil War in France*, in Tucker 1978, pp. 618–52.

McNally, D. (1993) *Against the Market*, London: Verso.

Meadows, D., D. Meadows and J. Randers (1992) *Beyond the Limits*, London: Earthscan.

Meadows, D., D. Meadows, J. Randers and W. Behrens (1972) *The Limits to Growth*, London: Earth Island.

Meeker-Lowry, S. (1988) *Economics as if the Earth Really Mattered*, Philadelphia: New Society Publishers.

Meisner, M. (1996) *The Deng Xiaoping Era*, New York: Hill and Wang.

Mellor, M. (1997) *Feminism and Ecological Polity*, Cambridge and New York: New York University Press.

Merchant, C. (1980) *The Death of Nature*, San Francisco, CA: Harper and Row.

Mészáros, I. (1996) *Beyond Capital*, New York: Monthly Review Press.

Mies, M. (1998) *Patriarchy and Accumulation on a World Scale*, 2nd edn, London: Zed Books.

Mihill, C. (1996) 'Health plight of poor worsening', *Guardian Weekly*: 5.

Mintz, S. (1995) *Sweetness and Power*, New York: Viking.

Miranda, J. (1974) *Marx and the Bible*, Maryknoll, NY: Orbis.

Mollison, B. (1988) *Permaculture: A Designer's Manual*, Tygalum, Australia: Tagari Publications.

Montague, P. (1999) 'Wrecking the oceans', *Rachel's Environment & Health Weekly*, #659, 15 July. http://www.rachel.org

Montague, P. (1996) 'Things to come', *Rachels' Environment and Health Weekly*, # 523, 5 December.

Moody, K. (1997) *Workers in a Lean World*, London and New York: Verso.

— (2000) 'Global labor stands up to global capital', *Labor Notes*, July: 8.

Morehouse, W. (1993) 'The ethics of industrial disasters in a transnational world: the elusive quest for justice and accountability in Bhopal', *Alternatives*, 18: 487.

Morris, W. (1993) *News From Nowhere*, Harmondsworth: Penguin.

Morrison, R. (1991) *We Build the Road as We Travel*, Philadelphia: New Society.

— (1995) *Ecological Democracy*, Boston, MA: South End Press.

Murphy, D. (2000) 'Africa: lenders set program rules', *Los Angeles Times*, 27 January: A1.

Murray, A. (1978) *Reason and Society in the Middle Ages*, Oxford: Clarendon Press.

Naess, A. (1989) *Ecology, Community and Lifestyle*, trans. and ed. David Rothenberg, Cambridge: Cambridge University Press.

Nahm, M. (ed.) (1947) *Selections from Early Greek Philosophy*, New York: Appleton Century Crofts.

Nathan, D. (1997) 'Death comes to the *Maquilas*: a border story', *The Nation*, 264 (2) (13–20 January): 18–22.

Needham, J. (1954) *Science and Civilization in China Vol. 1, Introduction and Orientations*, Cambridge: Cambridge University Press.

Norgaard, R. (1994) *Development Betrayed*, London: Routledge.

O'Brien, M. (1981) *The Politics of Reproduction*, London: Routledge and Kegan Paul.

O'Connor, J. (1998a) 'On capitalist accumulation and economic and ecological crisis', in J. O'Connor, *Natural Causes*, New York: Guilford.

— (1998b) *Natural Causes*, New York: Guilford.

— (2001) 'House organ', *Capitalism, Nature, Socialism*, 13 (1): 1.

Ollman, B. (1971) *Alienation*, Cambridge: Cambridge University Press.

Ordonez, J. (2000) 'An efficiency drive: fast food lanes are getting even faster', *Wall Street Journal*, 18 May: 1

Orleans, L. and R. Suttmeier (1970) 'The Mao ethic and environmental quality', *Science*, 170: 1173–6.

Parayil, G. (ed.) (2000) *Kerala: The Development Experience*, London: Zed Books.

Parsons, H. (1977) *Marx and Engels on Ecology*, Westport, CT: Greenwood Press.

Penrose, R. (1990) *The Emperor's New Mind*, London: Vintage.

Platt, A. (1996) *Infecting Ourselves*, Worldwatch Paper 129, Washington, DC: Worldwatch Institute.

Polanyi, K. (1957) *The Great Transformation*, Boston, MA: Beacon Press.

Ponting, C. (1991) *A Green History of the World*, Harmondsworth: Penguin.

Pooley, E. (2000) 'Doctor Death', *Time*, 24 April.

Pring, G. and P. Canan (1996) *SLAPPs: Getting Sued for Speaking Out*, Philadelphia: Temple University Press.

Proudhon, P. (1969) *Selected Writings*, trans. E. Fraser, ed. S. Edwards, Garden City, NY: Anchor Books.

Public Citizen (1996) *NAFTA's Broken Promises: The Border Betrayed*, Washington, DC: Public Citizen.

Purdom, T. (2000) 'A game of nerves, with no real winners', *New York Times*, 17 May: H1.

Quammen, D. (1996) *The Song of the Dodo*, New York: Scribner.

Rampton, S., and J. Stauber (1997) *Mad Cow U.S.A.*, Monroe, ME: Common Courage Press.

Rensenbrink, J. (1999) *Against All Odds*, Raymond, ME: Leopold Press.

Romero, S. (2000) 'Rich Brazilians rise above rush-hour jams', *New York Times*, 15 February: A1.

Rosdolsky, R. (1977) *The Making of Marx's Capital*, trans. Pete Burgess, London: Verso.

Rosset, P. and M. Benjamin (1994) *The Greening of the Revolution: Cuba's Experiment with Organic Farming*, Melbourne: Ocean.

Ruether, R. (1992) *Gaia and God*, San Francisco, CA: HarperSan Francisco.

Ruggiero, Renato (1997) 'The high stakes of world trade', *Wall Street Journal*, 28 April: A18.

Sale, K. (1996) 'Principles of bioregionalism', in J. Mander and E. Goldsmith (eds), *The Case Against the Global Economy*, San Francisco, CA: Sierra Club Books, pp. 471–84.

Salleh, A. (1997) *Ecofeminism as Politics*, London: Zed Books.

Sarkar, S. (1999) *Eco-socialism or Eco-capitalism?* London: Zed Books.

Schrödinger, E. (1967) *What is Life?* Cambridge: Cambridge University Press.

Schumacher, E. F. (1973) *Small is Beautiful*, New York: Harper and Row.

Sheasby, W. (1997) 'Inverted world: Karl Marx on estrangement of nature and society', *Capitalism, Nature, Socialism*, 8 (4): 3146.

— (2000) 'Ralph Nader and the legacy of revolt', three parts, *Against the Current*, 88 (4): 17–21; 88 (5): 29–36; 88 (6): 39–42.

Shiva, V. (1991) *The Violence of the Green Revolution*, Penang, Malaysia: Third World Network.

— (1988), *Staying Alive*, London: Zed Books.

Simmel, G. (1978) *The Philosophy of Money*, trans. Tom Bottomore and David Frisby, London: Routledge and Kegan Paul.

Slatella, M. (2000) 'Boxed in: exploring a big-box store online', *New York Times*, 27 January: D4.

Steingraber, S. (1997) *Living Downstream*, New York: Addison Wesley.

Stewart, B. (2000) 'Retrieving the recyclables', *New York Times*, 27 June: B1.

Stiglitz, A. (2000) 'What I learned at the world economic crisis', *New Republic*, 17 April.

Stille, A. 'In the "greened" world, it isn't easy to be human', *New York Times*, 15 July: A17.

Subcomandante Marcos (2001) *Our Word is our Weapon*, ed. Juana Ponce de León, New York: Seven Stories Press.

Summers, L., J. Wolfensohn and J. Skilling (1997) *Multinational Monitor*, June: 6.

Taub, E. (2000) 'Radios watch weather so you don't have to', *New York Times*, 30 March: D10.

Tawney, R. H. (1998) [1926] *Religion and the Rise of Capitalism*, New Brunswick, NJ: Transaction.

Thernstrom, A. and S. Thernstrom (1997) *America in Black and White*, New York: Simon and Schuster.

Thompson, E.P. (1967) 'Time, work discipline, and industrial capitalism', *Past and Present*, 38: 56–97

Thornton, J. (2000) *Pandora's Poison*, Cambridge, MA: MIT Press.

Tokar, B. (1992) *The Green Alternative*, San Pedro, CA: R.& E. Miles.

— (1997) *Earth For Sale*, Boston, MD: South End Press.

Trotsky, L. (1960) *Literature and Revolution*, Ann Arbor: University of Michigan Press, p. 253.

Tucker, R. (ed.) (1978) *The Marx–Engels Reader*, New York: W.W. Norton.

Turner, A. (2000) 'Tempers in overdrive', *Houston Chronicle*, 8 April: 1A.

Wald, M. (1997) 'Temper cited as cause of 28,000 road deaths a year', *New York Times*, 18 July: A14.

Watson, D. (1996) *Beyond Bookchin*, New York: Autonomedia.

Watson, J. (ed.) (1997) *Golden Arches East: McDonald's in East Asia*, Stanford, CA: Stanford University Press.

Weber, M. (1976) *The Protestant Ethic and the Spirit of Capitalism*, trans. Talcott Parsons, London: Allen and Unwin.

Website http://www.kenyon.edu/projects/permaculture/

Website: www.corporatewatch.org/bhopal/

Websites: http://www.brain.net.pk/diama; and egroups.com/groups/waterline

Weisman, A. (1998) *Gaviotas*, White River Junction, VT: Chelsea Green.

Wheen, F. (2000) *Karl Marx: A Life*, New York: W.W. Norton.

White, L. (1967) 'The historical roots of our ecological crisis', *Science*, 155 (10 March): 1203–7.

— (1978) *Medieval Religion and Technology: Collected Essays*, Berkeley: University of California Press.

Williams, A. (2000) 'Washed up at 35', *New York*, 17 April: 28ff.

Wolfenstein, E. (1993) *Psychoanalytic Marxism*, London: Free Association Books.

Woodcock, G. (1962) *Anarchism*, New York: New American Library.

Worster, D. (1994) *Nature's Economy*, 2nd edn, Cambridge: Cambridge University Press.

Zablocki, B. (1971) *The Joyful Community*, Baltimore, MD: Penguin.

Zachary, G. Pascal (1997) 'The right mix: global growth attains a new, higher level that could be lasting', *Wall Street Journal*, 13 March: A1.

Zimmerman, M. (1994) *Contesting Earth's Future*, Berkeley: University of California Press.

Index

Critical Acclaim for this Book

A challenging book, written with passion and eloquence. Its message is that 'capital cannot be reformed: it either rules and destroys us, or is destroyed, so that we may have a lease on life'. The underlying causes and their far-reaching implications are systematically explored. Rich in detail and insights and leading to much needed radical conclusions, this book should be read by all those who are concerned about the survival of the human species. **Istvan Meszaros, author of Marx's Theory of Alienation and Beyond Capital**

Joel Kovel has brought us a persuasive, passionate and hopeful ecosocialist manifesto. He shows how problems from toxic pollution to globalized poverty reflect the inner logic of capitalism, and extends the lessons of Marxism and other radical traditions to illuminate a path toward an ethical and ecological revolution. This book offers much food for thought to all who seek a systemic understanding of today's social and ecological crises. **Brian Tokar, activist and author of Redesigning Life? and Earth for Sale**

A necessary and timely book. Necessary because it openly declares capitalism as THE destroyer of the earth and all eco-systems. Timely, because it appears at a moment when more and more people are beginning to lose faith in capital's ability to solve the social and ecological crises. The book is a must for all those who are active in the international movement against corporate-driven globalization and who look for a perspective beyond capital's enslavement of nature and people. **Maria Mies, author of The Subsistence Perspective**

The Enemy of Nature exposes better than any other single work the extent and depth of capitalism's global ecological destruction. This master work by Joel Kovel then pursues the necessary implications – including the opportunity and need to imagine an ecological socialist society. Kovel shows that the core conditions of such a society are the accession of quality over quantity and use-value over exchange-value, with the emancipatory possibilities these imply. **James O'Connor, author of Natural Conditions**

Full of insights into the relationship between ecological degradation and capitalist expansion, this is a must read for thinkers and activists. **Walden Bello, Executive Director, Focus on the Global South, Thailand**

Joel Kovel has written a highly original and theoretically elegant argument that ecological crisis and capitalist exploitation of labour must be understood as two aspects of the same problem, and therefore remedies for ecological destruction require the destruction of capitalism. In the process, he puts forward an account of the ways the gendered separation of man from nature (woman) lies at the root of a masculinist capitalism. The abolition of patriarchy, then, becomes central to the ecosocialist project. In addition to this impressive reworking of Marxist theory, he offers a visionary program of practical political action. **Nancy Hartsock, Professor of Political Science, University of Washington**

Among the many benefits that have resulted from cessation of the Cold War is our freedom to criticize capitalism, openly and forcefully, without being labelled 'communists', or worse. Joel Kovel takes strategic advantage of this development by indicting capital's dismal ecological record in a book that is sure to spawn lively and sensible debate. **Mark Dowie, author and former editor of Mother Jones**